The Sephardim

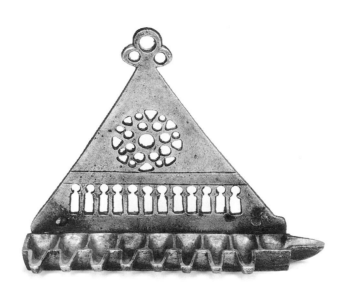

בָּרוּךְ • • שֶׁהֶחֱיָנוּ • וְקִיְּמָנוּ • וְהִגִּיעָנוּ • לַזְּמַן הַזֶּה :

The Sephardim

THEIR GLORIOUS TRADITION
FROM THE BABYLONIAN EXILE
TO THE PRESENT DAY

Lucien Gubbay

Abraham Levy

CARNELL LIMITED

LONDON

First published by
Carnell plc
28 Ecclestone Square,
London SW1V 1PU
© 1992 Lucien Gubbay
Reprinted 1996

British Library Cataloguing
in Publication Data
A catalogue record for this book is
available from The British Library

ISBN 1-8577-9036-7

Page 1

1 Hanukah Lamp
A 14th century Spanish-style brass
Hanukah lamp from Lyons in France.

Page 2

2 Spanish Haggadah
This scene from a 14th century Spanish
Haggadah depicts the Hazan (Cantor) of a
Spanish synagogue reading the Haggadah
(the story of the Exodus from Egypt) to
those members of his congregation unable
to do so for themselves in their own homes.

This page

3 Toledo
The former synagogue of Toledo, founded
in 1203.

Produced for Carnell plc
by Roger Davies, Darwen Press,
Green Street, Pleshey,
Chelmsford, Essex, CM3 1HT.
Designed by Roger Davies
and Gregory Taylor
Set on Ventura in Ehrhardt.

Origination and printing by
Butler and Tanner
The Selwood Printing Works
Frome, Somerset BA11 1NF

Contents

About the authors

Lucien Gubbay was educated at the Manchester Grammar School and Balliol College, Oxford. He is married, with two adult children, and lives in London. Lucien Gubbay has long been fascinated by religious history and is the author of books on related subjects, including 'Origins', 'Quest for the Messiah' and (jointly with Abraham Levy) 'Ages of Man' and its U.S. version 'The Jewish Book of Why and What'.

Abraham Levy was born in Gibraltar and educated at Carmel College, Jews' College London and University College London. He is married, with an adult son, and lives in London. Steeped in Sephardi tradition, Rabbi Dr. Levy exercises the position of spiritual head of England's longest established synagogue — the Spanish & Portuguese Jews' Congregation, London — with the title of Communal Rabbi. Rabbi Levy is one of the two ecclesiastical authorities of the Board of Deputies of British Jews, and a deputy-president of Jews' College. Author of 'The Sephardim: A Problem of Survival', Abraham Levy founded and directs the Jewish Preparatory School of London

This joint project was initiated by Abraham Levy. Lucien Gubbay did the writing, based on his own detailed research and on Abraham Levy's knowledge of Sephardi culture developed over many years.

Notes

Dates in general use are given in the Jewish style in the text. Thus:
B.C.E. (BEFORE COMMON ERA) is equivalent to B.C.; and C.E. (COMMON ERA) corresponds to A.D.

Abraham Levy was not involved in any of the descriptions of the Spanish and Portuguese Jews' Congregation, London; and the views expressed do not necessarily accord with his own.

Acknowledgements

Few scholars can claim mastery of the entire historical period covered by this book; and its authors are no exception. The subject matter, ranging as it does over so many countries of the world, is too vast in scope to be covered other than in outline. And this is what the authors have attempted, utilising the published work of a large number of fine scholars, together with their own knowledge, to distil the essential details of each individual community of the Babylonian/Sephardi diaspora and gather them together in a single volume.

The many books and papers consulted are too numerous for all to be named individually. The Bibliography lists those on which the authors relied most heavily for information and quotations. Much important data was also obtained from learned articles in standard reference books, and particularly from those in the Encyclopaedia Judaica.

Many of the photographs were provided by the Beth Hatefutsoth Museum of Tel Aviv, whose Director and staff are warmly thanked for their help in allowing access to their Photo Archive. Mr Alfred Rubens very kindly allowed the use of some of his unique collection of Jewish prints. Thanks are due also to the Israel Museum of Jerusalem, to the British Museum of London and to the Hon. Archivist of the Spanish & Portuguese Jews' Congregation of London for consent to use photographs from their collections.

Betty Naggar generously donated the photographs she took of some of the pictures. Estelle Levy worked the embroidery illustrated on the front cover and advised on the selection of other pictures. Joyce Gubbay contributed much to the final text by patiently criticising repeated drafts. Joanne Ison did the proof-reading and helped in other practical ways.

A great deal of help was readily given by many individuals, to whom the authors wish to express their gratitude. Though no list can ever be complete, special thanks are due to Esmond Ezra for details of London's Calcutta community, to Abraham Harounoff for his paper on London's Mashadi community, to Lord Kadoori for his account of the refugees from Shanghai, to Vivian Pereira-Mendoza for his unpublished history of the Wembley Sephardi Community, to Vicky Shammah for her account of childhood in Aleppo, to Simon Sibelman for his stimulating seminar on French Jewry, and to Leon Sassoon for his reminiscences of the Alliance Israélite Universelle and of life in Aleppo. Thanks too to many others who so readily helped with information and photographs, including Sam Arwas, Sidney Assor, Henry Azizolahoff, Manuel Cansino, Naim Dangoor, Asia Jaffet, Marlène Lerner, Jack Levy, Francis Mocatta, Sarah Orkin, Bunny Rogers, Cesare Sacerdoti, Ezra Sassoon and Judah Yeshooa.

It was a very great pleasure to have worked with Roger Davies, who designed the book's layout, and with John Mitchell who drew the maps.

The authors owe a special debt of gratitude to their publisher, John Gommes, both for his vision in undertaking the project and for his confidence during the book's many changes of content and form.

4 Bevis Marks Synagogue, London

This engraving of 1812 by Isaac Mendes Belisario is of the Spanish and Portuguese Synagogue in the City of London. It was opened in 1701 to replace the Congregation's first synagogue in a converted house in nearby Creechurch Lane.

Tradition has it that Queen Ann presented an oak beam from one of the Royal Navy's ships for incorporation in its roof; and that the builder, a Quaker, returned his profit to the Congregation, declining to benefit from the erection of a House of God. Oak benches from the Creechurch Lane building were used for part of the back row of seats. Four of the ten giant candlesticks and one of the great brass candelabra were donated by the Portuguese Synagogue of Amsterdam.

The original building stands almost unaltered and is still in regular use. It is the oldest synagogue in the kingdom.

Introduction

Six hundred years ago, more than half the world's Jews were Sephardim; and it was they who provided Jewry with the larger part of its leadership — secular, intellectual and religious. This book traces the origins and history of their own very special culture.

Their story started almost two thousand years before, when King Nebuchadnezzar sacked Jerusalem and carried its inhabitants off into exile by the rivers of Babylon. It was in Babylon that the foundations were laid for one of the two main divisions of the Jewish exile — the Sephardi Tradition.

Eight hundred years later, the underlying structure of modern Judaism was being forged in Babylon's great academies. The authority of their learned principals, the Geonim, was accepted by all Jews throughout the world. After many centuries, the tradition passed on from Babylon to North Africa and to Spain, where it was further enriched. From Spain it returned eastwards, to the Ottoman Empire, and it also established itself for the first time in Christian Europe and the Americas.

By the time of the Holocaust, fewer than one Jew in ten was Sephardi; and the influence of the Sephardim was greatly reduced. But that situation may be changing.

Today the proportion of Sephardim in the Jewish world is about one in six. But in Israel itself, which is the focus of Jewish hope, Sephardim now form half or more of the Jewish population.

Though the ancient Jewish communities of the Islamic countries have disappeared, probably for ever, those of their former members who did not emigrate to Israel have brought renewed life to previously declining Sephardi communities in Europe and the Americas. Others established outposts of Sephardi culture in places as distant as Australia.

Both in Israel and in the diaspora, individual Sephardim are again taking pride in their heritage and seeking deeper knowledge of their roots.

Sephardi thinkers, shedding their customary reticence, are beginning to suggest that the traditional Sephardi attitudes of accommodation and tolerance may have something to offer modern Jewish society, deeply polarised towards its extremes. They point out that the terms 'Orthodox' and 'Reform' are both Ashkenazi concepts — as indeed was the movement towards reform in response to the European Enlightenment, and the vigorous reaction against it.

In their better periods, Sephardim managed to achieve a rare synthesis between their own intense religious consciousness and the world around them. They led well-balanced lives, both as devout Jews and as members of society at large. This was demonstrated by the breadth of their learning and accomplishment — not only in Judaism but also in the full range of secular activity.

Sephardi interpretation of Jewish law was marked by an openness and tolerance which resulted from many generations of living at ease with their neighbours. It was free from those traces of isolationism and harshness that emerged among the Ashkenazim in reaction to two thousand years of relentless persecution, first under Roman and then under Christian rule.

The Sephardim attempted to practise a form of religion in which the requirements of Jewish observance did not inhibit their ability to play a proper part in the affairs of their host countries. Not for them was the notion of retreating ever deeper into tightly exclusive religious groups, increasingly separated not only from the outside world but even from fellow Jews whose standards deviate from their own supposed ideal.

For the purposes of this book, the adjective 'Sephardi' is used in its wider sense to describe all Jews whose traditions derived from Babylon — and not just those whose ancestors once fled from the Iberian Peninsula. In the story of The Glorious Tradition, Spain was just one — though a very important — episode in over two-and-a-half thousand years of exile. Indeed even the Hebrew word 'Sepharad', mentioned in the Bible and later translated into Aramaic as 'Ispamia', is now thought to have referred to Sardis, a town in Asia Minor, and not to Spain.

In Ottoman Palestine, Jews who were not Ashkenazim were classed as Sephardim. There was sense in that sweeping simplification, for most Jews can in fact be divided into the broad categories of Sephardim and Ashkenazim. The difference between them lies in their interpretation of some aspects of Jewish practice and law; and also in cultural patterns embracing social customs, food, music, synagogue ritual and other details of daily living.

Those in the Jewish exile who followed the Babylonian tradition — who derived their religious leadership and customs from Baghdad and then from Spain — became known as the Sephardim. Their culture was predominantly Mediterranean or Near Eastern.

Though all Jews in the diaspora accepted the Babylonian Talmud as their religious authority, there were always some who looked to the Land of Israel rather than to Baghdad or Spain for guidance. They were few and uninfluential compared to the Sephardim until the Middle Ages, when several inspired religious leaders emerged in Northern France and the Rhine valley — Rabbenu Gershom, Rashi and others. Those great scholars provided the impetus for the rapid growth of an alternative religious framework, different in some details from the Sephardi; and that was the real start of the Ashkenazim, who developed a distinctive North or East-European culture.

In the formative period, external political factors had maintained something like an 'iron curtain' between the followers of the two traditions. In Roman times, the world was divided between the Roman Empire in the West and the hostile Persian Empire in the East — with Palestine on one side, and Babylon on the other. Later, the division was between Islam and Christianity — with Baghdad, the Mediterranean basin and Spain in one camp, and North and Central Europe in the other. It is hardly surprising that two different traditions emerged among Jews; and almost miraculous that so high a degree of unity was always maintained between them.

Sephardim once contributed substantially to most aspects of Jewish life, both religious and secular. Their universality of spirit led to many great achievements; and they enriched the culture of their age in the fields of religious study, mysticism, philosophy, language, poetry, literature and science. With their ability to live at ease in the outside world, whilst continuing to develop their own religious identity, they pioneered the entry of Jews into Western society.

With their constant search for order and for clarity of thought and expression, Sephardi intellectuals were responsible for codifying Jewish law. At the other extreme, they retreated from arid rationalism by developing Kabbalah, the mystical tradition, thus endowing Judaism with another dimension. The sublime Hebrew compositions of the Spanish poets embellish the liturgy of the Sephardim; and their style of divine worship, with its emphasis on form, aesthetics and precision, can be remarkably inspiring.

Though swamped for the past few hundred years by the sheer weight of Ashkenazi numbers, and with their self-confidence shaken by the decline of some of the societies in which they formerly lived, Sephardim may still have something of special value to offer the Jewish world.

Sephardim are already beginning to take new pride in the splendid achievements of their ancestors; but time does not stand still. They will have to act now, and without delay, if they wish to preserve what was best in their history and then build a meaningful living tradition on what still survives of an unique heritage.

5 Cordoba Synagogue
The former Rambam Synagogue of Cordoba was constructed by Isaac Moheb ben Ephraim in 1315. This detail of its west wall shows the typical mudejar style of decoration, with quotations from the Psalms worked into its plasterwork.

PART ONE

THE
GLORIOUS
TRADITION

Ψ

*The
Beginning*

Mesopotamia, the once fertile strip of land between the rivers Tigris and Euphrates, now known as Iraq, was one of the cradles of human civilisation, possibly even pre-dating that of Egypt. As long as five thousand years ago, its people had already mastered the art of writing and were living in walled cities. Quite the most splendid was Ur of the Chaldees, capital of the Sumerian kingdom, situated on the river Euphrates within easy reach of the Persian Gulf. Its people had attained a high level of artistic achievement, as shown by the beautiful musical instruments, furniture and statues discovered in its ruins and now to be found in the museums of the world.

We know from the archaeologists that Ur was conquered and sacked by Elamite invaders from neighbouring Persia in about 1960 B.C.E. And that date has key significance in the history of the Jewish tradition for, according to the biblical book of Genesis, Mesopotamia was also the origin of the Jewish people.

The story is told in Genesis of how, some time before the destruction of Ur, Abraham's father and his family quit that city and moved to Haran in the north of the country. It was in Haran that Abraham had his vision of the one true God, the creator of heaven and earth. And it was from Haran that Abraham started on his epoch-making journey — in physical terms to establish his family, his followers and their descendants as a distinct people in the land of Canaan, later to be called Israel — and in religious terms, the journey that was to end in the adoption of at least a part of his remarkable insight by over two thousand million human beings.

The next great milestone in the history of the Jewish tradition occurred about eight hundred years later in Egypt, the other leading centre of ancient civilisation. Famine in Canaan had previously driven Abraham's descendants to leave that country and settle in the eastern part of the Nile delta, called the Land of Goshen in the Bible. And it was from Egypt that Moses led his people out into the desert for a momentous encounter with their God on Mount Sinai, and for a renewal of that revelation of the Divine previously granted to their ancestors Abraham, Isaac and Jacob.

Mesopotamia and Egypt, at each end of the Fertile Crescent where civilisation began, represented the two peaks attained by human society at the dawn of Jewish history. Abraham left the luxury and comfort of his homeland because of its spiritual decay. He and his followers emigrated to an unsophisticated new land — one in which they could live their lives and worship the one true God undisturbed by the corruption that had surrounded them. In similar manner, Moses later led his followers into the uncertain perils of the desert, departing from the splendour and moral laxity of Egypt without a backward glance.

Those migrations, at the very start of the Jewish tradition, were both prompted by the idealism which chose absolute, divinely-inspired values in preference to those compromised by luxury, conformity and security. And that, in essence, is the Jewish story.

6   **A Lady from Ur**
In this reconstruction from evidence found in the tomb of Pu-abi at Ur, the lady is shown as she was buried in all her finery.

7   **Life in Egypt**
In this Eighteenth Dynasty tomb painting from Thebes, guests are shown at a banquet. A servant offers wine and flowers. The guests have cosmetic cones in their hair, which melt during the feast, cooling and scenting them.

The Promised Land

Led by Moses's chosen successor Joshua, the Israelite tribes entered their promised land, the land of Canaan. They conquered parts of it and settled uneasily in the midst of the hostile peoples round about them. In time, the twelve tribes united under the leadership of an elected king. Saul attempted to weld the fiercely independent tribes into a single nation. He raised their first permanent standing army and for a time achieved a balance of power with their neighbours.

It was Saul's successor David who finally gained true independence by subduing the surrounding peoples. David and his son Solomon used military power and a shrewd network of alliances to expand their kingdom into a powerful empire, astride the main trade routes of the ancient world between Egypt and Mesopotamia. This resulted in a period of spectacular affluence for the nation. David established and embellished Jerusalem as his capital; and the magnificent Temple, built there by Solomon, immediately became the focus of the nation's worship.

The duration of David's empire was looked back to as a Golden Age by subsequent generations; but its glory did not last long. The empire was already coming to pieces before the death of King Solomon in 928 B.C.E. Then, when ten of the twelve tribes refused to accept Solomon's stupidly tactless son as his successor, it split up into the two separate kingdoms of Judah and Israel. The time of glory and prosperity was over; for neither of the two tiny and mutually hostile states was any match for the super-powers of the ancient world.

The Kingdom of Israel fell to an Assyrian army in the year 720 B.C.E. Its people — known thereafter as the Lost Ten Tribes of Israel — were deported and promptly disappeared from the stage of world history.

The Kingdom of Judah, still ruled from Jerusalem by descendants of King David, fared rather better than its sister kingdom. It was not until 598 B.C.E. that it was conquered by King Nebuchadnezzar of Babylon. The flower of its leadership was carried off to Babylon in captivity and Judah was reduced to a subject kingdom.

Twelve years later, the vassal King Zedekiah rashly rebelled against his Babylonian masters. That time King Nebuchadnezzar made no mistake. Jerusalem fell to his army in 586 B.C.E. and was razed to the ground. Most of its remaining inhabitants were deported to Mesopotamia.

When Gedaliah, the governor appointed by Nebuchadnezzar, was murdered by discontented supporters of the former king, Babylon intervened once again. Judah was almost completely depopulated. More of its people were transported to Mesopotamia; and the remainder fled to Egypt.

The Return to Zion

With the return of the Jewish people to its place of origin, the wheel of destiny appeared to have turned full circle. But it was not so; for far from turning their backs on their faith, the exiles deepened their understanding of its teachings under the guidance of the Hebrew Prophets; and many important developments in early Judaism, such as the institution of the Synagogue and the square Hebrew script still in use, can be traced back to the Babylonian Captivity.

Eventually a benevolent conqueror of Babylon, King Cyrus the Great of Persia, encouraged some of the exiles to return to Jerusalem and rebuild their ruined land and its Temple.

The hardship involved in that enterprise did not appeal to all of them, for most were by then well established and enjoying life in one of the most luxurious centres of the world. However, many of the more idealistic did seize the opportunity of returning to Zion between the years 528 and 428 B.C.E.

Under the leadership of Nehemiah and Ezra, Judah was slowly and painfully restored — this time not as an independent kingdom, but as a semi-autonomous province of the mighty Persian Empire. The Temple was rebuilt in Jerusalem and, profiting from lessons learnt in exile, the Jewish religion was further consolidated and developed by the Scribes and their successors.

The next three hundred years passed in a relatively tranquil manner. Alexander the Great's conquest of the Persian Empire caused little hardship; and the tradition, whether accurate or not, that Alexander himself offered a sacrifice in the Temple before conferring special privileges on Jerusalem's inhabitants is a good illustration of this. Conditions worsened after Alexander's death, with Judah becoming a self-governing province of his two successor empires in turn.

In the year 175 B.C.E., Antiochus 1V ascended the throne of the ruling Syrian-Greek empire and promptly attempted to unify his realm by banning the practice of Judaism on pain of death. The Jews of Judah revolted against their Greek masters and, under the leadership of the remarkable Maccabean family, eventually succeeded in gaining full independence from foreign rule.

The Jewish state established as the result of the Maccabean revolt expanded its borders; and many pagan inhabitants of the land were incorporated into the nation by mass conversion to Judaism. Judea, as the new state was called, managed to preserve its independence for eighty years.

In 63 B.C.E., two rival claimants to the throne of Judea made the disastrous mistake of appealing for help to a Roman army recently arrived in neighbouring Syria. Its general, Pompey, did not need to be asked twice. He promptly invaded the country and entered Jerusalem at the head of his troops. Temple Mount was besieged for three months before it was finally taken and thousands of its defenders killed. The Temple was sacked; and Pompey committed the ultimate sacrilege of entering its sanctuary, the Holy of Holies.

Judea was stripped of most of its territory and firmly incorporated into the Roman Empire. The truncated country was allowed a measure of local

8 King Cyrus the Great
Tomb of Cyrus at Pasargadae. King Cyrus described himself as 'ruler of all the world'. A watercolour by Robert Ker Porter.

autonomy under its former king, who lost his royal title. Life was hard and taxation heavy under the Romans. Having enjoyed freedom for the past eighty years, the Jews did not take kindly to foreign rule. They proved turbulent subjects; and they rebelled against their new masters again and again — but to no avail.

Conditions improved for a while when Judea became a vassal kingdom under Herod the Great, a trusted friend of Rome. But the country was fragmented again after Herod's death and the bad times returned once more.

Eventually, goaded beyond endurance, the Jews of Roman Palestine rose in armed revolt against the Romans. The war lasted for four years and cost Rome dear. But in the year 70 C.E., Jerusalem was totally destroyed. Its inhabitants were either killed or enslaved; and the Temple was burned to the ground.

9 **The Menorah**
This representation of the golden
candelabrum, which once stood in the
Temple of Jerusalem, was carved on the
Arch of Titus in Rome. This followed the
destruction of the Temple in 70 C.E. and
the looting of its sacred vessels by the
conquering Roman army. There is some
doubt concerning the authenticity of the
Menorah's pedestal depicted by the
sculptor.

From the ashes

The Temple had stood in Jerusalem with only one interruption of seventy years since the days of King Solomon, a thousand years before. For Jews it had become the centre of their national existence, the focus of their faith. God's presence had hovered in its sanctuary — a bare room considered so sacred that entry was restricted to the High Priest, and then only once a year at the climax of the service on the Day of Atonement. The destruction of the Temple was a catastrophe — a disaster so keenly felt that, almost two thousand years later, Jews still fast on each anniversary.

Yet for Judaism itself, seeds of renewal in a more vital form were also present at that terrible event. At the height of the siege of Jerusalem a leading Pharisee, Rabbi Yohanaan ben Zakkai, had his disciples declare that he had died of the plague. With great show of grief, they carried him in a sealed coffin for burial outside the city walls. Once beyond the ring of determined defenders, the rabbi emerged from his coffin and demanded to be taken to the Roman commander, General Vespasian. By some miracle Ben Zakkai persuaded Vespasian to give him permission to start a religious college in a small town remote from the fighting. Just why Vespasian, who became Emperor shortly afterwards, agreed to so bizarre a request in the middle of a brutal war will never be known. But Rabbi Yohanaan ben Zakkai did found his famous academy at Yavneh. From that new beginning, Judaism developed into a progressive and universal religion, no longer dependent on the Temple and the Holy Land for its continuation.

And that was just as well, for conditions in the Holy Land never completely recovered after the war, though they did improve for a while. The next major setback occurred in the year 132 C.E., when the Jews under their messianic leader Bar Kochba again rose up in furious rebellion and were again vanquished by the power of Rome. A period of harsh repression followed the defeat of that revolt; but better times came later, during the long and relatively peaceful patriarchate of Rabbi Judah the Prince, who was a personal friend of the Roman Emperor Marcus Aurelius. Rabbi Judah, in his Mishnah, for the very first time sifted and committed to writing the almost incoherent mass of oral law and tradition which had accumulated over the ages. This formed the core of both the Palestinian Talmud and the Babylonian Talmud.

The death of Rabbi Judah in about the year 220 precipitated the decline of the Holy Land as the prime centre of Jewish learning. Mesopotamia then gradually took over as the religious and cultural centre of the Jewish people, a position which it continued to occupy without challenge for the next seven hundred years.

PLATE II
Ivory pomegranate
Inscribed in ancient Hebrew script 'Belonging to the Temple, Holy to the Priests'. This may have been the tip of a sceptre used by the priests, and is probably the only surviving fragment from Solomon's Temple (8th century B.C.E.).

Babylon and Baghdad

J ews had first been deported to Babylon by King Nebuchadnezzar in the year 598 B.C.E., some eight hundred or so years before the death of Rabbi Judah the Prince. Advised by the prophet Jeremiah to work for the welfare of the country of their captivity and settle down and increase in number, many did just that. Though some of the exiles had returned to Zion to restore their mother country, others remained behind and built up the leading community of the Jewish dispersion.

After the first bitterness, the deportees were treated with tolerance by their new masters. Eventually they were even able to exercise a degree of local autonomy. The captive King Jehoiachin of Judah was released from prison in the year 561 B.C.E. and raised to a position of dignity in Babylon — exalted above all the other exiled kings there. And there is evidence to suggest that some of the sons of the Jewish nobility were groomed for service at the Babylonian court. The family and clan structure of the exiles was preserved; and communal leaders, known as the Elders of the Exile, maintained traditional authority.

Mesopotamia had by then become the core of the mighty Persian Empire which included Egypt. Its capital city, Babylon — with the massive walls, high towers and rectangular grid of streets revealed by the archaeologists — must have been the very centre of the world.

A fascinating glimpse into the lives of those early exiles was provided by the discovery of the records — written on clay tablets and stored in huge earthenware jars sealed with bitumen — of what must have been a leading Jewish business venture of the time. Founded in 587 B.C.E. by an exile from Jerusalem, the firm of Murashu and Sons lasted for at least one hundred and fifty years. Its head office was in Nippur and it claimed to have branches everywhere. It was an international bank which also dealt with personal loans at the then prevailing rate of interest of twenty per cent. The bank itself held the securities of those imprisoned for debt. It handled insurance and all kinds of legal transactions. Amongst the many deeds discovered was the conveyance of a large herd of cattle from a Jew to a Babylonian. Another was a twenty-year guarantee from two jewellers that the emerald would not fall out of a ring they had just sold to a customer.

On the whole, conditions for the Jews remained favourable throughout the centuries, enabling the community to strike deep roots in its adopted land and perform useful service throughout the Empire. Persian tolerance of the Jews and their religion is illustrated by a surviving letter of instruction to the Jewish garrison of Elephantine (Aswan) in Upper Egypt, instructing how Passover of the year 419 B.C.E. was to be celebrated. Though the letter was actually signed by Hananiah, Agent for Jewish affairs attached to the Persian governor of Egypt, it was issued in the name of King Darius II.

By the time of the Bar Kochba revolt of 132, the Persian Empire had been replaced by the Parthian Empire. The Jewish community had become largely self-governing, with its own courts of law and central administration. At its head was the Resh Galuta (Head of the Exile, Exilarch, or more grandly, Prince of the Captivity), always chosen from descendants of the

10 Rabbi Ashi teaching at the Academy of Sura in Babylonia
It was Rabbi Ashi (c. 335-427 C.E.) who began the monumental task of editing the Babylonian Talmud.
Detail from a modern ceramic relief.

11 A Persian Archer
Glazed brick panel from the palace of King
Artaxerxes II (404–359 B.C.E.) at Susa.

royal House of David. Such was the respect shown to the Resh Galuta that when he was 'called' to the reading of the Torah in synagogue, the scroll was brought to him instead of his having to go to the reading desk.

There is a rabbinic tradition to the effect that the office of Exilarch existed from the earliest days of the captivity, starting with King Jehoiachin; but there is no independent confirmation. The first documentary evidence of the existence of an Exilarch comes from the second century of this era. The Exilarch was sometimes accorded semi-royal honours by the kings of the country; and he governed the secular affairs of the community. Until the death of Rabbi Judah the Prince, the Babylonian community always looked to the rabbis of the Holy Land for its religious leadership.

Little is known about the culture of the mass of the people, mostly engaged in agriculture and trade; but we do have some evidence of an established Jewish nobility, well assimilated to the style and manners of the local aristocracy. Prominent Jews also participated in international commerce, particularly in the lucrative silk trade between China and Roman Empire.

Refugees from Judea were eagerly welcomed by the Jewish community. Those with learning were recruited into its courts and administration; and former pupils of Rabbi Judah the Prince founded religious academies near Babylon at Sura, Nehardea and Pumbeditha. The veritable explosion of Jewish learning that followed was centred on those famous schools. It was in them that the Babylonian Talmud, the underlying structure of modern Judaism, was compiled and written down between the years 200 and 500.

The rapid decline of the Jewish institutions of Roman Palestine from the early years of the third century did not leave an irreplaceable void; for the leadership of world Jewry was simply transferred to the worthy hands of the by then ancient community of exiles in Babylon — where it remained until the rise of new centres of Jewish learning and culture in North Africa and Europe.

The Jewish community of Mesopotamia was already well over a thousand years old when, in the seventh century, the Arabs burst out of Arabia with tremendous vigour. One result of their spectacular swathe of conquest, stretching from Spain to the borders of India, was that the great majority of the Jews found themselves living in an united Islamic world.

Baghdad, close to the site of ancient Babylon, became the seat of the Caliphs in the year 762. It reached the peak of its prosperity under the rule of Harun ar-Rashid in the early years of the following century when the city attracted to itself many of the riches and much of the learning of the known world. As described by travellers from comparatively barbarous Europe, it must have been truly splendid — with its pleasure gardens, peacock-blue tiled mosques and ornate buildings. It was also a great centre of commerce as well as of scholarship, science and the arts. For a time, Baghdad was unequalled in its wealth and culture.

After a decline because of persecution immediately following the Arab conquest of the eighth century, the condition of the Jewish population of Mesopotamia soon improved. The heads of the two great centres of Jewish

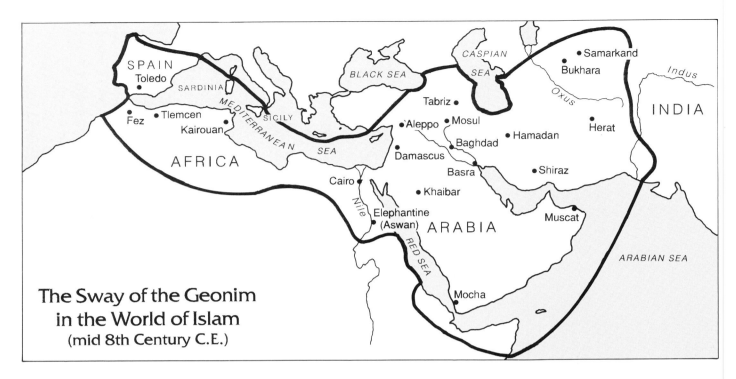

The Sway of the Geonim
in the World of Islam
(mid 8th Century C.E.)

learning, the colleges of Sura and Pumbeditha, were each addressed as Gaon (Excellency). The Geonim (plural of Gaon) helped the Exilarch to govern the community.

Because of the importance of Baghdad, the authority of the Geonim was accepted without question in all the lands conquered by Islam, from India in the East to Spain in the West. Copies of the Talmud were despatched to Jewish communities as far away as Spain; and scholars flocked to Sura and Pumbeditha from many distant places. The first legal codes to aid understanding and observance were developed in Baghdad and circulated; and the first complete prayer books were prepared specially for Jewish communities in Spain and Cairo.

Sa'adia ben Yusef was born in Cairo in 882. Summoned to Baghdad to become Gaon of the academy of Sura, he soon proved to be as independent of mind as he was brilliant as a scholar. He disagreed with the Exilarch on an important matter of principle; and, unlike the Gaon of Pumbeditha, he refused to be cowed. Sa'adia was sacked by the Exilarch; and he promptly retaliated by deposing the Exilarch in favour of his younger brother. Though this painful conflict — so typical of Jewish communal behaviour throughout the ages — was resolved eventually, his period of forced retirement enabled Sa'adia to concentrate on his writing.

In many ways the greatest of the Geonim, Sa'adia resumed the development of Jewish philosophy from where it had been left by Philo of Alexandria on his death in the year 50. In his books, Sa'adia attempted to persuade the doubters of his age that the validity of divinely revealed religious truth can be confirmed by the exercise of pure reason — also God-given. To him, there was no contradiction between revelation and reason. Both come from God.

Perhaps an even more important achievement of the Geonic period was the development of that method of extending the religious learning of the Talmud which is still in use today. The Geonim enlarged understanding of their faith by means of a long series of reasoned judgements on law and practice. These were called Responsa — for each one was written in response to a query from a Jewish scholar, sometimes from a far distant country.

The Babylonian academies began to decline after the death of Sa'adia in 942; and Baghdad's position of pre-eminence in Jewish scholarship passed to rising new centres of learning elsewhere. However, the material well-being of Mesopotamia's Jews continued almost undiminished until the country was devastated by Mongol invaders in the thirteenth century. The subsequent history of its Jewish community is traced in Parts Two and Three of this book.

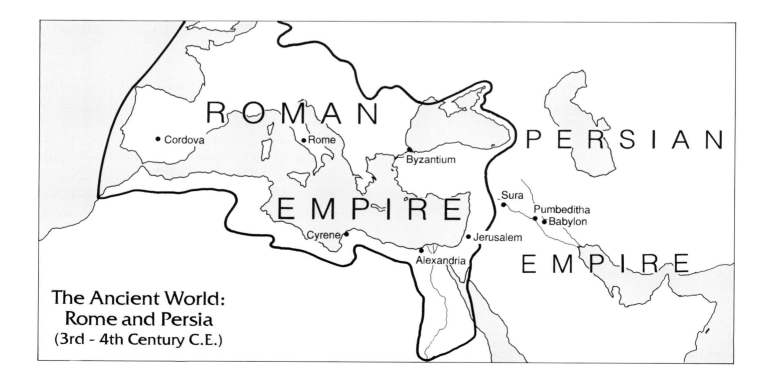

**The Ancient World:
Rome and Persia**
(3rd - 4th Century C.E.)

The rise of the Ashkenazi tradition

Though religious rulings from Babylon eventually came to be accepted as binding by all Jews everywhere, scholastic activity did not cease abruptly in the Land of Israel after the rise of the Babylonian academies. Its heroic rabbis laboured on for as long as they could. Despite relentless Christian persecution, they managed to complete their own masterwork, the Palestinian Talmud, about a century before its longer and more authoritative Babylonian counterpart.

In Roman times, the Jews of Palestine naturally gravitated westwards towards Europe — for Babylon and the East were then in the hands of Rome's great enemy, the Persian Empire; and something like an 'iron curtain' divided the two rival spheres of influence. Later, in the Islamic era, the Jews of Babylon readily travelled backwards and forwards along the established trade routes within the Islamic world — which included North Africa and Spain; but Christian Europe was still remote because of its alien rule and culture.

The Jews of Northern Europe, who had originated in the Roman Empire, naturally adopted Palestinian customs and attitudes where those differed from the Babylonian. Those around the shores of the Mediterranean remained loyal to their own Mesopotamian heritage with which they were in close contact. In some places, such as Egypt, tensions between the rival Babylonian and Palestinian traditions led to the establishment of separate congregations, each with its own synagogue.

The final split into distinct traditions occurred in Ashkenaz — the Rhine Valley and Northern France. There, at the edge of Christian Europe, the Exilarchs and Geonim of Babylon were far distant. Though communication did take place from time to time, no real leadership could be derived from the far-away heart of the Islamic world. Also, the lack of a local Jewish aristocracy with ready access to the Christian rulers caused a vacuum in the secular as well as in the religious direction of the community.

It was in the city of Mainz that an independent intellectual leadership arose for the first time in Christian Europe. Great luminaries such as Rabbenu Gershom of Mainz (c. 960-1028) — called 'the Light of the Exile' — and several of his contemporaries laid the foundations for what developed into the Ashkenazi branch of Judaism. They achieved this by sheer force of personality and by the authority that flowed naturally from their scholarship. Rabbi Gershom was followed by an even more brilliant scholar, Rabbi Shelomo Itzhaki — 'Rashi'; and from that time on the new path was firmly established.

The leadership in Ashkenaz still accepted the authority of the Babylonian Talmud; but it looked back more directly to the Land of Israel as the source of many of its traditions. Nor were its rabbis afraid to strike out on their own. Rabbenu Gershom, for example, issued the famous ruling that departed from Talmudic law by forbidding polygamy — but only to Ashkenazim of course, for Sephardim lived in Islamic lands where limited polygamy was sanctioned. In similar manner, he ruled that no woman could be divorced from her husband without her consent.

Though there are only small differences in the principal prayers of the

Ashkenazi and Sephardi rites, Ashkenazi prayer books depend heavily on the poetry of Kallir and others who were active in Palestine in the sixth and seventh centuries. They ignore completely the compositions of the poets of the Spanish Golden Age, such as Ibn Gabirol and Yehuda Halevi, which so enrich the Sephardi liturgy.

Migrating Ashkenazi Jews carried their culture with them into Central Europe. Jews were then invited by Polish kings to colonise the empty lands in the East. They enjoyed their own Golden Age of learning and culture in Poland and Lithuania between the twelfth and the seventeenth centuries, by which time the Ashkenazi brand of Judaism had become the norm in most of Europe except for the Mediterranean basin. It later spread further east to Russia and then west to the Americas.

The attitudes and traditions of Ashkenazi Jews were forged first in the cramped and hostile environment of Roman Palestine, and then under the harshly repressive regimes of medieval Christianity.

Sephardim, on the other hand, developed their way of life in the comparative freedom and prosperity of Babylon, and then later under the sometimes persecuting but more usually benevolent rule of Islam. Rarely excluded from participation in the affairs of their host countries, they were able to accommodate their own intense Jewish consciousness to the intellectual, cultural and political activities of their neighbours.

This ease and breadth of living became the hallmark of the Sephardim. It resulted in greater leniency and tolerance in Halacha (Jewish 'law') than that of the Ashkenazim; but it also contributed to their eventual decline.

A good example of this difference in emphasis is the famous ruling of Abba Arika (175-247), known simply as 'Rav', that 'The law of the land is the law' — meaning that Jews are obliged to obey the laws of their particular countries of residence. This appeared in the Babylonian Talmud; but, significantly, not in the Palestinian Talmud. In other words, the Sephardim were influenced by the good relations that often existed between Jew and gentile in their own experience, while the Ashkenazim had no choice other than to react to the prevailing hostility which surrounded them. This fundamental difference in attitude can best be expressed by the two words 'accommodation' and 'confrontation'.

The preoccupation of Sephardim with secular pursuits prevented them from spending as much time as Ashkenazim in the study of the Talmud. Hence the Spanish period saw a rapid development of the codification of Jewish law, designed as an alternative to the vast and unsystematic legal structure of the Talmud. The codification was both accurate and precise — though always biased towards the opinion of Sephardi scholars. This clear-cut method persisted throughout the centuries. It became a characteristic of later Sephardi Responsa, which rarely indulged in the hair-splitting arguments common to rabbis of German and East-European origin.

Spain

The Jewish communities of North Africa, Spain and Christian Europe gradually assumed the mantle of leadership that slipped from that of Mesopotamia.

But it was in Spain that Jewish experience of exile acquired a new dimension. Jews had first come to Spain with the Romans. Some thought themselves descended from captives taken by Titus in his sack of Jerusalem in the year 70; but others ascribed the origin of their community to very much earlier settlement. The Jews continued to live in peace under the Visigoths, who succeeded the Romans, until after their conversion from the Arian to the Roman Catholic form of Christianity early in the seventh century.

The beginning of what later historians described as 'The First Evil' occurred in 616, when all Jews were ordered to become Christians or submit to the confiscation of their property and expulsion from the country. Many thousands succumbed and accepted baptism — but they became Christians in name only and lost no opportunity to revert openly to Judaism as soon as circumstances allowed.

It was not surprising therefore that the Jews warmly welcomed the Arab invaders who crossed into Spain in 711. They helped them wrest control of the cities from the Christians, and held them safe for the Arabs afterwards.

Once Spain was securely incorporated into the Islamic world, it did not take long for its Jews to establish close contact with their brethren in Baghdad. Books and scholars, ideas and inspiration, all rapidly flowed into Jewish Spain as they had already into North Africa. Spain soon became an integral branch of the Babylonian tradition, then still under the direction of the Geonim.

The Legend of the Four Captives, which circulated in the Middle Ages, illustrates well the transfer of scholars from Baghdad to North Africa and Spain. According to this story, four rabbis on a mission to collect funds for the Babylonian academies were captured by pirates after their ship had set sail from Bari in Southern Italy on one leg of their voyage. The rabbis were ransomed by the Jewish communities of Alexandria (Egypt), Kairouan (Tunisia) and Cordova (Spain) — where each became the respected head of the community. (The identity of the fourth rabbi and his place of ransom was not related).

Spanish Jews participated to the full in the flowering of Arabic learning and culture that followed the conquest; and the Jewish community of Mohammedan Spain became the largest and most influential in Europe. Its leaders contributed much to the government and prosperity of the state; and its scholars, renowned for their piety and learning, took over the leadership of the Jewish world. It was indeed a Golden Age.

The very basis of Jewish life changed dramatically for the worse in 1148 when fanatical rulers from North Africa, who had been invited into Spain to check Christian attempts to re-conquer the North of the country, reversed the previous attitude of tolerance and offered all non-believers the stark choice of Islam or the sword. Large numbers were massacred or sold as

12 Detail
A capital in the Toledo Synagogue
(founded in 1203).

slaves. Others escaped by accepting Islam, by moving elsewhere in the peninsula, or by leaving for Algeria and other places overseas.

Like their forbears in Visigothic Spain, the new converts mostly cast off their assumed Islamic disguise as soon as they could, and were re-admitted to the Jewish fold. The most famous of these Anusim (Compelled Ones) was Rabbi Maimon ben Yusef, father of Maimonides, who fled from Cordova to Morocco with his family, where they were compelled to live for a time as outward Mohammedans.

The Christians, in their gradual re-conquest of Spain, did not at first differentiate between Arabs and Jews. They treated them both as enemies and burned down mosques and synagogues with equal enthusiasm. However, experience soon tempered the initial distrust as the rough, uneducated Christian rulers came to appreciate the valuable contribution that talented and learned Jews could make to their kingdoms.

The Jewish communities of Christian Spain then entered into a second, though lesser, Golden Age — a period that was looked back to with aching nostalgia in the centuries that followed, and which is still remembered today.

The Jews continued to govern themselves in separate communities under Chief Rabbis and Chief Justices appointed by the Spanish kings; and devoted much energy to developing their own religion and culture. None of this however inhibited them from entering wholeheartedly into the secular life around them. Their leaders served as courtiers, financiers, administrators, diplomats and physicians to the kings of the states into which Christian Spain was divided. The Jewish middle class earned its living from the land, from commerce and from manufacture; and lower down the social scale, Jews worked as skilled craftsmen and artisans.

The crowning glory of the Jewish community in its Golden Age was the contribution of its rabbis, scholars, philosophers and poets. Proficient in Arabic and other languages, Jewish scholars served as a channel through which the civilisation of the Arabs and that of the classical world before them, was transmitted to Christian Europe, just emerging from the Dark Ages.

The superb secular work of the Spanish Hebrew poets never lost its fascination for later generations; and is still being translated and published in other languages. Also their sublime liturgical compositions, many of which are now incorporated in Sephardi prayer books, remain unsurpassed.

Jewish philosophy too reached its zenith in the Spanish Golden Age. The leaders of the school — Solomon ibn Gabirol, Bahya ibn Paquda, Moses and Abraham ben Ezra, Moses Maimonides, Hasdai Crescas and Joseph Albo — were universal men, well versed in most branches of secular and religious knowledge. The philosophical method they developed, with its systematic approach to the codification of Jewish law and practice, enhanced the understanding of Judaism. However, philosophy had little direct long-term influence; and its masters are now remembered and admired more for their work in the field of Halacha (the laws and observances of Judaism), and for their poetry and Bible commentaries, than for mighty edifices of logical thought.

The same cannot be said for the task of codifying the Talmud, which is second in authority only to the Bible. The Talmud is a vast rambling compendium of human wisdom and knowledge, embracing subjects as diverse as religion, civil and criminal law, morals, medicine and astronomy. The Babylonian sages who compiled it had not been exposed to Greek influence; and they set little value on logical order or on clarity of expression. As a result, the Talmud is unsystematic in its arrangement, lacking ordered sequence. The same subject, for example, can be referred to in several different and sometimes unexpected places, and without cross-reference. Moreover it contains a bewildering welter of conflicting opinions — which the reader is left to sort out for himself without guidance. To make understanding more difficult, the deliberations of its many authors are expressed with extreme brevity, almost in a kind of shorthand. The Talmud cannot be mastered without the help of skilled teachers, and even then not before years of devoted study.

The process of attempting to summarise the contents of the Talmud for practical application started in the Baghdad of the Geonim. The first complete Code to appear outside Mesopotamia was written in Morocco by Rabbi Isaac of Fez (1013-1103), known as Alfasi. He simplified the Talmud by eliminating all argument and opinions with which he disagreed, and managed to produce a succinct summary of the law.

The work of codification was taken up eagerly by Jewish scholars in Spain, whose approach was dictated by the principles of reason. Rabbi Moses ben Maimon, known as the 'Rambam' to the Jews and Maimonides to the outside world, was the outstanding codifier of the time and one of the most brilliant men of his age. He fled with his family from persecution in Spain and finally settled in Cairo, where he became a famous physician and the head of its Jewish Community. An account of his life in Cairo is contained in the chapter on Egypt in Part Two of this book. Maimonides's monumental code, the Mishneh Torah, one thousand chapters long, was completed before 1184. Written with deep religious feeling and a clarity unusual for the period, it offered its readers an authoritative summary of developed Jewish law.

Another influential code was written by Rabbi Asher ben Yehiel (1250–1327), known as the 'Rosh' and also as Asheri — an Ashkenazi scholar who had escaped from Germany and settled in Toledo. His son, Rabbi Jacob ben Asher, also produced a valuable code called the Tur, after the rows of gems on the breastplate of the High Priest.

The most influential code of all was the Shulhan Aruch (The Prepared Table), first printed in Venice in 1565. Its author, Joseph Caro, was one of those forced to leave Spain in 1492. He finally settled in Safed in the Holy Land, where he wrote his masterwork, Beth Yosef, after twenty years of intensive study and comparison of previous codes. The Shulhan Aruch was written as a precis of that book. An Ashkenazi rabbi, Moses Isserles of Cracow, then prepared a Mappah (Tablecloth) for the Prepared Table, setting out all the Ashkenazi variations to Caro's rulings. The Mappah was printed alongside Caro's original text; and this modified version very soon became the definitive guide to Jewish law and practice that it still remains.

Kabbalah, or Jewish mysticism, was another activity which flourished in the heady religious and intellectual atmosphere of Spain. Comparatively few Jews indulged in actual mystical practice aimed at direct personal contact with God; and the main thrust of the movement was directed to attempting to explain the mystery of the hidden nature of the Divine and its relationship to man.

Kabbalah struck deep roots in the minds of Sephardi religious thinkers; and Kabbalistic theories rapidly developed new profundity and coherence. They came to encompass the very nature of existence and sought to explain how the hidden, unknown and unknowable God manifests himself in the world of creation — how the gulf is bridged between the Infinite and the finite. In these new theories, the imperfections of this world are attributed to a fundamental 'flaw' that followed the last act of the creative process, shattering the unity of God in his creation. Man's primary task is to correct that 'flaw'.

A view of existence is advanced in which each individual and the whole community of Israel are protagonists in a cosmic struggle between the forces of good and the forces of evil. Every Jew, through his actions and prayers, has a part to play in the divine purpose of hastening the advent of the Messianic Age and restoring the original harmony of creation.

The appearance of the Zohar (Book of Splendour) at the end of the thirteenth century was the greatest achievement of Spanish Kabbalah. Copies of the text were first distributed by Moses de Leon of Castile, who claimed to have discovered an original manuscript written by Simon bar Yochai in the second century. Some modern scholars believe that Moses de Leon wrote the book himself; others that he compiled it from a variety of more ancient sources. The traditional view however traces the substance and ideas of the work back to mystical doctrines revealed to Simon bar Yochai.

The Zohar takes the form of commentaries on parts of the Torah, the Song of Songs and the Book of Ruth. It deals with the nature of the Divine, with man's soul, with the problem of good and evil, and with the final Redemption. Knowledge of the Zohar spread steadily throughout the entire Jewish world during the three hundred years after its first appearance, until it came to occupy an unique position, ranking close to the Talmud in its influence and authority.

In Spain — both Mohammedan and Christian — Jews, for the first time in their history, managed to develop a genuine synthesis between their own religiously-based culture and the outside world around them. That synthesis was unique in the history of their exile. But the very success of the endeavour to live in both worlds nourished the seeds of its own destruction. The sight of Jews enjoying all the fruits of secular Spanish life, whilst at the same time maintaining a separate identity as resident aliens living under their own law, excited the envy of the less fortunate of their Christian fellow subjects. And for many Jews, peace and prosperity had lessened their sense of exile and their attachment to the faith of their ancestors.

The disturbance of the Crusades in France and the rest of Europe had its repercussions in Spain, especially in the North. Sporadic outbreaks of popular violence took place with increasing frequency and severity; and in 1328, for example, many Jewish communities in Navarre were massacred.

The Golden Age ended finally in 1391 when the pent-up jealousy of Christian mobs, whipped to fever pitch by determined priests, expressed itself in an outburst of public fury that at a stroke nullified the progress of

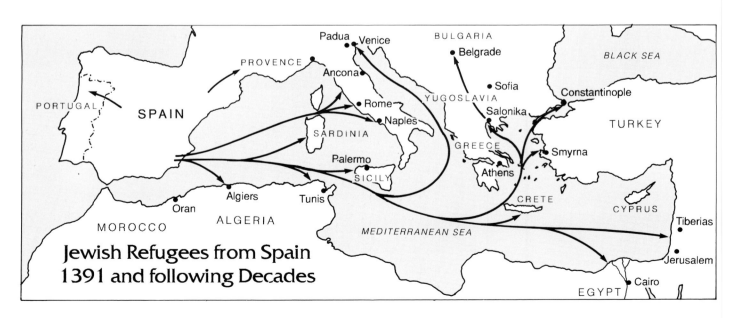

Jewish Refugees from Spain
1391 and following Decades

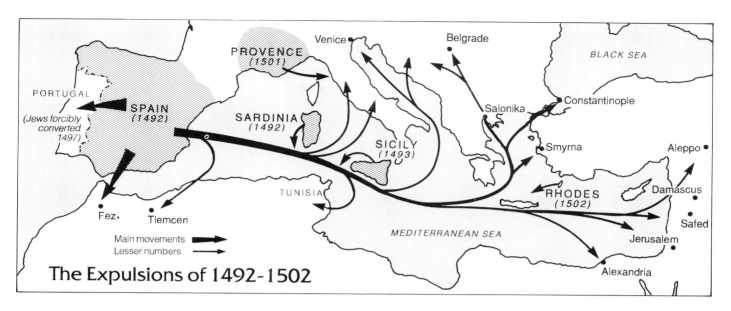

The Expulsions of 1492-1502

Main movements ➡
Lesser numbers →

centuries. The first pogrom broke out in Seville where, to quote a contemporary chronicler —

On 4th June thirteen hundred and ninety one, the Lord bent his bow like an enemy against the community of Seville... They set fire to the gates of the Jewish quarter and killed many of its people; and some of the women and children were sold as slaves... Some died to sanctify God's name... but many others violated the holy covenant and changed their religion to escape.

Jews were then massacred throughout Christian Spain and, one by one, their centres of population were destroyed.

Their persecutors offered the Jews the choice of baptism or death; and very large numbers chose to accept the Cross in preference to dying as martyrs — a few willingly, some with reluctance and most in sheer desperation. One third of all Spanish Jews perished or fled overseas in the decades that followed the first pogrom of 1391. A further third converted to Christianity; and only one third survived as openly professing Jews.

The glory and pride of the community departed, never to return. But the remaining Jews of the Iberian peninsula struggled on after the catastrophe, sustaining further losses through massacre and conversion, and also experiencing minor successes from time to time.

Finally, all openly professing Jews were expelled from Spain in 1492. At the end many opted for the Cross rather than leave their adopted homeland. It is estimated that fewer than two hundred thousand Jews actually quit Spain in 1492 — the remaining survivors of that once great community being lost to the sword or to the Cross.

Typical perhaps was the behaviour of the two most prominent leaders of the community, one secular and the other religious. Don Abraham Señeor, Chief Justice of the Jews of Castile, was the courtier who had helped arrange the marriage between Ferdinand and Isabella which united Aragon and Castile and precipitated the decree of expulsion. Señeor accepted baptism — with the King, the Queen and the Cardinal of Spain standing as his godparents. On the other hand, his deeply religious and learned colleague

in government, the great financier Don Isaac Abrabanel, had no hesitation in turning his back on Spain and going into exile.

It would be hard to exaggerate the impact on the entire Jewish people of the expulsion from Spain. The sudden end of the greatest, the best established and the most culturally assimilated Jewish community of Europe in the Middle Ages was a tragedy that seemed comparable only to the loss of their original homeland. In 1492, on the very anniversary of the destruction of the Temple by the Romans, the shattered and bewildered Spanish Jews entered into a further and deeper exile. Most found refuge in Portugal, only to meet an even worse fate in that country five years later. At roughly the same time, Jews were also expelled from Sicily, Sardinia and Provence.

A few exiles found temporary refuge in Naples and Venice. Others fled to Morocco, to other parts of North Africa, to Venetian colonies such as Crete and Cyprus, and above all to Turkey and the Ottoman Empire.

The refugees carried the culture of their beloved Spain with them into exile. They and their descendants long continued to cherish its customs, its music and its food. Proudly bearing Spanish or Portuguese family names, they carefully preserved the medieval Spanish language of their forbears and transformed it into Ladino — which still survives as a spoken language, though now only to a rather limited extent.

An epilogue. In October 1990 Crown Prince Don Felipe, son of King Juan Carlos of Spain, presented the Concorde Prize of the Prince of Asturias Foundation to a delegation of world Sephardi leaders. In his address, the prince expressed his deep regret and apologies for the actions of his ancestors in expelling the Jews from Spain. He praised the Sephardim for having spread Spanish culture in all the generations since the Expulsion; and voiced the hope that Spain would once again become a meeting place of the Spanish and Jewish traditions.

Though Spain had done much to protect Sephardi Jews from Hitler's clutches during the Second World War of 1939-45, as indeed had Portugal, almost five hundred years had passed before those royal words of apology and reconciliation. There is however no mistaking the genuiness of the retraction, nor the very real warmth of the resulting reconciliation.

Portugal

Significant numbers of Jews were living in Portugal as early as the year 300, long before the emergence of a separate Portuguese nation. It was not until the reign of King Affonso III in the twelfth century that Portugal attained full independence as a sovereign state.

Portugal's Jews enjoyed internal self-government under the rule of a Jewish court official known as the Arraby Mor (Chief Rabbi), who was appointed by the King. The community was divided into seven districts, each with its own judge selected by the Arraby Mor and facilities to hear civil and criminal cases. The selection of local rabbis was left to the people; but the Crown paid all salaries and could veto any appointment. The Elders who governed day-to-day life in each community were also elected locally.

The Jews prospered. By the fifteenth century, much of the country's trade was in Jewish hands; and the closeness of the Arraby Mor to the court — he often served as the King's treasurer — gave Jews great political influence.

As in Spain, envy and jealousy increased over the years and Jews became more and more unpopular. Heavier taxes were imposed on them as well as humiliating disabilities, such as having to wear special badges on their clothing. Riots ensued; and in the Lisbon pogrom of 1449, a number of Jews were murdered by the mob intent on sacking their homes.

Nevertheless, conditions seemed less hopeless than those in Spain. Many Spanish New Christians moved to Portugal to escape the attentions of the Inquisition. And after the expulsion of 1492, over one hundred thousand Spanish Jews sought refuge across the Portuguese frontier.

The Spanish refugees were admitted after paying a heavy entry tax. One very large group, with little ready cash, was given permission to stay for eight months only — during which time King John II undertook to arrange the necessary shipping for them to leave.

The King broke his promise and many of the group were not able to embark before the deadline expired. They were then arrested and enslaved by royal command. In one horrific episode, seven hundred children were separated by force from their parents and sent to colonise the wild African island of St. Thomas, where most of them perished.

The King died and was succeeded by Manoel the Fortunate, who promptly reversed his predecessor's policy and freed the newly created slaves. In 1496 however, the prospect of marriage to a daughter of the Catholic monarchs of Spain, Ferdinand and Isabella, caused King Manoel to change course once more and to devise a radical new policy.

In November 1496, all Portuguese Jews were given ten months notice to wind up their affairs and leave the country for good. In the event though, the Jews were actually subjected to a far crueller fate; and their expulsion never took place.

Guided by an apostate Jew, the King proceeded with cunning and ruthless efficiency. Despite opposition by the Council of State and leading churchmen, royal orders were suddenly issued requiring all Jewish children between the ages of four and fourteen to be presented for baptism the following Sunday. Those who did not appear were seized and marched to the nearest church. The King's officials were not too scrupulous about the age limit; and youths of twenty were also forcibly baptised.

Manoel's order applied to all Jews, regardless of position or rank; and Judah Abrabanel, the leading physician of the age, lost his son in that manner. According to the account given by Cecil Roth in his 'A History of the Marranos', scenes of indescribable horror accompanied the enforcement of the king's decree. Children were torn from the arms of their parents and distributed to Christian families as far away from their original homes as possible. Some Jews killed their own children rather than submit them for baptism. One such was the eminent Spanish scholar Isaac ben Abraham Zachin, who despatched himself and his children for the Sanctification of the Name. Even some Christians were moved by the plight of the unfortunate Jews. The terrible scenes he had witnessed were vividly recalled by Bishop Coutinho more than thirty years later:

> I saw many persons dragged by the hair to the font... Sometimes I saw a father, his head covered in sign of grief and pain, lead his son to the font, protesting and calling God to witness that they wished to die together in the law of Moses... Yet more terrible things that were done with them did I witness with my own eyes.

As the deadline for departure approached, about twenty thousand surviving Jews were concentrated in Lisbon. They were imprisoned without food and drink for long periods, while priests endeavoured to persuade them to embrace the Cross. The weaker ones soon gave way under pressure. Much of the remaining resistance crumbled after all the captives were declared slaves of the King. The process was not a gentle one, with an unknown number of Jews dying as martyrs for their faith. In the end, the remaining Jews had holy water sprinkled over them en-masse and were declared Christian, whether they liked it or not.

A remnant of the leadership led by Rabbi Simon Maimi, the last Arrabi Mor, continued openly to defy the triumphant priests. They were partly walled-up in a prison cell where Rabbi Maimi and two others died after a week of incarceration. Fewer than a dozen survivors were finally released by King Manoel and transported to North Africa in 1497.

Thus ended the smaller of the two Jewish communities of the Iberian Peninsula. But it was certainly not the end of the Portuguese Jews, who still had a strange but very significant part to play in the subsequent history of their people.

PLATE IV
The Arrabi Mor (Chief Rabbi of Portugal)
This detail from the painting 'The Veneration of St.
Vincent' by Nuno Goncalves, shows members of the
Court praying before the patron saint of Portugal.

The Marranos of Spain and Portugal

The forced conversion of Jews to Christianity or Islam was not new to Spain when that process started afresh in 1391. It had occurred before, under the rule of the Visigoths in the seventh century, and then again in 1148 when Mohammedan Spain fell under the sway of the fanatical Almohads from North Africa. In both periods, the 'Anusim' (Compelled Ones) were notoriously disloyal to their new religion and openly reverted to Judaism as soon as they could, whether in Spain or abroad.

In the fourteenth century, Jewish converts to Christianity were officially called Nuevos Christianos (New Christians), or simply 'conversos' (converts). They were also known as 'marranos' (pigs) by the coarser of their new brethren in Christ — a term chosen, no doubt, to indicate the contempt and even hatred with which they were regarded. It is important to appreciate that the New Christians included sincere converts within their ranks, as well as those who were reluctant but basically indifferent. But most were secret Jews who maintained their old faith in private and yearned to reassert their true identity. It is these we now describe as Marranos, transforming the word into a name of honour.

Many conversos, and especially those who had accepted the religion of Jesus with willingness, lost no time in making the most of the opportunities created by their baptism. Also quick to benefit were those who had been convinced by philosophy to distrust all religion and who felt that they had simply exchanged one cloak of superstition for another.

Freed at last from the restrictive shackles of a hated minority faith, New Christians quickly rose to occupy many of the top positions of Church and state. Some married into the aristocracy and penetrated the highest ranks of Spanish society. Eventually it was claimed that as many as one in three of the inhabitants of several cities of Southern Spain were of New Christian descent; and few noble families in certain areas could assert with truth that no Jewish blood flowed in their veins.

Some conversos went so far as to spearhead attacks on their former religion. But many, whilst punctiliously observing the outward ceremonies of the Catholic Church, remained Jewish in their hearts and in their private lives. They attached themselves to churches frequented by their own kind and confessed only to Marrano priests. They baptised their children; but then hurried home to wash the stain of baptism from their heads. They observed the Sabbath, the Jewish festivals and the dietary laws to the limited extent possible without arousing suspicion; and even the Church at first acquiesced in their aversion to eating pork. The Marranos gathered for a kind of abbreviated Jewish worship in the security of their own homes and in secret synagogues. They continued to maintain contact with openly professing Jews and, to some extent, married within their own group.

The conspicuous worldly success of the Marranos aroused the envy and hatred of the populace — for it was common knowledge that their Christianity was only assumed, and their allegiance to the Church no more than skin-deep. Almost equally disliked were the converso intellectuals who really believed in no religion at all. This was not only a problem for Marranos and intellectuals. Sincere New Christians suffered as well, for

15 The Holy Inquisition at work
This old print shows judgement being pronounced on Judaisers by the Inquisition in the Plaza Mayor, Madrid. Those 'relaxed' by the Inquisition were invariably burned alive.

16 The Inquisition at Goa
Goa, on the west coast of India, was a province of Portugal from 1510 to 1961. An Inquisition was established in 1560 to deal with an influx of Marranos and this remained active for almost two hundred and fifty years.

14 A Portuguese Marrano

the prejudice against them was too general and too deep to admit more than a few exceptions.

The Spanish Church, and later that of Portugal, refused to accept that conversions undertaken under duress could later be repudiated. It strove hard to eradicate what it regarded as the heretical Judaising tendencies of New Christians. The Church came to regard the New Christians as a large and influential fifth column, dedicated to the subversion of its loyal following.

Concern over the problem increased with the years. In 1434, the Council of Tortosa pleaded for steps to be taken to check what it described as 'the blasphemous duplicity' of the New Christians. Fifteen years later, Toledo debarred all New Christians from holding public office or bearing testimony against Old Christians; and many highly respectable judges, Christian clerics and other officials lost their positions. Riots directed against conversos spread; and these were sometimes accompanied by massacres. More and more decrees intended to separate New Christians from public life were promulgated in different parts of Spain from 1468 onwards; and only a few of the main centres of Marrano life — notably Seville — escaped without disturbance.

This time, there was no escape for secret Jews other than in flight. Having already been baptised, they could not take that way out again. Also the Church steadfastly refused to consider them other than vile heretics if they attempted to cast off Christianity on the ground that they had been compelled to accept baptism.

In 1480 Queen Isabella established an Inquisition in Seville and gave it unfettered jurisdiction over 'heretics and their accomplices'. Many New Christians, including some of the most eminent citizens were arrested, tried and condemned to death for heresy. Six men and women were burned alive at the first Auto-da-Fé in February 1481. This was followed by many more atrocities as the whole region was gripped by an orgy of denunciation and terror. Even the bones of the dead were dug up and then publicly burned after trial. By November of the same year, almost three hundred people had been burned at the stake and one hundred more condemned to perpetual imprisonment. Large numbers who confessed their error were heavily fined, debarred from holding public office and humiliated by being made to dress in coarse garments and parade as penitents through the streets. Some were made to appear as flagellants on six successive Fridays in turn. Such ferocity on the part of the Church was unprecedented; and even the Pope wrote to Queen Isabella expressing his disapproval of the methods employed.

But the Inquisition was popular; and what is more, it was good business. Its tentacles soon spread all over the country. Many thousands fell under its sway, either losing all their property or else submitting to heavy fines. The Inquisition waxed fat on the proceeds; and there were few connected with it who did not benefit greatly.

The Holy Inquisition, with its widespread network of informers, imposed a reign of terror on the secret Jews as well as on less committed but genuine New Christians. It tracked the secret Jews relentlessly, devising ever more

JUGEMENT de L'INQUISITION dans les grande place de MADRID

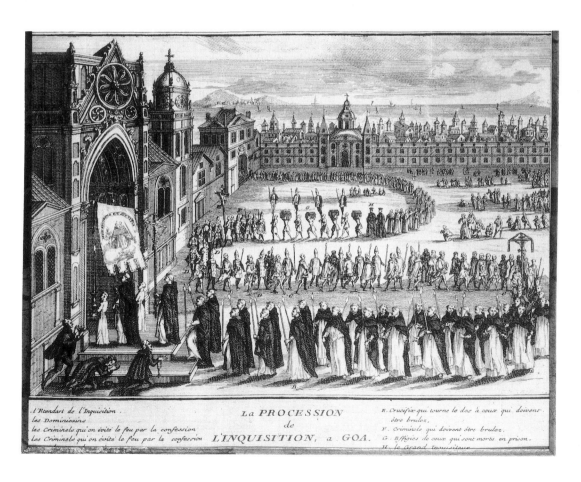

17 Auto-da-Fé
The title page of an account of the
Auto-da-Fé held in Seville in July 1722.

ingenious tests to discover them. Rooftops were scanned to see which chimneys were not smoking on Sabbaths and holydays. Even the act of changing the linen on a Friday (the eve of the Sabbath), or of turning the head to the wall in prayer at the moment of death, was sufficient to bring the heavy hand of the Inquisition to bear on the unfortunate suspects and their families. When identified, truly or otherwise, every effort was made to torture the crypto-Jews into submission; and they were put to death in large numbers.

Contrary to what might have been expected from their history, the determination of many Marranos to preserve their Jewish identity did not crumble under pressure but intensified with mounting persecution. They clung tenaciously to what they remembered of their ancestral faith, even when it had become so vestigial as to be barely recognisable. And many descendants of genuine apostates — those who had embraced Christianity of their own free will — tried hard to retrace their steps and return in secret to the religion of their people.

Many acts of great bravery were committed by victims of the Inquisition.

Quite padre que un palo a nadie salva (Take it away father for a piece of wood can save no one)

was the chilling response made by one Marrano, about to be burned to death in an Auto-da-Fé, when a priest snatched two pieces of wood from the kindling, made a rough cross and offered it to the condemned man as a last chance to save himself.

The more fortunate Spanish New Christians managed to leave the country. Their travels and subsequent history are traced later in this book.

Many Spanish New Christians moved to Portugal, where conditions were easier. In 1497 the entire surviving Jewish population of Portugal also became New Christians, having been suddenly and brutally forced to the baptismal font. These bewildered Marranos knew nothing of Christianity and cared even less for it than their Spanish brothers in misfortune. Even King Manoel recognised that by granting them a general amnesty for religious offences already committed, and immunity from investigation of matters of faith for a period of twenty years. He also strictly forbad them to leave the country without royal licence.

As in Spain, the Marranos flourished. They dominated the commercial life of the country and increasingly aroused the envy of the populace. In 1503, after a poor harvest which caused hardship, discontent against the Marranos led to a terrible massacre in Lisbon in which it is estimated that many more than two thousand New Christians were done to death.

In 1525 the swarthy, emaciated and dwarf-like David Rubeni arrived in Portugal with a warm letter of recommendation from the Pope. Though a charlatan and poseur, Rubeni seems to have been deeply religious and genuinely moved by the plight of Europe's Jews under Christian yoke. A year earlier, he had proudly ridden into the Vatican on a white horse and presented himself to Pope Clement VII as an ambassador from his brother, the king of a fabulous Jewish kingdom in Arabia which was peopled by three of the Lost Ten Tribes of Israel. Rubeni claimed to be the

18 Auto-da-Fé
The first page of the list of those "relaxed" to be burned alive at the Auto da Fe held in Seville in 1722.

commander-in-chief of a Jewish army of three hundred thousand choice warriors. He said that he had come to negotiate a treaty with the Pope by which his army would be supplied by the Christians with the firearms and cannon necessary to drive the Turks from Jerusalem. The Pope liked the idea of an anti-Turkish alliance. He received Rubeni with honour and kept him in Rome for the best part of a year before sending him on to the King of Portugal with a letter advising the King to supply Rubeni with the armaments.

King John III accepted Rubeni at face value. He received him with ceremony, not just as the emissary of a powerful foreign kingdom seeking a mutually profitable alliance, but as someone who had been highly recommended by the Pope. Rubeni was favoured with many marks of the King's personal regard; and whatever we may now think of his story, he certainly did command sufficient credibility to have convinced a pope and a king of his authenticity. A deal was struck during the year Rubeni enjoyed royal favour; and it was agreed that Portugal would provide the Jewish army with four thousand cannon and eight ships.

The Marranos of Portugal went wild with excitement. They flocked to kiss Rubeni's hand, convinced that he was either the Messiah or his forerunner. Though Rubeni did his best to remain aloof from the Marranos and dampen their excitement, the King became alarmed at the growing unrest among his New Christian subjects. When Diogo Pires — a gifted youth who was Secretary to the Royal Council and Clerk to the Appeal Court — had himself circumcised and fled the country, his worst fears seemed to have been confirmed. Negotiations were broken off and Rubeni was given two months' notice to quit the kingdom.

This episode was followed by disturbances and outbreaks of popular fury against the New Christians. King John attempted to set up an Inquisition on the Spanish model to deal with the New Christians once and for all; but his attempt was frustrated for five years by influential New Christians who paid massive bribes and engaged in intensive lobbying in Rome.

An Inquisition was finally established in 1536; but it was not until 1540 that the first Auto-da-Fé was held in Lisbon. From that time on, there was no turning back; and the New Christians of Portugal were gripped progressively by an Inquisition which pursued its aims with even more rigour and cruelty than that of Spain. The story of those Marranos who succeeded in fleeing the country is continued later in this book.

In time, the Inquisitions of both Portugal and Spain gradually lost their fervour and increasingly allowed New Christians to live their lives undisturbed. Though the Inquisitions were not actually abolished until the early years of the nineteenth century, the last converso to be burned at the stake perished in Lisbon at an Auto-da-Fé in 1775. Eventually tolerance accomplished what persecution had failed to do; and the New Christians melted away, merging into the general population.

Apart from a handful of surviving groups, the only traces of the Iberian Marranos that now remain are peculiar customs of undoubted Jewish origin, the meaning of which has long since been forgotten. Many of these survived

19 Title Page of Prayer Book
This 1687 Sephardi prayer book, printed in Amsterdam, was the first to include a special memorial prayer to be recited for Jews burned alive by the Inquisition 'Por santificamiento del nombre de Dios'.

until quite recently in parts of Spain and Portugal; and some still do today.

One such custom, described to the authors by a Majorcan, concerned his mother who always kept a side of bacon in her house — not to eat but to hang close to her window overlooking the street. A similar kind of Portuguese practice involved the lighting of a candle by the woman of the house in the cellar, or at the bottom of a deep jar, every Friday night, the eve of the Sabbath. The daughter of a good Spanish Catholic family, on learning the history of the Marranos for the first time from one of the authors, wrote that this might account for her own grandmother's seemingly eccentric, and previously inexplicable, refusal ever to do housework or listen to music on Saturdays.

The Marranos did not quite disappear from history after the abolition of the Inquisition. Some few communities survived, partly due to their own stubborn tenacity and partly because of the distrust of their supposed fellow Christians.

A few hundred of them, remembering fragments of Jewish practice and still leading furtive double lives, were discovered in a remote part of Northern Portugal in 1917; and some were helped back to the faith of their

20 The Kadoorie Synagogue of Oporto
The initiative for the erection of this synagogue, to serve those Marranos of Northern Portugal who wished to return to Judaism, was provided by Captain Barros Basto. The foundation stone was laid in 1929 and the synagogue finally opened in 1938.

22 **Captain Arthur Carlos de Barros Basto**
Captain de Barros Basto did much to rally the Marranos of Braganza, Portugal, in the 1920s and 1930s, and to bring their plight to the attention of the Jewish world.

21 **Three generations of a Marrano family**
Standing before the Ark of the Kadoorie Synagogue of Oporto, Portugal, in 1938.

ancestors. In 1989, thirty-two men of a Marrano community in Belmonte were circumcised in accordance with Jewish law, their leader declaring publicly that of several thousand Marrano families remaining in Northern Portugal, about two hundred were willing to return to Judaism. Curious too is the fact that, until the early years of this century, several thousand staunchly Roman Catholic Majorcans of converso descent were still maintaining a separate communal existence because of the inherited dislike of their neighbours.

To this day, the Spanish and Portuguese Jews of London solemnly recite the following prayer in their liturgy for Kal Nidre, the first service for the Day of Atonement:

May he who blessed our fathers, Abraham, Isaac and Jacob, Moses and Aaron, David and Solomon, bless, preserve, guard and assist all our brethren imprisoned by the Inquisition. May the King of kings bless them and make them worthy of his grace, hearken to the voice of their supplication and bring them forth from darkness to light. May such be thy divine will! and let us say, Amen.

Eventually perhaps, when Jews are no longer oppressed in any part of the world, that ancient prayer may at last be omitted.

The Redemption

The belief that God will intervene in human affairs to redeem his chosen people is deeply rooted in Jewish consciousness. Since the time of Maimonides in the twelfth century, it has been accepted as a fundamental principle of faith by all Jews, whether Sephardi or Ashkenazi. But from the destruction of the Second Temple in the year 70 C.E., much of the thought and speculation about the End of Days, and the cataclysmic events that will precede it, arose amongst followers of the Babylonian tradition.

Kabbalah, the mystical movement, took deepest root in Spain; and following the expulsion of the Jews in 1492, most of the actors in the tragic dramas of hope and disappointment associated with messianic expectation were Sephardim.

Belief in the coming of a Redeemer deepened amongst Jews during their first weary years of exile by the rivers of Babylon. The intense longing for national redemption, by a people struggling to preserve their freedom and purpose in conditions of adversity, was extended under the influence of the Hebrew Prophets to include a parallel yearning for the simultaneous redemption of all mankind. Inevitably, that event was projected into the future and viewed in terms of a culmination of human history. God would redeem Israel and the whole world at the end of time.

The prophets wrote moving descriptions of that ideal age. There was no need for speculation about the personality of the last king; for it was sufficient to know that he would be a mortal descendant of King David, a triumphant warrior who would restore Israel and then rule under the direction of the Divine Spirit. Isaiah, writing in Jerusalem in about 720 B.C.E., expounded his remarkable vision of the exiles of Israel and Judah returning to Jerusalem from the four corners of the earth, and of the gentile nations also flocking to Jerusalem to worship the one true God of Israel — and this under the rule of a king from the House of David, imbued with the spirit of the Lord and governing in peace and righteousness:

Then shall a shoot grow from the stock of Jesse
and a branch shall spring from his roots.
The spirit of the Lord shall rest upon him,
a spirit of wisdom and understanding,

Then the wolf shall live with the sheep
and the leopard lie down with the kid;
the calf and the young lion shall grow up together
and a little child shall lead them.

The word 'Messiah' (Annointed) acquired new and special significance during the era of oppressive Roman occupation of the Holy Land. It then came to be used as the title of the warrior king, descended from King David, who would be raised up by God to drive out the Romans, restore the fortunes of Israel and inaugurate the final utopian age of human history. Though Christians later attributed divine qualities to the Messiah, it must be appreciated that this was not a Jewish concept. Jews expect the Messiah to be human and mortal.

Jews never ceased to study the prophesies in their holy writings, and especially those in the Book of Daniel, in attempts to predict the actual date of the Redemption. Though repeatedly warned not to do so, few rabbis could resist the temptation of indulging in such speculation. Even Maimonides, the super-rationalist, once came close to disregarding his own advice to avoid calculating the End of Days.

A burst of messianic hope and activity followed the spectacular conquests of the Arabs that followed the death of Muhammad in the seventh century. Jews interpreted the humbling of the mighty Persian and Roman (Byzantine) Empires by the Arabs as necessary events preceding the coming of the Messiah.

In his book 'Beliefs and Opinions', Sa'adia — the great Gaon of Baghdad — summarised the beliefs of his age concerning the End of Days. After a series of catastrophic wars in which all the mighty empires of the world will be overthrown one by one, the Satan Armilus will conquer Jerusalem and drive the Jewish people out to starve in the wilderness. Only then, after the suffering has become almost intolerable, will the Messsiah appear to the well-sifted and purified remnant. He will slay the Satan Armilus, together with all the wicked of the world, and will restore the Kingdom. The righteous of all the peoples will then unite with the Jews in their worship of the one true God. Sorrow will become a thing of the past as the light of the Divine Presence shines on the Sanctuary for all to see for a period of two thousand years. Then the Day of Judgement will dawn, bringing with it the resurrection of the dead and the end of time.

As the year 950 approached, both Ashkenazi and Sephardi Jews became more and more excited that redemption was at hand. The Jews of the Rhineland even wrote to Jerusalem in 960 to inquire whether the Messiah had arrived, only to be rebuked in reply for their ignorance and credulity.

There is a strong tradition that Hasdai ibn Shaprut — the leader of Spanish Jewry and diplomatic advisor to Caliph Abdul Rahman III — in the same year sent a letter of inquiry to King Joseph of the powerful (Jewish) Khazar kingdom centred on the River Volga.

The relevant part of Hasdai's letter read as follows:-

...I ask my master the king to let me know whether there is any tradition among your people concerning the end of time for which we have been waiting these many years, and during which we have been going from one captivity to another and from one exile to another; for one must be very strong indeed not to inquire about it. How can I remain silent about the destruction of the Temple of our glory, and about the remnant of our people escaped from the sword and passed through the perils of fire and water. We who were many are now few, and are fallen from our former high estate and now dwell in exile...

Unfortunately King Joseph's reply can have afforded Hasdai very little comfort:

...our eyes are turned to the Lord our God and to the wise men of Israel in the academies of Jerusalem and Babylon, for we live very far from Zion. But we have heard that because of the sins of the people the calculations have gone astray, and we know nothing....We have nothing but the prophesy of Daniel. May the God of Israel hasten the Redemption and gather our exiled and scattered people in our lifetime and in yours.....

It was however the aftermath of the expulsion from Spain that proved most significant in the history of messianic speculation. To the bewildered exiles, and those who remained behind as reluctant New Christians, the date of the Redemption was no abstract theory but a matter of the most pressing urgency. Surely what they were enduring really were the travails prophesied to herald the coming of the Messiah — there could be no other explanation.

Also, knowledge of Kabbalah (the mystical tradition) had spread to ordinary people and gripped their imagination as never before. Kabbalah provided a complete explanation of what had happened in the world, what was happening and how it would all end. Mystical theory joined with messianic expectation after the Expulsion, one reacting to the other, to produce a climate of intense hope that was to have far-reaching consequences.

The ruin of David Rubeni's embassy to King John III of Portugal, by Diogo Pires in 1526, is described earlier in this book. Diogo was a handsome and gifted New Christian youth of good family, who had risen to become a favourite of the Portuguese Court. He must have studied Judaism and Kabbalah in secret, for Rubeni's visit caused him to become increasingly troubled by prophetic dreams connected with the Messiah and the Marranos. His visions grew in intensity after he had himself circumcised and assumed the Hebrew name of Solomon Molcho.

Molcho fled from Portugal and lived for a while in Salonica, where he was warmly welcomed by its Kabbalistic scholars. He consolidated his reputation for wisdom and prophetic insight and attracted a large circle of students and admirers. The great rabbi Joseph Caro, who had his own heavenly mentor to teach him the secrets of creation, became his friend and confidant.

In 1527 the Pope was forced to witness the sack of Rome by Charles V and the humiliation of the Church by the German Emperor's Lutheran army. For Jews, steeped in mystical teachings, the fall of Rome was the most important portent predicted before the coming of the Messiah. Thirsting for exposure and martyrdom, Molcho came to believe that he himself was the suffering Messiah of Kabbalistic theory. Seeking to fulfil an ancient rabbinic prophesy about the discovery of the Messiah, Molcho returned to Rome where, dressed in rags and abstaining from meat and wine, he sat for thirty days amongst the crowd of beggars outside the Pope's palace. He later described his experience in a letter:

...I left my horse and fine clothes with an innkeeper, telling him that I had come to visit a girl with whom I had been in love for many years. Though our two souls were bound together, her parents had forbidden her to see me; and she was so closely watched that I could only approach disguised as a beggar. I asked the innkeeper to obtain such a disguise for me.....and I dirtied my face and put on filthy rags...I walked through the city despised and rejected of men, like a man of sorrows acquainted with grief, until I came to the bridge over the Tiber close to the Pope's palace where the beggars and the sick of the city congregate. And I remained among them for thirty days, like one smitten by God.

Molcho's prophesies that Rome would be inundated by flood and that

Portugal would experience a severe earthquake had already come to the ears of Pope Clement VII, who granted him protection in 1530 and sheltered him in the Vatican. His reputation soared when Rome was indeed flooded later that year, and when an earthquake shook Portugal. Molcho emerged from obscurity and preached in the city's synagogues. He was honoured as a prophet by Jew and Christian alike; and the Pope's regard for him was openly demonstrated for all to see. The more cautious of the Jews, fearful for their safety, opposed Solomon Molcho and tried to discredit him. He was also hated as an apostate by some Christians. In the end though, not even the Pope's protective passport, nor the plea that he needed Molcho for a secret purpose, was sufficient to prevent him from being denounced to the Inquisition as a lapsed Christian. His papal passport was contemptuously torn from his hands. He was condemned for the crime of Judaising and sentenced to be burnt at the stake.

In what is perhaps the most curious incident of the entire episode, the Pope is alleged to have intervened in person to save his favourite. A shrouded wretch of similar build to Molcho was delivered to the executioner, and done to death in public before a large crowd, Solomon Molcho himself remained safely hidden in the Pope's palace until the coast was clear, when he obtained Clement's permission to leave Rome for Venice. If proof of Solomon Molcho's messiahship was needed, what could have been more convincing than his triumphant reappearance in Venice after his public execution in Rome. And even today, the story of Pope Clement's initiative in the plot to save Molcho's life seems almost as much of a miracle as if he had indeed risen from the dead.

Finally Solomon Molcho, together with David Rubeni, set out on a mission to Charles V at Regensburg — no doubt to persuade the Emperor of his claims. But from that point all went wrong. Both were arrested and Molcho was brought back and handed over to the Inquisition in Mantua. Opportunities to recant and return to the bosom of the Church were proudly rejected by Molcho, who declared that his only regret was that he had been a Christian in his youth. He was carried to the place of execution with a gag in his mouth to prevent spectators from being led astray by his powers of persuasion. When the gag was finally removed to enable him to reply to the Emperor's final offer to spare his life if he repented, Molcho proclaimed that he went gladly to his death as a martyr for the faith, trusting that the burnt sacrifice of his body would be acceptable as a sweet savour to the Lord.

Previous attempts to calculate the coming of the Messiah having all failed, Jews again turned to their sacred books and this time convinced themselves that 1648 was the promised year of the Redemption. But 1648 ushered in not the Messiah but a series of massacres of Jews in the Ukraine and Poland that were so terrible in their effect that the year was described by contemporary chroniclers as the beginning of the birth pangs of the Messianic Age. The scene was set for the imminent arrival of the Messiah. But when a 'messiah' did come, it was not from Poland as might have been expected but from the bustling port of Smyrna in Turkey where Jews lived contentedly under the benign rule of the Ottoman sultans.

It is tempting to suppose that it was news of the Ukrainian massacres of 1648 that started Shabbetai Zvi on his messianic career; for at roughly the same time as the first Polish refugees reached Turkey, Shabbetai's imagination shifted into a new direction. He heard a divine voice proclaim:

You are the saviour of Israel ... the true Redeemer

Shabbetai was a learned young rabbi, afflicted by a mental illness which might now be identified as manic-depression. He wandered for years through the main Jewish centres of the Near East, at first being welcomed

23 Shabbetai Zvi (1626-1676)
17th century engraving, Amsterdam.

24 Nathan of Gaza
Portrait of Nathan, sketched in Smyrna by an eye-witness in 1667.

when he was in calm mood, but then punished and driven out when the local rabbis became exasperated by his increasingly bizarre behaviour. At last he reached Gaza, where he went to the celebrated prophet Nathan to seek a cure for his troubled soul. Though the two men had never met, Nathan had seen visions in which Shabbetai figured as the Redeemer. Nathan therefore promptly fell to the floor before Shabbetai and hailed him as the Messiah.

It was shortly after that, in 1665, that Shabbetai announced his mission to the world. In this he was fully supported by Nathan who busied himself with reshaping the messianic tradition to fit the unsuitable figure of Shabbetai Zvi.

The result was a mystical messiah, far removed from age-old Jewish expectation. Nathan's messiah was not the all-conquering hero, come to lead his people to victory in battle against their enemies; but rather a man of suffering, whose mission was to wage a mysterious spiritual war against the powers of darkness.

A tidal wave of messianic enthusiasm swept over the Jewish communities of the Near East, and then over those of Europe. In the Ottoman Empire, men and women everywhere took to prophesying as they fell under the influence of strange spiritual powers.

Nathan's calls for immediate repentance to lessen the messianic woes evoked an overwhelming response in the hearts of Jews all over the world.

They succumbed to an orgy of penitence, coupled with rejoicing, the like of which contemporary observers claimed had never been seen before. Thousands fasted for days at a time and spent their normal waking hours, as well as most of their nights, in prayer. In the North, men rolled naked in the snow. They beat their bodies with thorns and nettles, as well as with leather scourges. Others wore layers of nettles under their clothes against their skins. Nettles were in such demand by Jews that in some places they had to be imported over long distances. Shops and businesses closed down,

25 Letter from Sephardim of Amsterdam
This letter, acknowledging the kingship of Shabbetai Zvi, was written and signed by the leaders of the Portuguese community of Amsterdam in 1666 but was never sent.

and workers neglected their tasks — for after all was not the End of Days
at hand? People tried to sell their immovable possessions in preparation for
the End, when they expected to be leaving to join the Messiah in Jerusalem.

A small minority held out against the tide. They urged that individuals
would be judged by the deeds they perform in this world rather than by
their faith in Shabbetai Zvi. But such opposition was submerged by almost
universal acceptance of the new creed; and even opponents found it hard
to ignore the positive features of repentance on so grand a scale.

Never before had the whole nation of the Jews — from the Holy Land
to Egypt, the Yemen, Persia, and Kurdistan — from Constantinople to
Salonika, Venice and Rome — from Vienna to Prague, Hamburg and
Amsterdam — from Poland and Lithuania to Alsace, Avignon and Morocco
— and even in England and the Americas — been engulfed by such a mood
of repentance and rejoicing. Never before had the rich and the poor, the
learned and the ignorant, the pious and the indifferent, so eagerly all
accepted the claim of such a pretender to the Messianic Throne. The
reaction to the appearance of the half-crazed Shabbetai Zvi was a phenomenon unique in Jewish history.

Flushed with success, Shabbetai travelled to Constantinople to seize the
Sultan's Crown and place it upon his own head. But the Turkish authorities
were waiting for him. Shabbetai was arrested, brought before the Grand
Vizier and committed to prison.

It was a strange sort of imprisonment. After the payment of hefty bribes,
Shabbetai was granted a fair degree of personal comfort, allowed to receive
visitors at will. He was even permitted to take ritual baths in the sea,
accompanied by crowds of admirers. During this period, he behaved as a
traditionally observant Jewish rabbi — though with Messianic pretentions.

On his transfer to the fortress prison of Abydos in Gallipoli, by order of
the Grand Vizier, Shabbetai's conduct reverted to its previous pattern.
Ignoring the prohibition against performing sacrifices outside Jerusalem,
he sacrificed a lamb on the eve of the Passover. He then consumed it with
its forbidden abdomimal fat after reciting his blasphemous benediction:

Blessed are you, O Lord our God, who permits that which is forbidden.

He perverted many other rituals and customs; and as the high point of
his innovations, he abolished the solemn Fast of Av, which commemorates
the destruction of the Temple and is the saddest day in the Jewish calendar.

By permission of his venal Turkish jailers who waxed fat on the proceeds,
and the liberality of his followers, Shabbetai lived the life of a king in
Abydos. He wore royal clothes, furnished his rooms with gold and silver,
dined off gold plate encrusted with gems and was attended by a bevy of
beautiful virgins. A retinue of learned Kabbalistic rabbis followed him
everywhere. He held court to thousands of visitors from all over the Jewish
world; and so numerous were the pilgrims to Gallipoli, that the Turks
complained of soaring food prices in the locality.

Messianic enthusiasm increased during Shabbetai's captivity. Expectations rose to dangerously high levels as fantastic stories of the wonderful

וַיִּקְּדוּ הָעָם וַיִּשְׁתַּחֲווּ ׃

doings of the King Messiah in his confinement, and those of new prophets who sprang up everywhere in the Jewish world, multiplied without limit.

The fragile edifice of hope was shattered beyond repair by the intervention of Nehemiah, a rabbi who arrived from Poland to visit Shabbetai in August 1666. Rabbi Nehemiah had a very literal mind; and he simply failed to understand Shabbetai Zvi's claim to be the Messiah. It was of course plain that Shabbetai, by his very nature, could not possibly fulfil the ancient prophesies regarding the Messiah — the warrior king who would lead the Jewish people to victory over their enemies. But he had always relied on Kabbalistic argument, on personal charisma and on his aura of manic illumination to cloud the issue and convince doubters.

The two debated furiously for three days and nights, during which they ate little and slept even less. In the end, the exasperated Rabbi Nehemiah rounded on Rabbi Shabbetai and accused him of lying and leading his followers astray.

Nehemiah rushed straight to the Turkish guards and declared his intention of becoming a Mohammedan. He immediately converted to Islam; and then denounced Shabbetai to the Turks as a dangerous imposter, bent on sedition.

The Turkish government reacted with alacrity to Nehemiah's denunciation of Shabbetai. All privileges at Gallipoli were abruptly cancelled. Shabbetai was taken under armed guard to Adrianople, one hundred and fifty miles away, where the Sultan was in residence.

It seems that Islamic authorities had advised against putting Shabbetai to death, thereby making a martyr of him; and so Shabbetai was brought to the Council Chamber, there to be confronted by a group of high officials. The Sultan himself observed the proceedings from behind a heavily latticed screen, as was his custom. To cut a long story short, Shabbetai displayed no heroism and very little dignity. On being offered the stark choice of the turban or his head, he chose the turban; and apostatized to Islam to save his life. He was graciously received into the Islamic faith by the Sultan, who allowed him to adopt his own name of Mehmed. The Sultan gave him new clothes and a purse of silver, appointed him to the honorary post of Keeper of the Palace Gates, and granted him a substantial pension.

In a resigned letter to his elder brother in Smyrna, Shabbetai commented sadly:

... and now let me alone, for God has made me a Turk

and he ended with a quotation from Psalm 33:

For he spoke, and it was done; commanded, and it stood fast.

Most Jews turned their backs on Shabbetai with revulsion after his apostasy, feeling themselves betrayed. But an influential minority, called 'believers', refused to accept that Shabbetai Zvi had been a fake, or even that he had been deluded. To them it was inconceivable that God could so cruelly have deceived the righteous and led his people into fraud. For some who had already tasted the bliss of redemption — if only in their own minds — things could never be the same again.

26 Letter from Shabbetai Zvi
This letter, very probably in Shabbetai's own hand, was written in 1676, the last year of his life and ten years after his apostasy. In it, he asks a nearby Jewish community to send him prayer books for the coming High Holydays. The letter is signed 'The Messiah of the God of Israel and Judah, Shabbetai Zvi', with no mention of his new Islamic name.

Refusing to submit to the sentence of history, they embarked on a secret inner life of their own whilst outwardly professing conventional Judaism. The 'believers' were sustained by a mystical theology developed by Nathan of Gaza and those who came after him. This explained the mystery of the apostasy in terms that prepared the way for Shabbetai's Second Coming and the Redemption.

Nathan never doubted Shabbetai, insisting from the first that a sacred mystery lay behind the apostasy. He taught that it was not possible for the Messiah to attain perfection until he had first descended into the realm of evil and arisen unscathed. The Messiah was not bound by the ordinary rules of the world, but governed by a more profound mystical purpose.

At the heart of Sabbatean belief was the disturbing doctrine, present just below the surface of most messianic movements, that a new Age had dawned in which laws previously given by God to men were no longer valid. Extremists never found difficulty in extending that idea to include a positive obligation to break the old laws in order to sanctify the new epoch. Believers in Shabbetai Zvi were not slow to follow suit, their crazier elements assuming with glee that they had been commanded to follow their Messiah into the realms of sin. The paradoxical notion of 'redemption through sin' became popular in radical Sabbatean circles, especially among the apostates. It caused great scandal when details of ceremonies involving group adultery and incest leaked out.

In general though, the vast majority of believers in Shabbetai Zvi remained within the Jewish fold, differing from other Jews only in their secret beliefs and hopes. The underground movement was widespread and included influential rabbis.

This hidden messianic movement survived within Judaism until the beginning of the nineteenth century.

A few Jews followed their Messiah by outwardly converting to Islam during his lifetime. Their number was increased shortly after his death by the mass apostasy of two to three hundred entire families. They were recognised as a separate group within Islam by the Turks, for its members kept themselves apart from other Mohammedans and only married amongst themselves. The Doenmeh, as they were called by the Turks, practised a heretical form of Judaism in secret, while maintaining an unblemished Islamic front to the outside world.

With the passing of time, the Doenmeh grew moderate and respectable. Salonika became their centre of activity; and some ten to fifteen thousand were living there in 1914. In 1920 they gave evidence to the International Commission that they wished to be sent to Palestine. This was disregarded; and they were expelled to Turkey in the exchange of populations that marked the end of the war between Turkey and Greece.

The sect was very greatly weakened by assimilation following its dispersion from Salonika. A remnant has managed to survive in Turkey to this day. Unfortunately no outsider has yet managed to penetrate the veil of secrecy with which it cloaks its existence; and so its present size cannot even be estimated.

The Ottoman Empire

Sephardi Jews fleeing from Spain and Portugal were welcomed with open arms by the Turks, who found it hard to believe their good fortune in acquiring so many talented, cultivated and useful subjects. Indeed Sultan Bayazid II even sent two of his own ships into Lisbon harbour to take off Jewish refugees in 1497.

The Ottoman Turks, it should be remembered, were a highly successful nation of warriors. It was beneath their dignity to engage in occupations other than the army, the government or the Mosque; and they despised commerce and crafts. They also disdained to colonise their far-flung empire or settle in its cities.

The Jews provided the Ottoman Empire with the nucleus of a new middle class — one that was free from political ambition and on which the Turks could rely for a degree of loyalty they were unable to obtain from the newly conquered subject peoples of their huge empire. To the Turks, the Jews were by far the most productive and stable non-Turkish minority in their domains.

As followers of the religion of Abraham, the People of the Book, Jews and Christians were accorded the status of dhimmis (protected persons) in all Islamic lands. This ensured state protection for their lives and property, freedom for them to follow their own religion on condition they did not insult Islam or attempt to convert Mohammedans, and exemption from military service. In return, dhimmis had to accept restrictions and humiliations as second-class subjects. They had to pay a special poll tax, wear distinctive clothes and refrain from building new synagogues and churches without permission. Their evidence in court was not accepted against that of a Mohammedan; nor could a Mohammedan be put to death for killing a dhimmi. Fortunately many of the restrictions, except for the paying of the tax, were not always imposed — or if they were, not strictly. They served mainly to preserve the subservient status of the dhimmi in Islamic society. On occasion though, and in bad times, they were applied with rigour; and then they could be humiliating in the extreme.

As dhimmis, communities of Jews and Christians formed many separate millets (nations) in the Ottoman Empire. Each millet was largely self-governing, with its own laws and administration. It levied and collected its own taxes; and was ruled by a Chief Rabbi or Patriarch directly responsible to the Sultan. This system suited the Jews very well, especially in the early days when humiliating restrictions were not imposed on their lives.

Rabbi Moses Capsali was first to be appointed head of the Jews of Constantinople in 1461; and it was reported that he and the Christian Patriarch occupied seats of honour in the presence of the Sultan. However the post of Chief Rabbi of Constantinople lapsed in 1527 because of discord between the different Jewish communities of the capital; and it was not filled again until 1837 when the first Haham Bashi was appointed as the result of Turkish government reforms.

In the interval of over three hundred years, the special interests of the Jews were represented at court by the great Jewish merchants of the day such as Dõna Gracia Mendes, Don Joseph Nasi (Duke of Naxos) and

Solomon ibn Yaish (Duke of Mitelene). Moses Hamon, personal physician to Suleiman the Magnificent, must also have wielded powerful influence — for it was he who obtained the firman of 1553 in which the Sultan forbad the bringing of blood-libel accusations against Jews.

Under the benevolent sway of the Grand Turk, the Iberian Sephardim joined existing Jewish communities all over the Ottoman Empire. They settled around the shores of the Mediterranean, penetrating up through the Balkans towards central Europe, and eventually across Turkey to Baghdad and beyond. Usually superior in education and culture to the local Jews in whose midst they settled, the Sephardim at first jealously preserved their separate identity, forming themselves into a kind of aristocracy. In time though, they either succeeded in absorbing the older-established resident Jews or else merged into them.

The Sephardi Jews who found their way to the Land of Israel transformed that country's Jewish community. They soon became a majority in Jerusalem. In Tiberias, sponsored by Doña Gracia Mendes and Don Joseph Nasi of Constantinople, they participated in a grand venture to rebuild the town as a refuge for oppressed Jews. Under the influence of the Sephardi rabbis, mystics and poets who settled there, Safed (in Galilee) became a spiritual centre of world Jewry — and, in particular, the focus of the Kabbalistic (mystical) movement which came to dominate Jewish thought after the Expulsion from Spain.

Turkey was then approaching the peak of its power as the leader of a vast Islamic civilisation. The Turks' kindly treatment of their own Jewish populations and their warm welcome to the refugees ensured that, from that time on, the fate of most Sephardim would be closely bound to that of their Islamic hosts. As Turkey prospered, so did its Jews. And Ottoman Jews soon became the financiers, the tax farmers, the merchants, the diplomats, the interpreters and the physicians of the Empire.

Nor did the Jews neglect industry and the crafts. Indeed the Christians of Europe were soon to complain bitterly that Spanish Jews had introduced the manufacture of cannon and gunpowder into Turkey and had taught the Turks the art of modern warfare. The textile industry in all its aspects, from raw materials to the making of garments, became a Jewish speciality — and, in places, a near monopoly. As in Europe, the great Jewish commercial houses, run as close family businesses with widespread networks of trusted contacts all over the world, dominated international trade to an extent difficult to visualise today.

However the comparatively backward Christian countries of Europe were not asleep. Their tiny sailing ships managed to round the Cape of Good Hope to reach India, while others crossed the Atlantic to discover the Americas. By means of sea power and advanced technology, the Christian West gradually succeeded in outflanking the serene, land-bound world of Islam. Eventually it came to dominate the globe; and, what is more, to impose its own values upon it.

Turkey itself began to decay from within. The sultans who succeeded Suleiman the Magnificent (1520-1566) generally lacked the ability of their

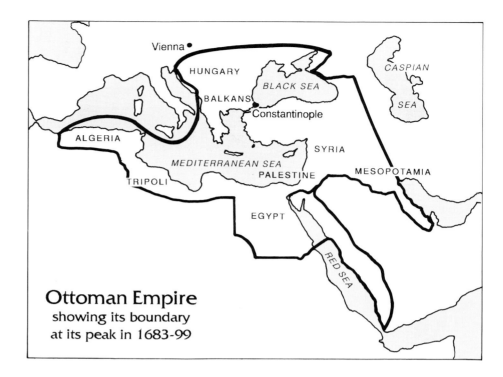

Ottoman Empire
showing its boundary
at its peak in 1683-99

brilliant predecessors. Spoilt by the wealth that seemed so effortlessly to flow in their direction, they grew increasingly decadent and devoted far more of their energies to court and harem intrigue than to governing their empire. Their grip on government relaxed. Some of its important posts became hereditary; and others were openly sold to the highest bidder. Corruption and nepotism flourished as the huge bureaucracy became increasingly inefficient.

Taxation was increased to ruinous levels. Economic troubles and inflation followed, with large price increases. Crop yields fell sharply as more and more peasants moved into the towns from the countryside. Greater competition from Christian Europe, particularly in textiles, had a bad effect on trade. Military reverses lead to a progressive crumbling of the edges of the Empire; while within it, chaos and lawlessness gradually became usual.

In time not only did Turkey decline in wealth and power, but the relatively privileged position of its Jews was also eroded. This was partly the result of the weakening of central Ottoman control over the far-flung provinces of the Empire — which led to an increasing degree of autonomy for the local governors, who often proved lazy, greedy and corrupt. Another important factor was the failure of the Jews to maintain their own formerly high standards of education and culture in the decaying Islamic environment.

The Jews somehow seemed to lose the will to rise above the torpor that progressively paralysed a society that had lost confidence in its own worth. Eastern Sephardim shared in the decline of the Islamic world just as they had previously shared in its success; but they did even worse.

Eventually the Jews were forced to yield their prominent position in Ottoman affairs to another but more thrusting minority, the Christians.

These Christians — Italians, Greeks and Armenians — became far better educated in European ways and languages than the Jews. They were able to maintain many more trading and diplomatic contacts in the increasingly dominant Christian countries of Europe, and could rely on sympathetic Christian powers for protection. Increasingly isolated from Europe, the Jews lost the ability to compete.

In 1826 the Sultan moved to reassert his direct control of affairs. In an action that proved terminal for the dwindling Jewish influence in Constantinople, he massacred his entire corps of Janissaries. The Janissaries had effectively ruled Turkey in the Sultan's name; and in their fall from power they dragged down with them the last few prominent Jewish families in the city.

The condition of the Jews of the Ottoman Empire deteriorated steadily until its lowest point was reached in the first half of the nineteenth century, when their degradation was movingly described in many accounts written by European travellers to the Near East. Paradoxically, it was the Sultan's destruction of the Janissaries that turned the tide; for his subsequent reforms resulted in a tightening of central control over the provinces, with consequent benefit to their Jews.

Another very important factor in the improvement of the Jewish condition was the establishment in 1860 in Paris of the Alliance Isráelite Universelle. The Alliance created a network of European-type Jewish schools throughout the Near East. It was those schools that enabled Jews to acquire the rudiments of a secular education for the first time, as well as some knowledge of French and English. Once again they were able to start competing with their Christian rivals; and for the first time they began to look to the West, not just with nostalgia but as the key to survival and worldly success.

Despite its splendid work, the Alliance was criticised in some religious quarters for alienating its pupils from their Jewish roots. In its enthusiasm for all things French and European, for the new world ahead, it was accused of failing to foster appreciation for the old, of tending to diminish respect for religion and of opening a gulf between secularly educated children and their more pious parents.

The Alliance schools certainly were very different from the traditional religious schools of the poverty-stricken Jewish areas of North Africa and the Middle East. But it must be said that, as well as secular subjects, the study of Judaism and Jewish history always constituted an important part of the curriculum, both at local level and at the college for teachers established in Paris.

However part of the inevitable price paid for the Alliance's tremendous achievement in liberating so many Ottoman Jews from obscurity and poverty was that some of its graduates became vulnerable to assimilationist pressure when removed from their closely-knit communities.

A similar dilemma was faced by Shneur Zalman of Lyady, founder of the Lubavich Movement (Habad), when asked to support Napoleon's invasion of Russia in 1812. Zalman accepted that the French would bring

27　Teachers and Rabbis of the Alliance's School, Tunis 1886
The teachers are wearing European dress. The number of rabbis, wearing turbans, illustrates the prominence of religious instruction in the school's curriculum.

emancipation and great material improvement to the oppressed and poverty-stricken Jews of Russia; but for the sake of religion, he opposed emancipation for the Jews and brought all his influence to bear in favour of the Czar and against Napoleon.

Not only did the Alliance schools help to bring the long isolated Sephardim of the Near East back within sight of the mainstream of European life, but its European-trained teachers and inspectors ensured that Jews could no longer be oppressed by local Turkish governors in secret. From the date of the Alliance's foundation in 1860, the full glare of international publicity was brought to bear on cases of wrong-doing, with beneficial result.

By that time, the Islamic world had started to open embassies in the capitals of Europe; and through those embassies, pressure by prominent European Jews and Christians could more easily be brought to bear on the Turkish authorities to counter anti-Jewish excesses.

England, partly because of genuine Old Testament sympathies, and partly as a lever to exert influence in the declining Ottoman Empire, began to interest itself in the plight of Turkey's Jews. Sir Moses Montefiore's visit to Palestine in 1843 and its influence on its Jews was noted with approval by the British government. At about the same time, Lord Shaftesbury's proposal to repatriate the Jews, so that they could build themselves a National Home in Palestine under British protection, found favour with Lord Palmerston and the government. Not surprisingly, it was rejected out of hand by the Sultan.

As far back as the year 1580, a British envoy to Constantinople had won a grant of Capitulations from the Sultan, governing the conditions in which British subjects could trade in the Turkish Empire. These Capitulations, modelled on those granted to France some years previously, protected British subjects and their goods from molestation by the Turks, except for lawful customs. They also provided for the appointment of consuls to regulate the relationship of the British merchants with the Ottoman authorities.

Taking full advantage of this system of Capitulations, the European powers wielded considerable influence in Turkish affairs. They gained trade advantages by extending 'protection' to members of Christian minority groups within the Ottoman Empire. Thus Russia protected Orthodox Christians, while France and Austria extended their patronage to Roman Catholics and Maronites. Such 'protected' persons were no longer subject to Ottoman law; and could only be brought to justice in courts held in the consulates of their protecting power.

Britain was at a disadvantage here, for there were few Protestants to whom protection could be extended. Some Jews therefore were adopted as British-protected subjects in the nineteenth century; and if justification was needed, the Turks were told that the families in question had originated in British India — as indeed was the case for a few. Other European powers also adopted Jews, but to a lesser extent.

Just how far the fiction of Indian descent was believed by the local British consular officials is hard to determine. But study of the correspondence of the British consulate in Aleppo, Syria, for example, indicates that by the

28 A Turkey merchant
One of the first European traders in the Ottoman Empire is shown in this 1593 engraving by de Bry.

end of the nineteenth century its records were in such confusion that all attempts to regulate them on a rational basis had been abandoned. The Consul was well aware that many of the so-called British Jews had in fact lived in Aleppo since time immemorial. Thus Consul Jago, writing to his ambassador in Constantinople in 1890, reported that:

> There are more than four hundred Europeans in Aleppo, leaving out large numbers of native Arab Jews ... who by some means or other have acquired British nationality... The vast majority of persons enjoying (British) consular protection are Arab Jews of an alleged Indian origin ....

It was therefore through secular European-style education and increasing contact with merchants from Europe — for whom Jews often acted as agents — that Sephardim of the Ottoman Empire began to trade and travel to the West. Some few of the leading families were helped by acquiring European nationality, but by no means all. The more energetic started moving to countries such as British India and cosmopolitan Egypt, where European influence was strong. Others migrated directly to Western Europe and to North, Central and South America.

It must be remembered that only a proportion of the Jews of the Ottoman Empire was exposed to the European influence of the Alliance schools; and even then, most parents were not able to afford to keep their children there for more than three or four years of elementary education. A small minority only of the children was able to proceed from the Alliance to higher French or other European schools, or else was educated wholly in foreign (usually Christian) schools — and it largely constituted the Jewish upper class.

The remainder, trained only in traditional religious schools (Talmud Torah), emerged with little secular knowledge and no command at all of French or of English. Unfortunately, as the chapter on New York in Part Three of this book will describe, they were very ill-equipped to face the great migrations to which they were subjected after the collapse of the Ottoman Empire and the later thrust of modern Arab nationalism. On the positive side though, it must be said that however poor and however ignorant in a secular sense they may have been, they were mostly people of genuine piety untinged with fanaticism — modest folk, God-fearing and with a high standard of morality. Their like may not be seen again.

In the middle decades of the twentieth century the earlier emigrants were followed to Europe, to Israel and to the Americas by the remainder of their brethren, fleeing from the rising tide of Arab nationalism which culminated in the total destruction of their ancient communities. There are now very few Jews left in the Arab world; and the story of their subsequent wanderings is told later in this book.

Unfortunately those Sephardi Jews who remained in the European part of the former Ottoman Empire — mainly Salonika, Rhodes and the Balkans — fared far worse. They suffered horribly in Hitler's Holocaust during the Second World War of 1939-45. They were not allowed to emigrate; and their communities were destroyed by deportation and mass-murder on a scale that even surpassed that endured by their ancestors in Spain and Portugal. It is a tragic story.

Western Europe

The Inquisition came very much later to Portugal than to Spain. Taking advantage of the easier conditions there, many Spanish New Christians had crossed over the frontier into Portugal where their beliefs and religious practices were not at first subjected to close scrutiny. It must be remembered that the New Christians included sincere converts in their ranks; and that even those had to endure the same distrust and disabilities heaped on secret Jews.

Those who wished to return to Judaism moved even further afield to parts of Italy, North Africa and above all to the Ottoman Empire. From the end of the fourteenth century, many Mediterranean ports were sheltering forced converts who had fled from the Iberian peninsula.

Having been forcibly and brutally converted to Christianity within the space of a few months, the Marranos of Portugal were even more passionately devoted to their Jewish past than their brethren who had remained behind in Spain. It was not until forty years after this mass conversion that an Inquisition was established in Portugal; but once started on its course, it lost no time in gripping that country's New Christians with full intensity.

Strictly forbidden to leave without a royal licence, only comparatively few of Portugal's New Christians managed at first to slip away and seek refuge overseas. Antwerp, which though under Spanish rule had no Inquisition, attracted some who settled there under the protection of a safe-conduct issued by Emperor Charles V in 1526.

An escape route through Antwerp was established for Marranos who could obtain permission to leave Portugal for Flanders. They then proceeded overland — sometimes through Italy and the Balkans — until they could take ship for freedom in Turkey. A boatload of such refugees arrived in Ragusa (Dubrovnik) in 1544; and by 1564 it appears that there were few Italian cities in which Marranos could not be found. The Ottoman Empire remained the prime goal for those wishing to return to Judaism; and Rhodes, conquered by the Turks in 1522, became a transit destination for New Christians and a place in which many Marranos returned to their preferred religion.

Those among the New Christians who feared the Inquisition, but lacked the burning desire to renounce their baptism, sought asylum in other places where they might simply dwell in peace. They spread out from Antwerp into Germany, settling in Cologne, Hamburg, Emden, Altona and Glückstadt; and some penetrated to Scandinavia. At first they all continued to live as Christians; though some eventually returned to Judaism.

Five prominent and wealthy New Christian families had settled in Cologne by 1578; and others joined them. It was partly due to their presence that Cologne first attained the status of an international financial centre in the 1580s.

In 1612 some one-hundred and fifty Portuguese New Christians were given the right to remain in Hamburg for five years — but only as Christians. The first evidence of secret Jewish worship came five years later, when the Lutheran Church protested to the city's Burgomasters; and it was not until 1623 that a Jewish community was granted tacit toleration by the authorities. By 1646 numbers had grown to some five hundred strong; but opposition to Jewish settlement had also increased.

France was another country which attracted New Christian families, some arriving even before the expulsion from Spain. In the year 1475 King Louis XI granted extraordinary privileges to foreign merchants, including New Christians, who had settled in Bordeaux. These were confirmed by Henri II in his Letters Patent of 1550, after which New Christian settlement in France gained momentum.

It was not until well over one hundred years after the expulsion from Spain that larger numbers of Marranos began to find their way to Holland. The Union of Utrecht, which in 1579 had established the Protestant Dutch provinces in their independence from Spanish Catholic rule, included freedom of conscience as one of its terms. Once beyond the reach of the dreaded Inquisition, the Marranos lost no time in casting off their mask of Christianity and openly returning to Judaism. By that time they no longer knew any Hebrew, nor did they remember more than vestiges of Jewish practice; but they were eager to learn. Amsterdam became home to a flourishing Jewish community; and its fine synagogue and system of religious education were admired all over the world.

Amsterdam was the principal staging post for those Marranos who wished to revert to Judaism. It also served as the power-house of Western Sephardim through the efforts of its Jewish merchants who, participating

29 Dutch Jewish merchants of Amsterdam
By Rowlandson, 1796.

30 The main entrance of the Portuguese Synagogue of Amsterdam

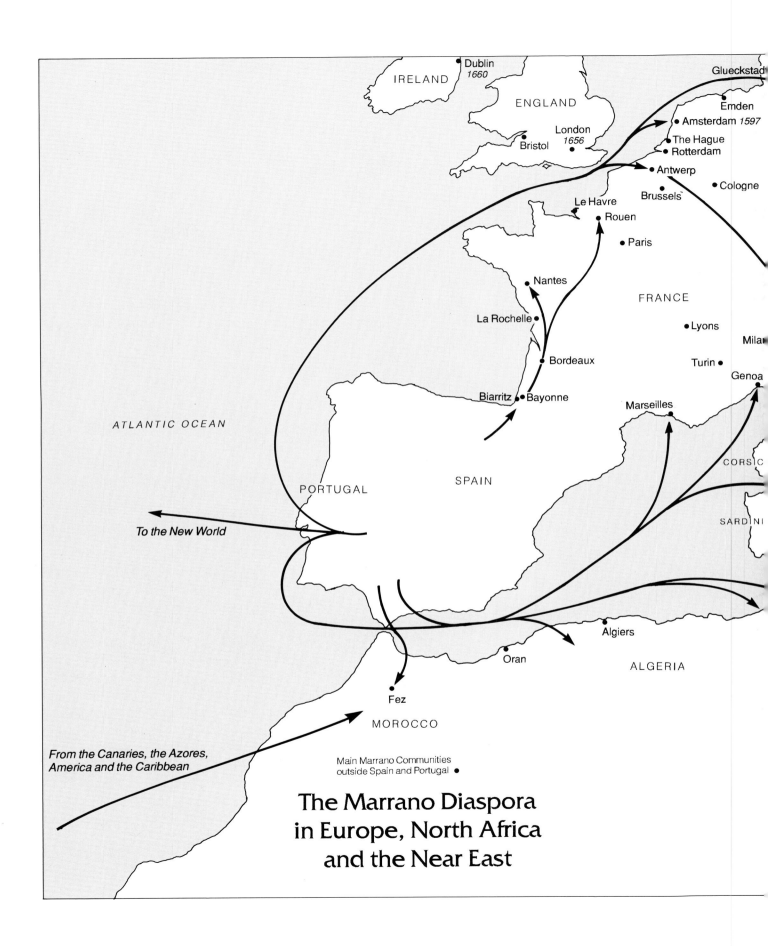

Dublin
1660

IRELAND

ENGLAND

Glueckstad

Emden

Amsterdam *1597*

London
1656

Bristol

The Hague
Rotterdam

Antwerp

Cologne

Brussels

Le Havre

Rouen

Paris

FRANCE

Lyons

Mila

Nantes

La Rochelle

Bordeaux

Turin

Genoa

Biarritz

Bayonne

Marseilles

CORSIC

ATLANTIC OCEAN

SARDINI

PORTUGAL

SPAIN

To the New World

Algiers

Oran

ALGERIA

Fez

MOROCCO

*From the Canaries, the Azores,
America and the Caribbean*

Main Marrano Communities
outside Spain and Portugal ●

The Marrano Diaspora
in Europe, North Africa
and the Near East

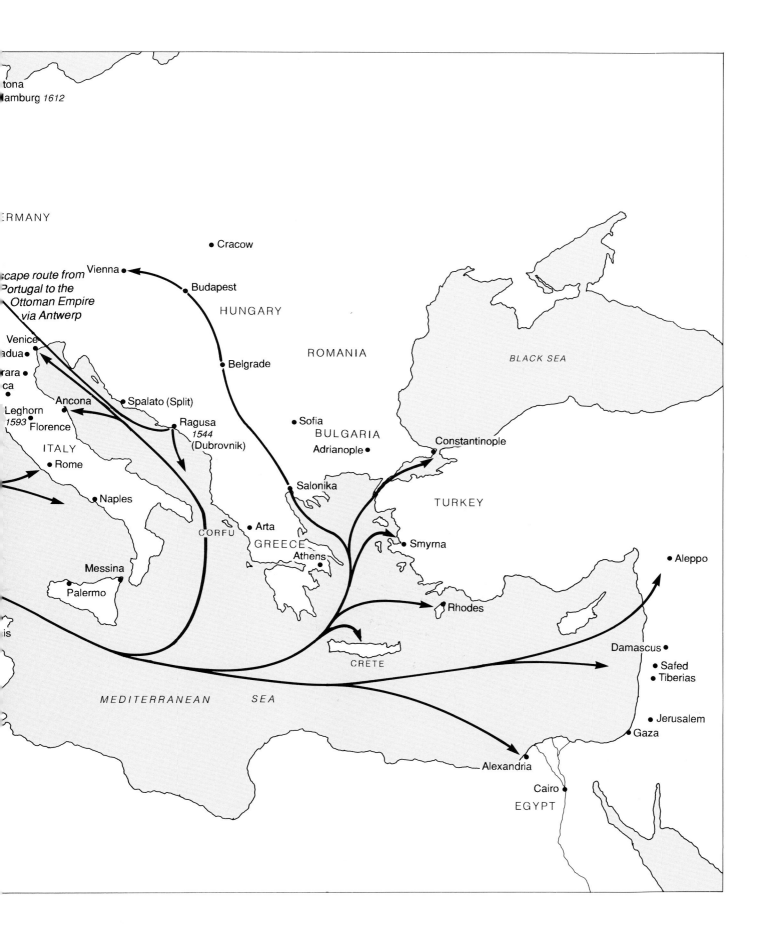

tona
Hamburg *1612*

GERMANY

• Cracow

*scape route from
Portugal to the
Ottoman Empire
via Antwerp*

Vienna •

Budapest •

HUNGARY

Venice •
adua •
rara •
ca •

ROMANIA

BLACK SEA

Belgrade •

Ancona •
Leghorn •
1593 Florence •

Spalato (Split) •

Ragusa
1544
(Dubrovnik)

ITALY
• Rome

• Sofia
BULGARIA
Adrianople •

Constantinople

• Naples

Salonika •

TURKEY

CORFU

• Arta
GREECE
Athens •

• Smyrna

• Aleppo

Messina

• Rhodes

Palermo

Damascus •

• Safed
• Tiberias

is

CRETE

MEDITERRANEAN   SEA

• Jerusalem
Gaza •

Alexandria

Cairo •
EGYPT

to the full in the world-wide trading activity of the Dutch Republic, were able to maintain close but secret contact with the New Christian communities of Portugal, France, Northern Germany, Scandinavia and the New World.

The Jewish community of London, for example, owed much to its roots in Amsterdam. Its twenty or so Marrano families were helped by the celebrated Amsterdam rabbi Menasseh ben Israel to cast off their Catholic disguise and openly embrace Judaism. The Sephardim opened their first synagogue in London in the year 1656; and Benjamin Disraeli, Queen Victoria's favourite Prime Minister, was the son of one of its members.

Livorno (Leghorn) in Italy was another of the very few towns of Christian Europe where Jews could live openly and without pretence; for in 1593 Grand Duke Ferdinand I issued a proclamation inviting all persecuted people to come and live freely in his new port. Many Marranos came direct from the Iberian Peninsula, and other Sephardi Jews flocked there from Venice and from parts of the Ottoman Empire when conditions there began to deteriorate. By 1645 it is estimated that there were more than two thousand Jews in Livorno out of a total population of nine thousand.

Portuguese remained for many years the day-to-day language of the Marrano diaspora; and Spanish, though still remembered, was used mainly for commercial dealings with the outside world and as a language of literature and prayer. The Marranos were proud to preserve their identity as a self-styled Portuguese 'Nation' in exile; and indeed, in most of Europe, Asia and the Americas the very word 'Portuguese' became synonymous with 'Jewish'.

The Marrano merchants, with their widespread but closely knit family businesses and their network of trusted contacts in most of the trading centres of the world, operated what amounted to an international credit system. This gave them a disproportionately large share of the world's commerce and a virtual monopoly of products such as sugar, tobacco, coral and gem stones. In time, some of them also became prominent in the emerging financial system of Western Europe and on its exchanges.

Perhaps the greatest contribution of all to Jewish life in Western Europe was the part played by former Marranos in the re-establishment of Jewish communities in many of its countries. These Jews, though foreign and Portuguese-speaking, wore the same dress and had the same kind of manners as the upper classes of the lands of their adoption. Once they had been admitted and recognised as Jews, it became harder to exclude their Ashkenazi brethren — some of whom were far stranger and more uncouth in their habits and dress. Though, to their discredit, the Sephardim did not always do as much as they might to welcome the Ashkenazi immigrants who followed them — sometimes even the reverse — nevertheless they were the forerunners. It was they who paved the way for the acceptance of the very much larger Ashkenazi immigration into Western Europe that came after their own settlement.

The New World

Christopher Columbus embarked on the first of his epoch-making voyages of discovery within a day of the deadline set for the final expulsion of the Jews from Spain in July 1492. Though there is no evidence that Columbus himself was of Jewish descent, as is sometimes claimed, it is thought that up to six members of his crew may have been. Indeed the expedition's interpreter Luis de Torres — the first man actually to set foot in the New World — was a Jew who had accepted baptism shortly before his departure. Other Marranos must have followed the explorers, for one was brought back from Hispaniola to Seville in 1515 to face trial by the Inquisition.

Large scale Spanish settlement on the mainland of America started with Cortes's conquest of Mexico in 1521 and Pizarro's conquest of Peru eleven years later. Spanish colonies were then planted all over Central and South America — except for Brazil, which was left to the Portuguese. Some Marranos must have crossed the Atlantic with those early settlers, for we know that two of Cortes's own conquistadores were accused of heresy in Mexico City and burned at the stake in 1528. However numbers remained small at first, for both the King and the Pope did their utmost to prevent New Christians from settling in America.

Portuguese policy started rather differently. The first Auto-da-Fé to be held in Lisbon took place in 1540; and from 1548 onwards, penitent New Christians were actually deported to Brazil after trial for religious offences. The King of Spain took over Portugal thirty two years later, temporarily uniting the two kingdoms. The growing grip of the Inquisition, coupled with the coming of Spanish rule, caused large numbers of New Christians to cross the Atlantic and seek haven in the Spanish colonies, where the Inquisition's scrutiny of their beliefs and practices was less thorough. In fact, King Philip II even accepted a hefty bribe in 1601 in exchange for his consent for New Christians to emigrate freely to America.

Spanish control of Portuguese immigration to their colonies having

31 Kingston, Jamaica

Jamaica was discovered by Columbus in 1494, during his second voyage to the New World; and there were Marranos amongst the first Spanish settlers. Marranos helped the British wrest the island from Spain in 1655, after which Jews were able to practise their religion freely. Other Sephardim from Brazil, Surinam, Curaçao, Barbados, Holland, England and France then came to live in Jamaica. This photograph of a painting entitled 'Spanish & Portuguese Synagogue' may well be of the first synagogue, erected before 1750, of which no details have survived.

PLATE VII
Facing page
Psalm 67 in the shape of a Menorah
This device, sometimes found in Sephardi
prayer books, shows the letters of the psalm
formed into the shape of the Menorah, the
seven-branched lamp of the Temple. It
symbolises the substitution of words of
prayer for the former Temple rituals. This
particular 'Shiviti' was made for Moses
Sequerra in 1869 by Solomon Halawa in
the Holy Land.

32 Petition to the Queen of England
dated 1692, from eight Jews of Jamaica

33 Tombstone
From the Jewish cemetery of Hunt's Bay,
across the harbour from Port Royal,
Jamaica. The stone is dated 1729. The
lettering is in Hebrew and Portuguese.

slackened, it was not long before Marranos who had remained loyal to their ancestral faith were observing at least some of the practices of Judaism all over Central and South America — from Mexico to Argentina, and from Brazil to Chile and Peru. Those Marranos, with close links to their brethren in Antwerp, Amsterdam, Livorno, Turkey and the Iberian Peninsula, dominated many aspects of European trade with the colonies; and they prospered accordingly.

It was when the Dutch invaded Brazil in 1624 and again in 1630, and offered freedom of conscience to all, that some local Marranos returned openly to the Jewish faith; and these were soon joined by many professing Jews who came over from Holland. By 1638, it is thought that about half the total white population of twenty-two thousand in the Dutch territory was of Jewish origin.

The Dutch evacuation of Brazil in 1654 was a disaster for its Jews; but the Portuguese did at least grant an amnesty for three months during which Jews could depart. Rather than submit to Portuguese rule, many returned to Holland. The remainder founded a series of settlements all over the West Indies. Curaçao was by far the largest; but Barbados, Jamaica and Martinique also hosted viable congregations, as did several of the smaller islands.

There was another wave of Sephardi immigration to Brazil after that country finally gained its independence from Portugal in the 1820s. This time the settlers came directly from Morocco, attracted by the economic opportunities of the rich new land.

It was in 1654 that twenty-three Jews, fleeing from Recife in Brazil, first

To the Queen..s Most Excellent Majesty:

The humble peticon of Isaque Fernandez Diaz, Isaque Moses
Baruk-Isaque Nunez, Phineas Abarbanel, Isaque Rodriquez de Souza,
Aron Jacob Soarez, Samuel de Cazerez, Jacob de Roblez
Isaque Mendes Gutierez. Jews Late of Jamaica, Merchants
humbly sheweth:

That whereas your peticoners having inhabited for Severall
years in your majesties Island of Jamaica and by that most
terrible Earthquake which happened there on ye 7th of June
Last have Lost all they had in the World humbly begg your
majesties favour to be made free Denizons.

At the Court at Whitehall
Aug ye 30th 1692

From the "Calendar of State Papers, Colonial Series,
America and West Indies 1689/1692"
Public Record Office, London

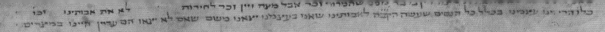

18

עַל שׁוֹ שֶׁמָּ

שֶׁמְּרוּ

אֶת חַיָּי

בְּמִצְרָיִ

אֶת הַחַיֵּיהֶם

קָשֶׁה בְּחֹמֶר

וּבְכָל עֲבוֹדָה

כָּל יְבוֹרָתָם

שֶׁאָנוּ אוֹכְ

עַל שׁוּם

הַמִּצְרִים

אֲבוֹתֵינ

שֶׁנָּ וַיְמָרְד

בַּעֲבוֹרָה

וּבִלְבֵנִים

כְּשֶׁרָה אֶת

אֲשֶׁר עֲבְרוּבָהֶם בְּפָרֶך

וְרֵד חַיָּיב אָדָם לִרְאוֹת

אֶת עַצְמוֹ כְּאִלוּ הוּא יָצָא

מִמִּצְרָיִם שֶׁנֶ' וְהִגַּדְתָּ לְבִנְךָ בַּיּוֹם הַהוּא לֵאמֹר בַּעֲבוּר

41 From a Spanish Haggadah
An artichoke is shown as the bitter herb in this 14th century Spanish Haggadah — a custom unknown to Ashkenazim.

set foot in New Amsterdam — later to become New York. Peter Stuyvesant, the Dutch governor, wanted to turn them away; but he was ordered to give them refuge after the intervention of the Jews of Amsterdam. From that small beginning grew the mighty Jewish community of the United States.

Forty-two Jews, including two Ashkenazi families, were sent by ship to Savannah by the London Sephardi Congregation in 1733. The first Sephardi congregation of Charleston was established in 1750; and its synagogue, opened in 1795, was considered the most splendid in America. The Sephardi synagogue of Newport, Rhode Island, was founded in 1763 by families from Barbados, Curaçao and the Iberian Peninsula. And, in the same period, Sephardi communities were also established in Philadelphia and Richmond. Jews were granted citizenship of New Amsterdam in 1655. A synagogue was functioning by 1700; and the first purpose-built structure was opened thirty years later. The community was able to appoint the American-born Gershom Mendes Seixas as its Spiritual leader in 1768; and

34 Shearit Israel's first synagogue
The first synagogue in Mill Street, New York City, built in 1730.

35 Shearit Israel's second synagogue
The synagogue in Mill Street, New York City, shown here as it was rebuilt in 1818.

36 Second cemetery of Shearit Israel
In this early picture, the cemetery at Chatham Street, Manhattan Island, is shown marked "D".

A. CATIEMUTS HILL	E. RUTGERS FARMHOUSE	H. ROAD TO THE CITY
B. THE FRESH WATER	F. BOWERY ROAD	I. ROAD TO ROLCK POND
C. THE FRESH WATER BRIDGE	G. ROAD TO THE FERRY	J. CITY COMMONS
D. THE JEWS BURYING GROUND	(PRESENT PEARL STREET)	K. WALPHERTS MEADOW

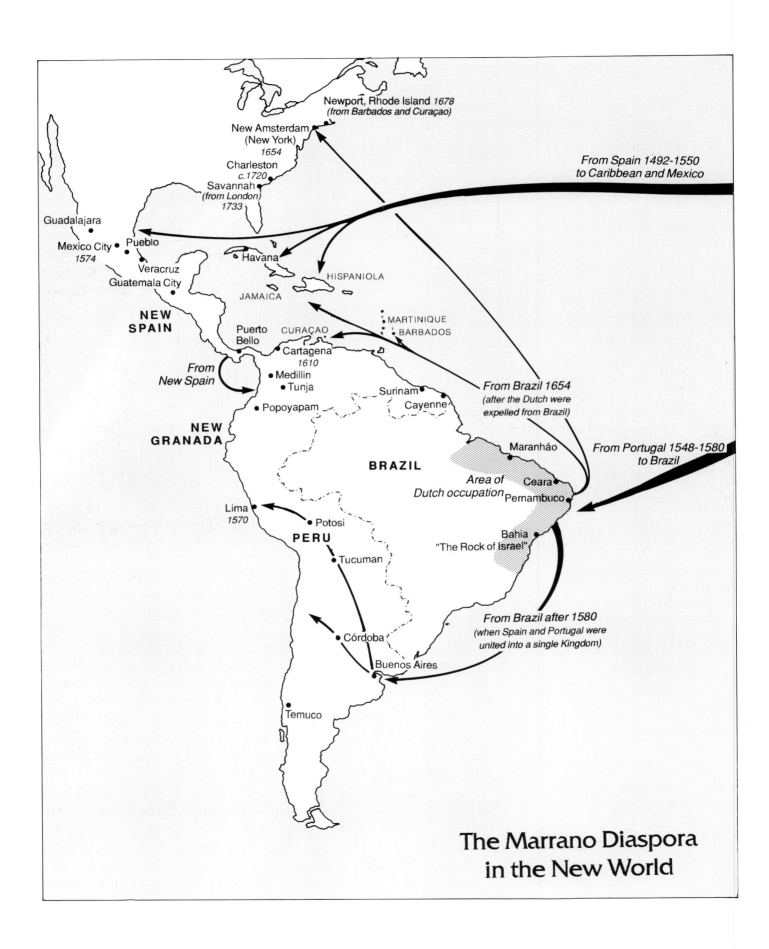

Newport, Rhode Island *1678*
(from Barbados and Curaçao)

New Amsterdam
(New York)
1654

Charleston
c.1720

Savannah
(from London)
1733

Guadalajara

Mexico City
1574

Pueblo

Veracruz

Guatemala City

Havana

HISPANIOLA

JAMAICA

From Spain 1492-1550
to Caribbean and Mexico

NEW SPAIN

Puerto Bello

CURAÇAO

MARTINIQUE
BARBADOS

Cartagena
1610

Medillin

Tunja

Surinam

Cayenne

From New Spain

Popoyapam

From Brazil 1654
(after the Dutch were
expelled from Brazil)

NEW GRANADA

Maranháo

BRAZIL

Area of
Dutch occupation

Ceara

Pernambuco

From Portugal 1548-1580
to Brazil

Lima
1570

Potosi

PERU

Tucuman

Bahia
"The Rock of Israel"

Córdoba

Buenos Aires

From Brazil after 1580
(when Spain and Portugal were
united into a single Kingdom)

Temuco

The Marrano Diaspora
in the New World

37 The Synagogue of Newport, Rhode Island
This was built in 1763 for the Sephardi Congregation of Newport. Its interior is modelled on that of the Portuguese Synagogue of Amsterdam.

Seixas commanded sufficient respect to be invited to President George Washington's inauguration in 1798. The synagogue was rebuilt in 1818 with financial help from a number of overseas communities including those of Curaçao and Barbados.

From its early days, Ashkenazim formed a substantial part of the American Jewish community. They did however prove curiously reluctant to start their own synagogues and preferred to join the Sephardim. Indeed Sephardi ways proved so attractive that Ashkenazim even founded a Sephardi synagogue in Baltimore, where no Sephardim lived. In time, Ashkenazim came to outnumber Sephardim in most Sephardi synagogues, maintaining the Sephardi prayer book, services and music — but in an American rather than in a traditional Sephardi context.

These so-called Sephardim of the United States long enjoyed high prestige and formed themselves into a kind of Jewish aristocracy. They maintained their leadership of the Jewish community unchallenged, until events in 1840 caused them to yield their position to the by then far more numerous Ashkenazim.

The Damascus Affair of 1840, described in the chapter on Damascus

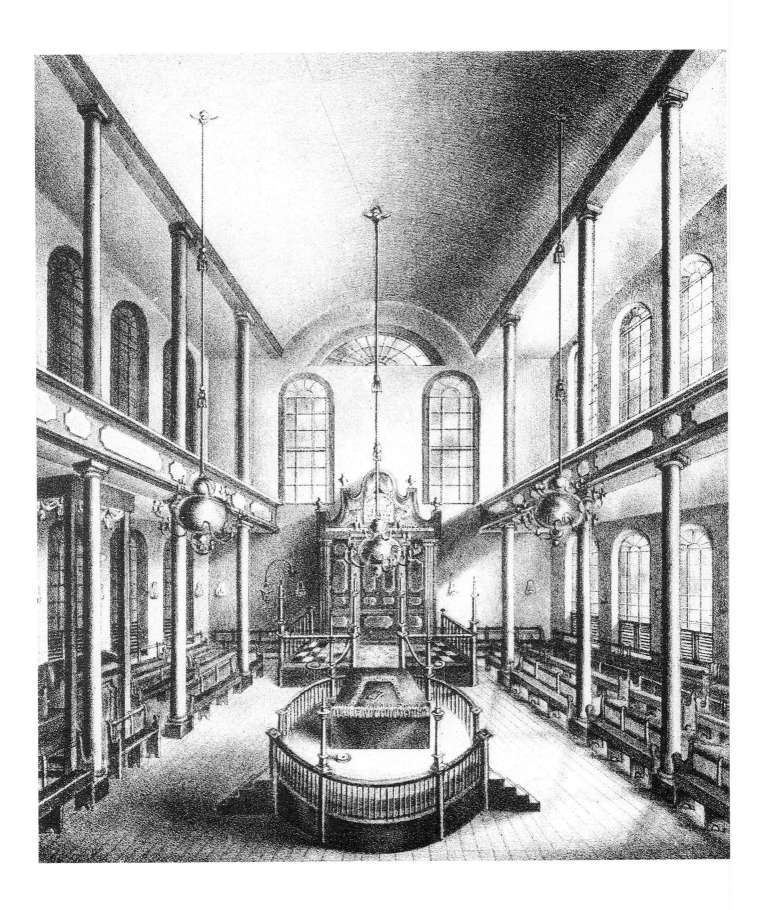

39 Gershom Mendes Seixas (1746–1816)
The first native-born Jewish minister in the United States. Seixas, who served at Shearit Israel, New York and at Mikveh Israel, Philadelphia, was invited to President George Washington's inauguration in 1789.

40 Extract from George Washington's letter
Part of the reply to a message of encouragement and support, delivered by Moses Seixas on behalf of the Congregation of Newport, Rhode Island, during President George Washington's visit to the town in 1790.

Facing page
36 Charleston Synagogue
The Sephardi Community of Charleston, South Carolina, was founded in 1749. This lithograph by Solomon Carvalho is of the synagogue opened in 1795 and destroyed by fire in 1838.

The Government of the United States, which gives to bigotry no sanction, to persecution no assistance requires only that they who live under its protection should demean themselves as good citizens, in giving it on all occasions their effectual support.

It would be inconsistent with the frankness of my character not to avow that I am pleased with your favorable opinion of my administration, and fervent wishes for my felicity. May the children of the Stock of Abraham, who dwell in this land, continue to merit and enjoy the good will of the other Inhabitants; while every one shall sit in safety under his own vine and figtree, and there shall be none to make him afraid. May the father of all mercies scatter light and not darkness in our paths, and make us all in our several vocations useful here, and in his own due time and way everlastingly happy.

G. Washington

later in this book, involved the Jews of Damascus being accused of murdering a Capuchin friar for ritual purposes and being badly persecuted as a consequence. Jews in America wished to protest and influence their government to intervene on behalf of their Syrian brethren. However the Elders of the Spanish and Portuguese Synagogue of New York flatly refused to allow a protest meeting to be held on their premises, not wishing to associate themselves with 'noisy intervention' on behalf of a group of foreign Jews.

The meeting was held in a nearby Ashkenazi synagogue. The subsequent letter of protest to the President was cordially received with the assurance that the Secretary of State had already taken action in the matter. This was a significant lesson for the Ashkenazi majority, who learnt for the first time that their voice could be heard with respect in America. From that time on, they rightly took the lead in communal affairs, relegating their 'aristocratic cousins' to a picturesque backwater.

Of the original Sephardi congregations of the United States, only those of New York and Philadelphia survive. Ashkenazim and those of mixed descent now form a substantial part of their membership.

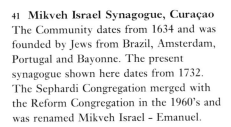

41 Mikveh Israel Synagogue, Curaçao
The Community dates from 1634 and was
founded by Jews from Brazil, Amsterdam,
Portugal and Bayonne. The present
synagogue shown here dates from 1732.
The Sephardi Congregation merged with
the Reform Congregation in the 1960's and
was renamed Mikveh Israel - Emanuel.

Alan Corré, in a perceptive analysis of the problem of Sephardi survival
in North America, (in the book 'The Western Sephardim'), has pointed to
neglect of Jewish learning and education as the prime reason for that failure.
According to Corré, without the stimulus of Jewish study, the Sephardim
of the United States, few in number and far from their European roots,
had only three viable choices.

The first was to adapt completely to life in the New World by abandoning
their traditions and changing into Reform Congregations — which is what
happened in Savannah, Charleston and New Orleans, as well as Curaçao
and Jamaica in the West Indies. The second choice was extinction — which
was the fate of Richmond. And the third course, adopted in New York and
Philadelphia, was to stress the aesthetics of the Sephardi minhag, to cultivate
its history, its archives and the quaint ways and rules of the founders —
and in the process to risk forgetting their true meaning. It is a sad story
— but one which is being repeated in several other Sephardi communities
today.

The Sephardi population of North, South and Central America increased
sharply in the early years of the twentieth century because of a flood of
new immigrants from the old Ottoman Empire and, later, from Persia and
the Arab world. In mid century, the final destruction of the ancient Jewish
communities of the Near East provided what will probably be the last wave
of Sephardi immigration to the New World.

This fresh immigration certainly gave a new breath of life to the
Sephardim of the United States; and its impact will be described in Part
Three of this book.

PART TWO

THE HISTORIC COMMUNITIES

Ψ

Baghdad

As described in Part One of this book, a Jewish presence in Mesopotamia had been continuous since King Nebuchadnezzar first carried a large part of the population of Judah into exile by the rivers of Babylon in the sixth century B.C.E. Many hundreds of years later, after the decline of Jewish life in the Holy Land because of Roman oppression, Babylon again took over as the intellectual centre of the Jewish world. Its scholars produced the Babylonian Talmud — the underlying structure of the Jewish religion today.

Baghdad, close to the site of ancient Babylon, was founded by Arab conquerors in 762 C.E. The seat of the Mohammedan Caliphs, it rapidly grew to become a fabulously splendid city. As described earlier, its Jewish community governed itself through the Resh Galuta (Exilarch, or Prince of the Captivity), descended from the royal House of David. He was assisted in this by the Geonim, the heads of the two great Jewish learned academies which eventually moved to Baghdad.

The Geonin acted as the supreme religious authorities for all Jews everywhere until the final decline of their institutions in the tenth and eleventh centuries, after which leadership shifted to the rising new centres of Jewish learning in North Africa, Mohammedan Spain and Christian Europe.

In the year 1039 the Spanish poet Solomon ibn Gabirol marked the death of Hai Gaon — principal of the Academy of Pumbeditha, then in Baghdad — in a moving elegy:

Weep my people....
Break all the instruments of music and song.
For Rab Hai our master, the last remnant
Left to us in this world has gone....
And for what shall we first grieve and mourn?
For the ark which now lies hidden in Zion,
Or for Rab Hai buried in Babylon?

But the days in which the Caliphs ruled the Islamic world from Baghdad, and the Geonim ruled the Jewish world also from Baghdad, were fast drawing to their close. As Baghdad fell prey to a succession of foreign conquerors and usurpers, as it decayed into decadence and corruption, so too was its Jewish leadership gradually destroyed through nepotism and strife. So too did the Jewish community's intellectual level decline sharply.

On the material plane though, Baghdad's Jews continued to prosper for a while longer. In the twelfth century, the powers and dignity of the Exilarch were greatly increased and he was again accorded semi-regal honours by the Caliph. As noted at the time:

Horsemen, Jewish and non-Jewish, escort him every Thursday when he goes to visit the great Caliph. Heralds go before him proclaiming 'Make way for our lord the son of David, as is his due'. He is mounted on a horse and dressed in robes of embroidered silk.... the Caliph rises and places him on a throne ...and all the Mohammedan princes rise up before him.

In the year 1170 Benjamin of Tudela reported that forty thousand Jews were living peacefully in Baghdad, including many wealthy people. The community possessed no fewer than twenty-eight synagogues and ten theological colleges. Other sources refer to physicians, perfumers, shopkeepers, goldsmiths and distinguished scholars among the Jews of the city. However, only a few decades later, another Jewish traveller to Baghdad reported that the community had sunk into degradation, with its synagogues and colleges in ruins.

Hulagu — a grandson of Ghengiz Khan, the Scourge of God — finally put an end to old Baghdad in the year 1258. He conquered the city at the head of his Mongol army and massacred most of its population without mercy. It is recorded that he spared the lives of Baghdad's Jews and Christians; but they too were utterly ruined by the devastation wrought by the implacable Mongol conquerors.

The pagan Khans at first favoured their newly acquired Jewish subjects; and a Jew was even appointed to the post of supreme governor of Mesopotamia. But his eventual downfall, followed by the conversion of many of the Mongols to Islam, signalled a very long period of intermittent persecution during the course of which most Jews either perished or left the city.

In 1401 Baghdad was sacked again, this time by another dreaded Mongol, Timur the Lame (Tamberlane); and it was said that the havoc he wrought was only less than that of Hulagu before him because there was so much less left to destroy. We know little of what actually happened to the Jews of Baghdad, other than that their synagogues and dwellings were burned to the ground and that many lost their lives or were converted to Islam.

From that time on, there is no longer any mention of the Exilarch or the Geonim in surviving records. There can have been few if any Jews left in Baghdad between the end of the fourteenth century and the early years of the sixteenth century. Some historians maintain that the continuity of Jewish settlement was never interrupted; but there is no evidence, one way or the other.

It was not until the sixteenth century that Jews began to trickle back to Baghdad in appreciable numbers. But the Baghdad to which some of the Spanish refugees eventually found their way was no longer the fabulous city of the Caliphs of Islam. It was only a shade of its former self. The learned academies with their illustrious Geonim had long since disappeared; and the grand, semi-royal, office of Exilarch had been replaced by the more prosaic one of 'Nasi' — merely the president or head of the community.

Baghdad itself still occupied a pivotal position astride several of the world's major trade routes. Goods reached its markets from the East, either overland or up the Persian Gulf. They then travelled westwards along the main caravan route across the desert to Aleppo in Syria, and then on to the Mediterranean and Europe. The city was able to maintain its status as an important trading centre even though its formerly fertile countryside — once the granary of the East — had been reduced to a series of barren and swampy wastelands by the Mongols, who had destroyed all the ancient irrigation and drainage systems.

The fortunes of Baghdad's Jews improved considerably under the rule of the Ottoman Turks. When Sultan Suleiman the Magnificent entered Baghdad in 1534, he was accompanied by his Jewish physician as well as by a number of other Jewish scholars, and was warmly welcomed by the resident Jewish population. In time though, the administration of the outlying provinces of the Ottoman Empire was more and more left to local governors; and the personal attitude of each became crucial to his Jewish community. Some were tolerant; but others were vicious. Though a measure of prosperity was often achieved in Baghdad, the former glory of the community was never fully revived. Even in religious matters, its rabbis often had to turn to those of Aleppo and Safed for rulings — a far cry from the days when it was Baghdad which set the standards for the Jewish world.

Even more devastating than the sporadic persecution of Baghdad's Jews by their Mohammedan overlords were the succession of epidemics of cholera and typhoid, and the floods that periodically inundated the city. It is thought that disease may have been brought to Baghdad by burial traffic from Persia to the Shia shrines nearby; but for whatever reason, the epidemics spread like wildfire, often wiping out large sections of the population.

The plague of 1742, for example, claimed as its victims most of Baghdad's rabbis and its entire Beth Din (Ecclesiastical Court). A new Haham (Chief Rabbi) had to be imported from Aleppo; but he too died in the epidemic of 1773. Fifty Jewish families from Aleppo, including some of Spanish descent, accompanied the new Haham to Baghdad at that time and helped re-populate the city. The worst outbreak of all, which occurred in 1831, was compounded by a great flood which destroyed a large part of the town. It is estimated that two-thirds of the total population of one hundred and fifty thousand perished in that episode; and the city was virtually emptied of inhabitants for some time after.

Far from the restraining influence of Constantinople, Jews were also occasionally molested by the Ottoman governors. After one particularly outrageous incident, they had to appeal for help to the Sultan, to the Board of Deputies of British Jews in London, to the Alliance Israélite in Paris and to the Sassoon family before obtaining the belated recall of their governor.

The venerated Haham Abdallah Somekh died in the cholera epidemic of 1889; and the governor's written permission was obtained to bury him in a Jewish shrine outside the city. The Mohammedan gatekeeper demanded a huge bribe to unlock the gate of the shrine for the burial procession and gravediggers; and when this was refused, Jews broke in and commenced the burial. They were set upon by local officials and severely beaten. On complaining to the police the following day, many community leaders, including rabbis, were arrested and arbitrarily imprisoned. To their great distress, Jews who had left the city were not allowed back because of quarantine regulations, though Moslems and Christians could pass freely. Those leaders who later signed the telegrams of protest to Constantinople and abroad were also cast into prison. The British Consul of the day found little unusual in this treatment of the Jews, reporting that:

42 A Jewish Merchant from Baghdad in traditional dress. Photographed in about 1900.

43 David Sassoon (1792-1864)
David, founder of the Sassoon dynasty and
family fortune, was unjustly imprisoned in
1828 by Daoud Pasha, Governor of
Baghdad. Released from gaol after the
payment of a huge ransom, he prudently
fled to Bushire in Persia. He eventually
made his way to Bombay in British India,
where he set up in business in 1832.

The prescriptive right of doing as he pleases with a Jew is here held to belong, in virtue of his natural and religious superiority, to every Moslem.

In the face of so many natural and man-made disasters it is hardly surprising that the Jewish population of Baghdad fluctuated greatly in numbers, diminishing sharply in response to hostile governors and natural disasters; and reviving again after the passing of the worst epidemics and especially during periods of political stability. At such times the immigrants even included Jews from Central and Northern Europe who arabized their Germanic names to suit their new surroundings.

Perhaps the worst of all Baghdad's governors was Daoud Pasha, who ruled between 1817 and 1831. It was during and shortly after this period that the first Jews began to leave Baghdad for India and Persia to the east and for Aleppo to the west — before eventually making their way to England, to the countries of Western Europe and to the Americas.

By that time, rabbinic scholarship in Baghdad had revived. Beth Zilkha, a small institution of higher learning, was established in 1840 and many distinguished rabbis studied there before taking up posts in other parts of the Near East. Most recent Sephardi Chief Rabbis of Israel, for example, were of Baghdadi origin.

However, this revival of learning did not extend to the masses. Despite continuing decay of the traditional religious schools, the rabbinic leaders grew increasingly introspective and made no attempt to replace them with a viable modern alternative. Consequently the standard of religious education was low.

The Alliance schools, with their European type of education, did tremendous work in equipping many of Baghdad's Jewish children for the new Western-style life to come; but despite their efforts and good intentions, the introduction of secular subjects inevitably resulted in some cases in a weakening of attachment to their religious heritage. The role of the Alliance Israélite Universelle is described in the chapter on the Ottoman Empire in Part One of this book.

The Turkish government reforms of 1908 granted equal rights to the Jews, who took full advantage of their new opportunities. Jews were elected as delegates to the Turkish Parliament and accepted official posts in the administrations of Baghdad, Basra and Mosul. Jewish merchants extended their trading activities and became prominent in international commerce. For the first time in the Islamic world, Jews could glimpse a future in which they need no longer remain as second-class citizens, dependent for their welfare on the whims of their Mohammedan masters.

By the time Great Britain assumed its mandate over Mesopotamia after the First World War of 1914-18, and created the Kingdom of Iraq, Jews constituted twenty-five per cent of the population of Baghdad and dominated the city's trade. The new King Faisal, under British influence, proclaimed

Freedom of religion, education and employment for the Jews of Baghdad, who had played such an important part in its welfare and progress.

44 Shaoul Nawa and his wife
Traditional Baghdadi dress of the early
20th century.

The Jews, better educated than their neighbours and speaking some
English because of the Alliance Schools, were favoured by Faisal and his
British advisors. Many were appointed to high positions in government;
and several served as representatives in Parliament and in the Senate. It
was as good a period for the Jewish community as it was for Iraq as a whole.

King Faisal died one year after Iraq gained its full independence in 1932.
He was succeeded by his young son Ghazi, best described as a drunken
ignoramus. Significantly, Hitler came to power in Germany that same year.
"Mein Kampf" was translated into Arabic and a German embassy was
opened in Baghdad. The new government lost no time in proceeding against

45 A Jewish family of Baghdad
Note the change to European-style dress amongst the younger members of this family in the above photograph taken in 1928.

its minorities. The Christian Assyrian community was decimated by massacre and many Jews were dismissed from their official positions.

The Iraqi government was overthrown by a military coup in 1936. Disabilities against the Jews multiplied as the Iraqis became increasingly drawn to Nazi Germany and its ideas. Restrictions were placed on Jewish entry to colleges of higher learning. Anti-semitism increased everywhere. Bombs were planted in Jewish centres and several Jews were killed in riots. Denials by community leaders of any sympathy with Zionism were all in vain as the situation of the community steadily deteriorated.

The Iraqis even set up their own youth movement, modelled on the Hitler Youth. The pro-German Grand Mufti of Jerusalem, virulently anti-Jewish in thought and deed, fled to Baghdad in 1939 where he was warmly welcomed. A climax was reached in 1941, when Raschid Ali's Nazi-inspired revolt against the pro-British government collapsed after much fighting. The Mufti escaped to Berlin, where he remained as Hitler's ally and guest for the rest of the war.

A vicious pogrom erupted in Baghdad following the suppression of Raschid Ali's revolt. It lasted for three days, during which much property was looted and destroyed. Nearly two hundred Jews were brutally murdered and many more were injured. British troops stationed nearby refused to intervene, supposedly because of lack of orders.

That incident prompted a large number of Jews to leave the country, most fleeing to India and Persia. Those, wise enough to have done so then, were at least spared the further years of misery awaiting their brethren who remained behind, vainly hoping for better times to come.

The very last episode in a long history, which included some splendid periods, was associated with the events that followed the establishment of the State of Israel in 1948 and the intense wave of Arab nationalism that accompanied it.

The community was virtually liquidated — once and for all — with the

46 **King Feisal I with the leaders of the Baghdadi Jewish community**
King Feisal is flanked by his Chief Chamberlain and the Governor of Baghdad. In the front row, from right to left, are Haham Sasson Khedourie (Ab Beth Din) and Haham Ezra Dangoor.

vast majority of its members leaving for Israel. Some of the richer Jews lingered in Iraq for a while before eventually emigrating to Europe and North America. Thus, apart from a few hundred survivors, Mesopotamia was at last emptied of its Jews, who had lived there for a thousand years before the Arabs first entered the country, and whose ancient tradition maintains that it was from Mesopotamia that they had first set foot on the world's stage some four thousand years before.

47 Jewish musicians of Baghdad 1933
Saleh al Kuwaiti is holding the violin. His brother, David al Kuwaiti, is holding the oud (lute).

48 Ancient Jewish cemetery of Baghdad
The memorials are of brick, covered in bitumen; and the larger structures are those of famous rabbis. The cemetery was destroyed by government order to make way for a new road.

Aleppo

The Jewish community of Aram Zova in Northern Syria — otherwise known as Halab or Aleppo — had ancient roots. It was certainly in existence shortly after the destruction of the Temple in 70 C.E. and possibly was even older. Local tradition maintains that Ezra the Scribe paused there on his way from Babylon to Jerusalem; and that he built the synagogue which still stands in Tedef, a few miles distant from the city.

Halab's own ancient synagogue, burnt down in the pogrom of 1947, was built in the fifth century when Syria was still part of the Byzantine Empire. Two Hebrew inscriptions on its walls survived the sacking of the synagogue by the Mongols and its subsequent restoration. The synagogue's greatest treasure was the Keter (Crown) — otherwise known as the Aleppo Codex. This Hebrew Bible was written by a Palestine scribe in the ninth century and had its vowels added by Aharon ben Asher the Masorete. Before the discovery of the Dead Sea Scrolls, the Keter was the world's oldest surviving biblical manuscript. It was closely studied by Maimonides in the twelfth century; and being accepted by Jews as the authoritative version of the Bible, it is an object of veneration.

Halab's 'native' Jewish population was enlarged by an influx of Sephardi refugees, including some outstanding rabbis, following their expulsion from Spain at the end of the fifteenth century. It was further augmented by another influx of 'Francos' in the eighteenth century, this time mainly from Italy and Austria. The immigrants merged with the local Jews so completely as to leave only their Spanish family names and a few words of Ladino in the local dialect as a memorial to their origins.

Aleppo was once a great city. A main caravan route linked it to Baghdad

49 Aleppo in the eighteenth century
The famous citadel dominates the view of the city.

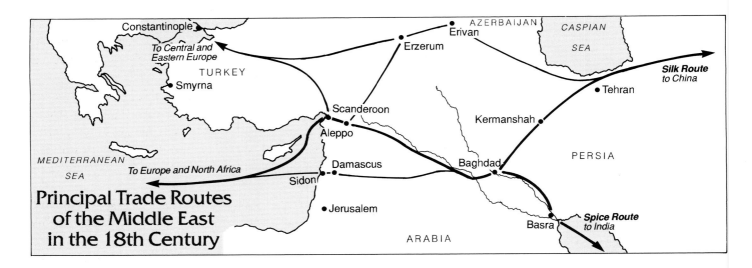

Principal Trade Routes of the Middle East in the 18th Century

and Basra; and goods from the East passed through its famous markets on their way to the Mediterranean coast and Europe, meeting others travelling in the opposite direction. It attracted many European merchants for, as described by a British chaplain in 1675, Aleppo was one of the pleasant cities in the Levant, comparing favourably with most in Europe:

...from hence all the city shows most beautiful...the buildings all of stone and flat on top look white and very beautiful. Next you see the cupolas, which are in abundance not only on their mosques but on many of their great buildings, rising up over the rest of the buildings like so many pretty mountains over the plains...Another adorning are the cypress trees, which are high and green all over the town, which make a very pretty show. And last of all the castle, which though it stands on the south side of the city...seems to stand in the very midst of all...About the town are brave gardens and pleasant plantations...being made more fruitful by a small brook which runs close by the town.

By the middle of the eighteenth century, the lot of the European merchants of Aleppo was pleasant indeed. According to Henry Maundrell, chaplain to the British community, social life consisted of a continual round of visits to other Europeans, as well as to the houses of Turks, Jews and Armenians. Their tables were well stocked with a marvellous assortment of game and fish; and much of their spare time was spent in feasting and hunting, in games and in picnics in the delightful countryside.

The European merchant colonies established in Aleppo did, to some extent, insulate its leading Jews from some of the worst pressures of life in the Ottoman Empire. Aleppo Jews co-operated to the full with the foreigners, often acting as factors or agents for the eastern end of the lucrative trade with Europe. They also worked for the Europeans as interpreters and in other supporting roles. Of course, Jewish merchants traded extensively on their own account too, buying silk, dyes and spices from Persia and India, and sending them on to Europe.

The Sephardim from Italy (mainly Livorno), France and Austria who came to settle in Aleppo in the eighteenth century, on the heels of the European merchants, were able to rely on the consuls of their countries of origin for protection. So too did Jews from India (originating in Baghdad) obtain British protection in a similar manner. Some "native" Jews also managed to acquire foreign nationality in one way or another. (The system of Capitulation treaties governing such extra-territorial rights is described in the chapter on the Ottoman Empire in Part One of this book).

By those means, many of the prominent Jewish families of Aleppo were able to enjoy the status of foreign subjects; and were thus freed at a stroke from the whims and exactions of the local Turkish governors, who periodically made life impossible for their brethren in other cities of the Empire. Aleppo thus became the most prosperous and important centre of Jewish life in Syria.

Fascinating glimpses of Jewish life in the Aleppo of the eighteenth century were provided by Alexander Russell, doctor to the English colony, in his book on the town.

It seems, at the time, that the Jews all lived close to their synagogue; and, being very much under the eye of their Haham (Rabbi), they were religiously observant and well behaved. Russell comments in explanation that, for Jews, it was

...more difficult to conceal debauchery than it would be among a more numerous nation.

The community included poor people as well as prosperous bankers, merchants and shopkeepers. Russell explains that kasher meat (slaughtered and prepared in accordance with Jewish law), was not often available; but that when it was, the richer members subsidised its price for the benefit of the poor — otherwise they subsisted on poultry and vegetables.

Such was the influence of the Jewish merchants and bankers on the town's commercial activity that trade ceased altogether on Jewish holydays when

...even the Bashaws and other Grandees are sometimes obliged to postpone the dispatch of their own affairs when it happens to interfere with the Jewish holydays.

and the departures of important trans-desert caravans had to be postponed if they clashed with the dates of Jewish festivals or fasts.

The festival of Succot (Tabernacles) made the greatest impression on the English doctor. Each family, however poor, had its own succah.

Turkish ladies at this season stroll in troops among the Jewish houses to see the tabernacles, and are seldom refused admission. Such as are acquainted with the family are entertained with coffee, sweetmeats and sherbets; the others, after satisfying their curiosity, retire without ceremony....They entertain hospitably at their houses, send presents of various kinds of sweetmeats to their friends, and all business is suspended.'

Within their own community, women were not segregated from men nearly so strictly as were the Mohammedans. Their social centre was the hamam (bath house), where they met together for a gossip on Friday afternoons after they had finished preparing for the Sabbath. It was only in the hamam that they could meet, show off their fine clothes and talk freely to strangers between baths and massages. Unmarried girls were on their best behaviour there; for it was in the hamam that mothers often selected likely brides for their sons. All marriages were, of course, arranged by the parents — but only rarely were unwilling girls and boys forced

50 The Tebah of Aleppo's great Synagogue
The synagogue was built in the fifth century. It was rebuilt in the 9th century and restored again after the Mongol devastation. It was finally burned down in the pogrom of 1947. The Reader's Desk (Bimah) was, as shown, a roofed structure in the open courtyard.

51 Ezra Ruben Gubbay (1845-1916)
Ezra Gubbay is shown wearing his uniform
of Hon. Consul. He was an Aleppo
merchant of British nationality, whose
family had originated in Baghdad and come
to Aleppo via Calcutta in British India.

together. After the formal engagement ceremony, the young couple was
closely chaperoned until the wedding and never left alone.

Polygamy, though not forbidden to Sephardim, was only resorted to when
a wife refused to live with her husband, in cases of childlessness after a
ten-year period of waiting or, more rarely, where there was no male heir
born to the marriage. In such circumstances, the taking of a second wife
did occur —though usually only with the consent of the first wife — and
that custom continued in the East at least until the end of the nineteenth
century.

Russell reported that it was considered scandalous to take more than one
wife in the absence of such cause — which seems to imply that it did
happen sometimes. But, despite the amusing anecdote he quoted in support,
he was wrong in stating that the practice of taking a second wife was frowned
upon in all circumstances.

In one case a person, of low condition, on account of his wife's barrenness had taken a
second wife; and soon had the mortification of seeing both become pregnant. Both wives
continued for several years to bring one child every fifteen months, which the pious
Hebrews considered as a punishment for not trusting to God's providence.

Another custom mentioned by Russell was that of visiting the sick.

.... the men, on their return from synagogue in the forenoon, go in parties together from
house to house to visit the sick; and it is sufficient for a person to be considered sick if
he does not make his appearance at public worship. People, though really indisposed, often
make an improper exertion to go to synagogue in order to avoid the fatigue of ceremonious
visits.

The formal visiting of all senior relatives by the many members of their
respective families on the afternoons of Jewish holydays was another
pleasing Aleppo custom which survived in Manchester and New York until
quite recently. Each such visit — and there could be very many in the
course of an afternoon — could only be terminated after the sipping of a
cup of Turkish coffee served by the host. The arrival of the coffee at each
house was, understandably, often awaited with some impatience.

Aleppo's period of great affluence was affected by the development of
the Cape route to India in the early part of the nineteenth century, and
then by the overland route to India across Egypt to the Red Sea. It was
finally ruined by the opening of the Suez Canal in 1869. Much of the highly
profitable Eastern trade was then diverted from the desert caravans to and
from Aleppo, to the cheaper sea route. The prosperity of Aleppo declined
accordingly; and in 1890 British Consul Jago reported to his superior that
'The Suez Canal gave the death blow to the commerical prosperity of
Aleppo'. It should be noted that this was at a time when, again according
to Jago, 'Trade and commerce is almost exclusively in the hands of the
Christians and Jews'. In the same year the Consul also reported that there
were still over four hundred (Christian) Europeans resident in Aleppo.

In 1904 Henry Barnham, British Consul in Aleppo, estimated the
population of the Vilayet (or province) of Aleppo to be 116,000, of which
80,000 were Mohammedans, 27,000 were Christians, and 9,000 were Jews
who lived mostly within the city. A letter he sent to his ambassador in

52 Jewish orphanage in Aleppo, 1919

Constantinople, dated 27th January 1904, deserves quoting in full because of the light it sheds both on the economic situation of the country after the opening of the Suez Canal, and on the movement of the more energetic of its Jews to the West:

I have the honour to call Your Excellency's attention to the steadily increasing exodus of young men from this city and neighbourhood in consequence of the poverty of the country and the difficulty of finding employment.

The fact has been brought to my notice especially in connection with the grant of annual registration certificates to our own protégés, Christian or Jewish, and I estimate that during the nine years of my tenure of this Consulate, fully one fifth of the males on our register have left the country. After obtaining an imperfect knowledge of French, or still less of English, in the Franciscan school or that of the Alliance Israélite, they remain here until they come of age, then take a certificate of registration and leave, the greater part for Egypt, the remainder for North or South America. They seldom return, but if, as often proves the case, they succeed in their new life, they send for their families to join them.

There are others who do not leave Aleppo from necessity, who after having established a successful business in Manchester, for instance, return to Aleppo in the course of years, purchase land, and become rooted to the place. Their sons carry on the same business in Manchester and, in their turn, come back. Those however are exceptions to the prevailing condition of things here. The number of those in easy circumstances can be counted upon the fingers. The others who have any education to speak of have little capital and are compelled to emigrate.

The collapse of the Ottoman Empire and its replacement by French colonial rule between 1920 and 1945 brought much benefit to the country. With the French came law and order as well as the principles of liberty, fraternity and equality, noticeably absent in British colonies. The potentially fertile countryside recovered after centuries of neglect; and once again great flocks of sheep and fields of cotton and wheat provided exports which enriched the Arab farmers and landowners.

Trade with the West, in which Jews took a full part, was the key to prosperity and a comfortable middle-class life for many hundreds of Jewish families, far removed from their poverty-stricken brethren still penned in the Jewish quarter of the old city. In the 1930s, graduates of the Alliance schools started to go on to the French Lycée for further education; and these in turn produced the community's first doctors, lawyers and other professionals.

Victoria Shammah's account of Jewish life in the Aleppo of the early 1930s, seen through the eyes of a young girl, evokes something of the flavour of a bygone age in which Jews and Mohammedans were on good terms, the local Christians being hostile to both.

People in Aleppo did not travel much prior to the Second World War. We were happy in our own self-contained world and did not bother too much with what was going on outside. We had an uncle who lived in Istanbul; and I always remember the great excitement of meeting him and seeing him off again on the Taurus Express.

There was no welfare state or big charitable organisations in Aleppo. It was left to the rich to take care of the poor.

A few of the young men emigrated to New York where they prospered. As soon as they became established there, they would ask one of their relatives in Aleppo to choose a bride for them. The young man would then buy the trousseau, send this back to Aleppo, and marry the girl by proxy. Amazingly, most of the marriages turned out really well.

In Aleppo we kept Shabbat to the letter — no cooking, writing, etc. but just reading. A rabbi called at the house regularly to teach my brothers; but as this was not considered necessary for girls, we never learned any Hebrew.

The most wonderful food was served for Shabbat lunch after the men returned from synagogue. We had our own pet beggars who came to the house to be fed every Saturday after the family had finished lunch.

We celebrated all the Jewish holidays meticulously. At Purim we were given lots of presents and had a lovely time riding in horse-drawn carriages and singing our heads off.

Jews and Mohammedans were often good friends in Aleppo; and many became partners in business. Gozem was the Mohammedan partner in my father's firm. We used to send the Gozems trays of Turkish delicacies (cakes and sweets) at the end of Ramadan; and the Gozems would send us similar trays at the end of Passover.

Those were happy days!

The Jews of Halab remained loyal to their roots throughout the countries of their dispersion. For the first hundred years or so, wherever they settled—in Manchester, New York, Buenos Aires, Mexico City or elsewhere—they maintained their closely-knit communities and married their own kind, marriage partners often being specially exported from Halab for the purpose. They preserved their original customs; and the food of Aleppo, fragrant with almonds, pistachios, apricots and rosewater, accompanied them everywhere. Only in recent years have the bonds rapidly begun to unravel, and the former Halabis merge with Ashkenazi Jews and, sadly, even with the Christians of their new environment. Indeed, New York is the only place where the Aleppo tradition has survived almost undiluted to this day; and an account of that vibrant but inward-looking community will be found in Part Three of this book.

The Jewish community of Aleppo received its death blow in 1947, on the day following the decision of the United Nations to partition Palestine. All Aleppo's synagogues and Jewish institutions were burned to the ground in a violent pogrom which shook the city. Even the Keter was badly damaged, though part survived and was smuggled out to Israel. The community rapidly dispersed.

Damascus

Described in the Talmud as the 'Gateway to the Garden of Eden', because of the fertility of its orchards and vineyards, Damascus was host to an important Jewish community in Roman times. Saul of Tarsus, later to become the Christian apostle Paul, was on his way from Jerusalem to visit the Jews of Damascus when he is said to have experienced the vision described in the New Testament.

The fortunes of the Jewish community fluctuated as the tides of history swept over Syria and, in the Arab period, according to the alternating policies of tolerance and repression of the Mohammedan rulers.

Many Jews from Baghdad settled in the town at the end of the tenth century and had their own separate synagogue. The Palestinian Academy moved close to Damascus when Christian Crusaders conquered most of the Holy Land.

In 1173 Benjamin of Tudela reported that the community numbered some three thousand souls and included physicians, intellectuals and poets as well as small traders and craftsmen. In 1286, the community was ruled by an Exilarch on the Babylonian model, who claimed descent from the Royal House of David. He wielded sufficient authority to excommunicate several Jews of Acre who had criticised the work of Maimonides. Damascus and its Jews suffered severely when Timur (Tamberlane) the Mongol occupied the city in 1401 and exacted a huge ransom from its population.

Spanish refugees started to arrive in Damascus shortly after the Expulsion of 1492; and their numbers swelled when Damascus was incorporated into the Ottoman Empire in 1516. It was reported in 1521 that there were five thousand refugee families in the city, which by then had separate synagogues for those of Baghdadi, Spanish and Sicilian origin—each with its own Rabbi and Beth Din (religious court).

Nathan of Gaza was welcomed to Damascus after the apostasy of the false messiah Shabbetai Zvi; and, as a result of Nathan's teaching, many in the city long continued to believe that Shabbetai was the Messiah.

The commercial history of Damascus is generally similar to that of Aleppo, already described in detail in the last chapter, but with important differences. Though Damascus was also on an established caravan route between India and the Mediterranean, it never attained the same degree of prosperity as Aleppo.

Damascus, an asssembly point for many thousands of pilgrims to Mecca from the Balkans and Turkey, was notorious for its intolerance and fanaticism. So extreme was the behaviour of its Mohammedan population to foreigners, that it was not until the nineteenth century that the town could be entered safely by anyone wearing European clothes. Indeed, Damascus was the last major city in the Ottoman Empire to admit foreign consuls.

This meant that Damascus always lacked the large colony of European merchants present in Aleppo from the seventeenth century onwards. Consequently its Jewish community was denied the opportunity to participate fully in the East-West trade so abundant in Aleppo. Also the Jews had no alternative other than to lead their lives in a fully Ottoman and

Islamic environment, largely untouched by things European—and this was to their detriment.

The Jewish population of Damascus, so very much less cosmopolitan than Aleppo, was fully exposed to occasional blasts of Mohammedan intolerance. Its low point came in 1840 with the infamous 'Damascus Affair' in which Capuchin friars in league with the French Consul accused the Jews of murdering one of their number for ritual purposes.

Many Jews were arrested and tortured in this revival of the medieval Christian Blood-Libel. Some were put to death in a most barbarous manner as the result of the accusation; and sixty-three Jewish children were seized and held hostage. After a storm of international protest at the behaviour of the Islamic and Christian mobs, unleashed with the tacit support of the authorities, a Jewish delegation from Europe, led by Sir Moses Montefiore, travelled first to Egypt and then on to Constantinople to secure the release of the hostages and the protection of the community.

From time to time Jews were able to play a prominent part in local Ottoman affairs. A group of them became official bankers to the Turkish governor of Damascus in the 1740s; and they and their descendants acted in similar banking and administrative roles for the next hundred years.

The most eminent was Haim Farhi who entered the service of Jazzar Pasha, Governor of the Province of Sidon. He was responsible for financial administration and played a prominent part in the defence of Acre against Napoleon in 1799. Haim later ruled both the provinces of Sidon and Damascus on behalf of their Turkish governors until his eventual downfall and execution at the peak of his power in 1820. The famous Farhi Bible was once in his ownership; and the central square of Acre (now Acco in Israel) is still called Place Farhi in his honour.

In 1848 it was estimated that there were about four thousand Jews in Damascus, mostly working as petty traders, craftsmen and artisans. There were also a few wealthy merchants who lived in splendid houses. Isabel Burton—wife of the British Consul, and a lady with deep prejudice against Jews—described the two grandest Jewish houses of the city in her book 'The Inner Life of Syria', published in London in 1875 —

Now we will ride to the Jewish quarter, and visit Khawaja Lisbona, one of the wealthiest of his wealthy faith; he has the most beautiful house, save one, in Damascus. We shall be received with the greatest hospitality—the whole family will be equally pleased to see us. You will again remark the mean doorways, the narrow, winding passage, perhaps a stable-yard, which precede riches and beauty. Lisbona affects less of this contrast, yet even in his establishment a mean entrance is a shabby outer court, and a second poor doorway masks the beauty which flashes upon the stranger. The house is in the form of a square, and appears to be all as richly ornamented. A beautifuly paved Court stands before us, with large marble fountains and their goldfish, orange and lemon trees, jessamine and other perfumed shrubs, springing from a tesselated pavement, and kept moist by two or three little jets d'eau. Flowering creepers and shrubs are trained about the lattice work, shedding shade and sweets. The apartments open into the court. The Ka'ah, or open alcove, with raised floor and open front, looks on the court; the stone pavement and raised dias are covered with velvet and gold cushions on three sides. The walls are a mass of mosaics in gold, ebony, and mother-of-pearl, with tiny marble columns and many alto relievos. The reception-room inside is similar, but richer, we shall all sit round a beautiful white marble

53 Interior of a Jewish house in Damascus
This late 19th century photograph is of the inner courtyard of a house belonging to a Jew from Constantinople.

fountain, whose bubbling is most refreshing in the parched weather.

Khawaja Ambar, another Jew, is also building a palace, but it is in more modern style, and therefore less pleasing to me. The fashionable luxury is rich, but too rich; Lisbona's is tasteful as well as old. However, no one can find fault with Khawaja Ambar's idea of comfort. He has attached to his house a private synagogue and Turkish bath, and he is buying up all the old tenements around him to spread his establishment over as much ground as he can; unhappily he is also burning their carved wood and ancient ornaments, in which he sees no grace and beauty, and laughs at me for my heartache.

As in Aleppo, the Alliance schools and the coming of French colonial rule in 1920 brought order, stability and a measure of prosperity to the city.

Most of the five thousand strong Jewish community fled from Damascus to Beirut in 1948 after the establishment of the new state of Israel. Those remaining were oppressed by the authorities. A bomb was planted in their synagogue in 1949, causing yet more to quit the city.

Only four thousand Jews now remain in the whole of Syria. They lead a fearful existence — isolated, oppressed, and forbidden to leave the country.

Though overlooked by a Christian world obsessed with the plight of Palestinian refugees, it must never be forgotten that the obliteration of the ancient Jewish communities of the Near East was part of the heavy price exacted by the Arabs for the establishment of the modern state of Israel.

54 Jazzar Pasha Condemning a Criminal

F.B.Spilsbury was surgeon to the flagship of Admiral Sir Sidney Smith, who successfully defended Acre from Napoleon in 1799. Spilsbury accompanied the admiral on his visits to the Ottoman rulers and sketched the scenes he witnessed. These were later engraved in London, coloured and published. Seen holding the bill of indictment in his hand is Haim Farhi, who co-operated in the defence of Acre. Haim was later to become the virtual ruler of the provinces of Sidon and Damascus on behalf of their Turkish governors.

Calcutta

The origins of the two really ancient Jewish communities of India—the Cochinis and the Bene Israel—are shrouded in antiquity. Many claims are advanced for each, some plausible and others more fanciful, ranging in date from the sixth century B.C.E. to a time hundreds of years after the destruction of the Second Temple. Though refugees from Spain also came to Cochin after their expulsion in 1492, both groups were effectively isolated from the mainstream of Jewish tradition until comparatively recently.

The small community of Calcutta, on the other hand, dates only from 1798. It was a natural continuation of the far older communities of Aleppo and Baghdad, its founders having been attracted to India by economic opportunities waiting to be grasped under British rule. Baghdadi Jews also settled in Bombay where they were greatly outnumbered by the Bene Israel living there, and where the Sassoon family added lustre to their history.

The early immigrants to Calcutta brought with them the religion, language, way of life and dress of their native cities. They had mostly reached India in the years before Aleppo and Baghdad came under the influence of the network of Alliance schools which taught European languages and secular subjects as well as Jewish religion and history. The pioneers spoke Arabic and knew little or no English. More significant, they were pious; and the effect of that genuine piety could still be observed in their descendants who came to England in the 1950s. They had remained far more religiously observant than the immigrants who also arrived in England directly from Baghdad at roughly the same time.

Calcutta is chosen for special mention in this book because of the history of its two founders. This provides rare insight into the lives, customs and attitudes of mind of the Eastern Jews of the time, as well as information on their migrations. Their full story was told with great charm by Flower Elias and Judith Elias Cooper in their book 'The Jews of Calcutta'. They obtained copies of two diaries and a memoir left by those remarkable men; and the passages quoted below come directly from their book. Esmond Ezra—a descendant of Moses Duek—and Rabbi Mushleah also include much valuable detailed information on Calcutta's Jews in their own books on the subject. Though the story of the two founders of the Calcutta community may have been embellished by legend, much of it comes directly from the pens of Shalom Cohen and Moses Duek, its first leaders.

In 1789, at the age of twenty six, Shalom Cohen left his home in Aleppo and his wife to seek his fortune in the East. After visiting Baghdad, Basra and Bombay, he ended up in Surat — then India's leading port and home to a thriving colony of sixty five Arabic-speaking Jewish merchants. Shalom established himself quickly in Surat and was recognised by the East India Company as the 'Chief Jewish Merchant' and spokesman for the colony.

Legend relates that Shalom then sent back to Aleppo for his wife Sathie, only to be rebuffed by her parents:

Even if you were to pave the way from Aleppo to Surat with gold and precious stones, we would still not send you our daughter.

If true, that refusal seems inexplicable in the context of Jewish family

55 The David Sassoon Library
Erected in Bombay in 1847 by David Sassoon.

custom of the period unless it was prompted by a deeply unhappy marriage.

The following year, the frustrated Shalom took a second wife, as permitted by Sephardi Jewish law. He chose Najima, the sister of his business partner in Baghdad.

Two years later, Sathie's parents having relented, Shalom was re-united with his first wife in Baghdad; and he finally escorted her home to Surat. Najima is said to have embraced Sathie at the entrance of the house and handed over its keys saying:

You are my elder sister so must keep the keys. We will live together in love and peace.

Sathie died after giving birth to her first child. The infant was suckled and reared in love by Najima, who had given birth herself a few months earlier. The two half-sisters were married from their father's house on the very same day in 1815. They and their husbands then set up home together in the kind of extended family so common in the East at that time.

In 1796 a monopoly controlling the shipping of goods into and out of Calcutta was lifted and Shalom Cohen, accompanied by his shohet (ritual slaughterer) and cook, set out to investigate business prospects. The date of his arrival in 1798 is traditionally regarded as that of the birth of Calcutta's Jewish community. Before long, Shalom was joined by his wife and daughters and by several friends who accompanied them from Surat.

From that small start, the Jewish population of Calcutta steadily increased as more immigrants arrived from Aleppo and Damascus, from Baghdad and Basra, from Yemen and Persia and from even more distant places. It reached its peak of just under four thousand in the early 1940s, declining again after the granting of independence to India, until by 1990 fewer than one hundred Jews remained.

Shalom Cohen was the acknowledged leader of the Jewish community in its early years. The synagogue was in his house and he acted as its hazan (reader/minister). He prospered in business at first; but his life was far from uneventful. Lengthy and mutually ruinous litigation with a former partner, the bitterness of which must have divided the Jewish colony, caused him to accumulate so many debts that in 1812 he moved to Chinsura to avoid his creditors.

Far from being discouraged by misfortune, Shalom eventually made his way to Lucknow where he was appointed Court Jeweller by the (Moslem) Nawab of Oudh. He was presented with the Robe of Honour and even

56 An English Officer
This gouache, by a Bengali artist, was produced in 1775, shortly after the British conquest of Bengal.

57 Moses Duek
In this etching of 1839, Moses Duek is
wearing traditional Baghdadi dress, though
a native of Aleppo, thus demonstrating
Baghdadi dominance of the Calcutta
community.

given the unique distinction of being permitted to ride with the Nawab on
an elephant. It seems that Shalom fell out of favour with the Nawab, for
he departed from Lucknow in some haste two-and-a-half years later; but
when he did leave, it was with a retinue of thirty soldiers, twenty-five
chokras, seven carriages, seven palanquins, sixty household servants, ten
personal servants and twenty three porters. He was rich indeed.

After the death of the Nawab, Shalom later returned to Lucknow to serve
his son and successor. In the meantime he had acted as Court Jeweller to
the (Sikh) Maharaja Ranjit Singh. In Amritsar it is said that he was once
asked to value the 191-carat Koh-i-Noor diamond, later presented to Queen
Victoria. Shalom earned the Maharaja's praise when he declared that, as
such a jewel could only be acquired as a gift or by the shedding of much
blood, it was priceless!

Shalom Cohen died in Calcutta in 1836. He was buried in the cemetery
that he had himself presented anonymously to the Jewish community, which
by then numbered three hundred.

Shortly after his eldest daughter Luna's twelfth birthday in 1806, Shalom
wrote to his old friend and brother-in-law in Aleppo, asking him send one
of his sons to Calcutta to marry Luna. The letter was received with joy
and an enthusiastic reply returned:

... my dear son Moses, the light of my eyes, the crown of my head, choicest of young men,
is yours. And I trust in your affection that you will keep your eye on him. And from this
day on, he is your son ....

Moses Duek obediently set out for India, where he encountered his new
family for the first time. Arriving at Shalom's house at midnight, he later
recalled that:

...we met and I bowed before him and kissed his hand; and he also kissed and embraced
me as a father his son. And so did all the other relatives living in the house....and in the
morning we rose early to the synagogue of my father-in-law, the crown of my head, which
was in the house....and I gave praise and thanksgiving for life and peace and for my having
arrived. Blessed be He who does good and deals kindly....Amen.

Two months after her thirteenth birthday, Luna was married to Moses.
Again, in the words of his old age quoted in Flower Elias's book,

...And I stayed in quiet and peace in the house of my father-in-law; and God, blessed be
He, set me favourably in his sight and in the sight of his family... I married my bride, my
dove, my perfect one, Miss Luna—of women in the tent may she be blessed—daughter
of my father-in-law, the crown of my head. And I lived with her and she found favour in
my eyes; and she also loved me as her own soul. And I give thanks to His great name for
all the above that I had experienced...And after the wedding, my father-in-law gave into
my hands and possession all his affairs. And all his secretaries and servants were under
my control...and he was pleased with my efforts.

Moses Duek had already taken over the leadership of the community by
the time Shalom left Calcutta in 1812. Though lacking the flair of his
father-in-law, Moses was sufficiently successful in business to enable him
to devote much of his time to communal service.

Appalled by the inept circumcision of his eldest son, when

...the blood was flowing and the baby went on weeping until he was silenced by the great weakness, pain and danger,

he taught himself how to perform the rite. It was with great pride that Moses later claimed to have carried out three hundred and forty three circumcisions during his lifetime.

Not only was Moses the head of Calcutta's synagogue, with full responsibility for its running and maintenance, but he also read the services, performed the circumcisions and marriages, wrote the marriage contracts and other legal documents, and arbitrated in disputes. Only in matters of divorce did he refuse to become involved. In best Sephardi tradition he claimed:

58 Magen David Synagogue of Calcutta
This was built in 1884.

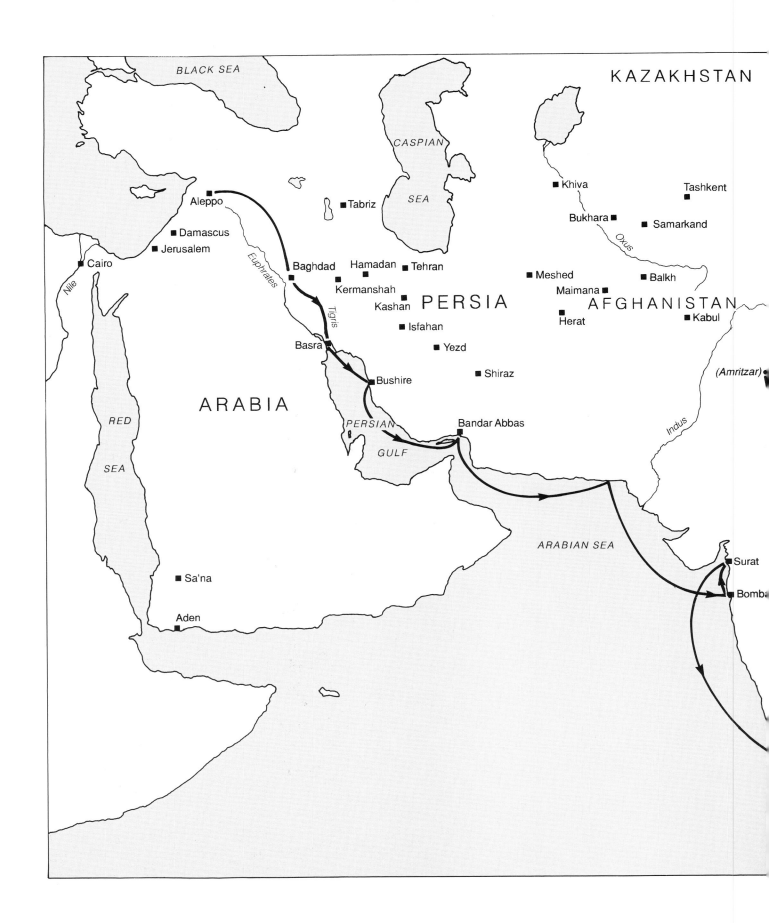

BLACK SEA

KAZAKHSTAN

CASPIAN

Aleppo

SEA

Tabriz

Khiva

Tashkent

Damascus

Bukhara

Samarkand

Jerusalem

Oxus

Cairo

Euphrates

Baghdad

Hamadan

Tehran

Nile

Meshed

Balkh

Kermanshah

Maimana

AFGHANISTAN

Kashan

PERSIA

Herat

Kabul

Tigris

Isfahan

Basra

Yezd

(Amritzar)

ARABIA

Shiraz

RED

Bushire

SEA

PERSIAN

GULF

Bandar Abbas

Surat

ARABIAN SEA

Bomba

Sa'na

Aden

Indus

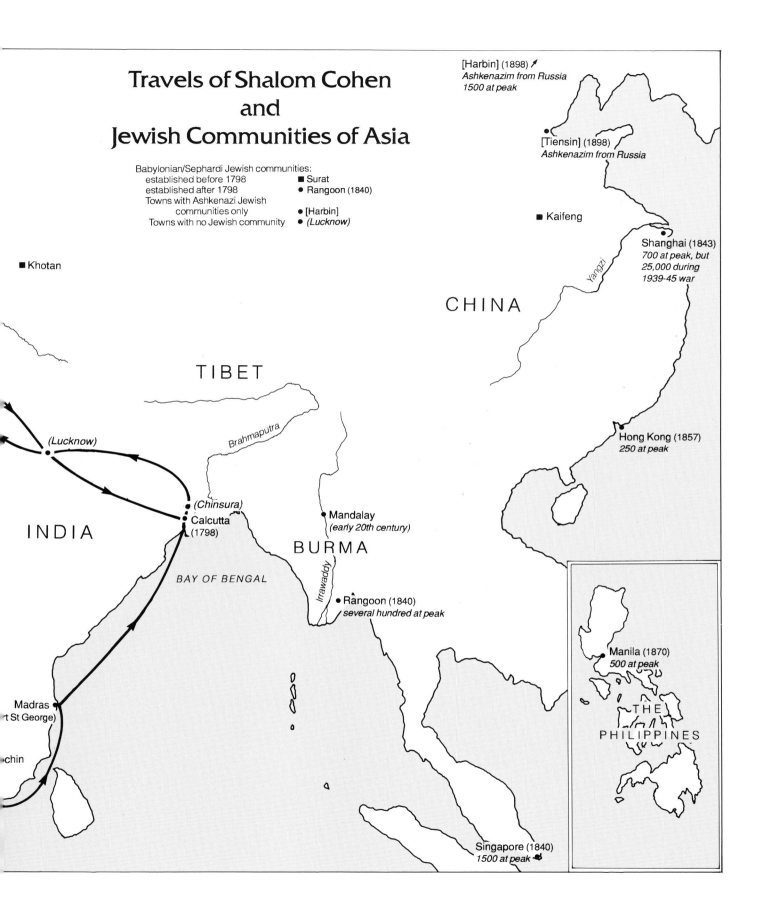

Travels of Shalom Cohen
and
Jewish Communities of Asia

Babylonian/Sephardi Jewish communities:
established before 1798   ■ Surat
established after 1798   ● Rangoon (1840)
Towns with Ashkenazi Jewish
  communities only   ● [Harbin]
Towns with no Jewish community ● *(Lucknow)*

■ Khotan

[Harbin] (1898)
*Ashkenazim from Russia
1500 at peak*

[Tiensin] (1898)
Ashkenazim from Russia

■ Kaifeng

CHINA

Shanghai (1843)
*700 at peak, but
25,000 during
1939-45 war*

Yangzi

TIBET

Brahmaputra

(Lucknow)

INDIA

(Chinsura)
Calcutta
(1798)

Hong Kong (1857)
250 at peak

● Mandalay
(early 20th century)

BURMA

Irrawaddy

BAY OF BENGAL

● Rangoon (1840)
several hundred at peak

Madras ●
rt St George)

chin

Manila (1870)
500 at peak

THE
PHILIPPINES

Singapore (1840)
1500 at peak

...and I have not forsaken any matter as far as my poor abilities would allow...Further, all my days, through the grace of God the Exalted, I have received no fee or material benefit for any of my work.

After Moses's death in 1861 his place was taken by other pious merchants, including his own grandson who served with much distinction for many years. No paid rabbi was available or was engaged until well into the twentieth century—the community being content to rely on those devoted men and to turn to the rabbis of Baghdad and Jerusalem for guidance on matters outside their competence.

That spirit of devotion to communal service, whether in the synagogue or in the rich endowment of so many charitable institutions, became the hallmark of Calcutta's Jews— and indeed of wealthy Middle and Far Eastern Jews as a whole. It also had its drawbacks; for the rich virtually ruled their communities by means of their generosity to synagogue and other causes. As a consequence, many descendants of the Eastern communities today lack a developed tradition of democratic communal responsibility and endeavour. Even the idea of paid synagogue membership—an important basis of Jewish identity in the West—was unknown to them before leaving the East.

The merchants of Calcutta flourished under British rule, as did those of Bombay. Many made great fortunes by trading in opium and indigo. Opium, it must be realised, was a respectable commodity in those days. Indian farmers were compelled to sell all their produce to the British Indian government, which then re-sold it by public auction for export. Later on, the Jewish merchants shifted to the textile trade. Many also became very wealthy by shrewd investments in property (real estate) in booming Calcutta.

As trade opportunities beckoned, enterprising merchants moved outwards from centres such as Calcutta and Bombay, founding smaller Jewish communities wherever they settled—in Rangoon, Shanghai, Singapore, Hong Kong and Malaya.

An interesting incident, relating to the Kadoorie family (of Baghdadi origin), illustrates well the personal responsibility for the entire community gladly undertaken by wealthy Eastern Jewish merchants. Just before the Second World War, many European Jews found sanctuary from Hitler's minions in the free port of Shanghai, which was one of the few places in the world where entry visas were not required. After the Japanese conquest of South East Asia, all Jews found there, as well as those of Japan, were concentrated in Shanghai, where they managed in one way or another to survive. After the end of the war, Kuomintang China was steadily overrun by the communist Red Army. The Jews of Shanghai had to get out before Shanghai fell to the communists; and so it was that, at the end of 1947, some five hundred and fifty of them obtained visas for Australia. Horace Kadoorie in Shanghai arranged for the American 'Joint' to ship the refugees direct to Australia.

Something went wrong. Lawrence (later to become Lord) Kadoorie—one of the eleven-strong Jewish community of Hong Kong—was suddenly

תאר זן עַרוס בן שׁלֹמוֹ

notified by his brother that the refugees would be arriving in Hong Kong, where they needed to land for two days before being trans-shipped to Australia. War-ravaged Hong Kong was then under military administration and desperately short of food and water. No civilians, and especially not women, were admitted at that time. Lawrence appealed in person to the military government, which most reluctantly granted permission for the refugees to land for two days only, and on the strict conditions that Lawrence Kadoorie himself assumed personal responsibility for their accommodation and behaviour, and that they did not work.

In Lord Kadoorie's own words:

In due course the group arrived and was escorted to the Peninsula Hotel where I was to put them up—all the women in one ballroom and all the men in the other. This in spite of noisy protestations from individuals who did not wish their families to be separated. The refugees were a varied lot —Germans, Poles, Russians, etc.—embracing every section of society. The British troops who then occupied the hotel lobby looked on this invasion of strange people, speaking a variety of languages, with much curiosity.

The day before their ship was intended to sail, I received a cable saying that it would not be coming to Hong Kong to pick up the refugees after all, thus making me responsible for supporting the entire group until other arrangements could be made.

To make a long story short, it was not long before many of them set up a mini-industrial centre in the lobby of the Peninsula Hotel — rabbis, tailors, music teachers, card-sharpers (who complained that they could not work because it would spoil the sensitivity of their fingers when dealing!). I reported to the military administration saying that it would solve my problem if they arrested me and dealt with the matter themselves. They, however, declined. It took considerable effort to find and charter alternative shipping and it was six months before we were able to say 'goodbye' to the last member of the group.

After that digression, back to Calcutta. The city also contained comfortable middle-class Jews as well as the fabulously wealthy. There was a disreputable element too, some of whom it seems earned a reasonable living by begging. Members of the Jewish community owned slaves, as did the other peoples of India until that practice went out of favour with the British in the middle of the nineteenth century. Jewish slaves were, however, given their freedom in accordance with Jewish custom and law; and many were converted to Judaism.

Though ever grateful to the Indian people, who always treated them with tolerance and regard, the Jews were advised by Gandhi to remain aloof from pre-independence politics. As a community they no more fully identified with the Indians than they did with their British masters. India's gaining of independence from Britain in 1947 was viewed without enthusiasm by Calcutta's Jews. The community began to disperse from that time on, until there were fewer than one hundred left by 1990. Many of them came on to London and their story is continued in Part Three of this book.

Central Asia

Bukhara Mashad Afghanistan

Jews have lived in that part of Central Asia straddling the present borders of Iran, the former Soviet Union and Afghanistan since early times. Local legend identifies Bukhara (Republic of Uzbekistan) with the Biblical town of Habor; and ascribes the foundation of its Jewish community to the Lost Ten Tribes of Israel. The community of Bukhara was certainly in existence by the thirteenth century; and we do know that it increased in size following the sack of Samarkand in 1598.

According to local guide books for tourists, several of Afghanistan's leading Mohammedan tribes proudly claim to be descended from the Lost Ten Tribes of Israel—and also from King Saul through one of his wives. The Jewish communities of Afghanistan and Bukhara came under the jurisdiction of the Babylonian Exilarchs; and it is recorded that unsuccessful candidates for office in Baghdad were sometimes exiled to Afghanistan because of its remoteness.

Jews were encouraged to move to Meshed (Mashad in Arabic), in the extreme north of Persia by Nadu Shah in 1740. Once settled, they built up a vibrant community during his lifetime.

Islamic fanaticism in the area grew alarmingly during the end of the eighteenth century, when many restrictions were heaped on its Jews. In Bukhara, the payment of the obligatory poll tax levied on Jews was accompanied by a humiliating slap across the face to emphasise their inferior status. Many were forcibly converted to Islam.

In Meshed, a holy city of the Shi'as, the concept of ritual uncleanness was applied to Jews with dire consequences; and again, many were compelled to accept the Crescent. A violent pogrom erupted in 1839. The synagogue was burned to the ground and much Jewish property was destroyed. The Jewish community only escaped being butchered by the enraged mob by promising its Sheikh to embrace Islam.

However, like the Jews of Spain and Morocco before them, neither the Bukharans nor the Mashadis ever accepted the religion of Muhammad with sincerity. They continued to practise their ancestral faith in secret. In their shops, forced to open on the Sabbath, they quoted ridiculously high prices so as to avoid making a sale; and even on pilgrimage to Mecca, some claimed to have secreted miniature tefillin (phylacteries) inside their Islamic turbans.

In a continuous wave of migration, they quit the places of their oppression for more tolerant parts of the region—particularly Afghanistan, where they joined the local communities. They also travelled further afield to Teheran, Bombay and Jerusalem.

In 1868 Imperial Russia conquered most of the area and incorporated parts of Bukhara, including the cities of Samarkand and Tashkent, into Russia. The Russians attempted to placate the local population and all anti-Jewish restrictions were abolished. But conditions remained very much the same in the rest of the Emirate of Bukhara, where the Emir was granted local autonomy. The converted Jews from Bukhara and from Meshed in Persia—called the 'Anusim' (Compelled Ones) — moved into the more tolerant Russian areas whenever they could escape. They then openly returned to Judaism; and in the process, many added the Russian ending

59 **Succah in the Bukharan quarter of
Jerusalem**

'off' (meaning 'son of') to their names—like 'Davidoff' for example.

The Russians unsuccessfully tried to stop this movement of Mashadi and Bukharan Jews into their territory by making distinctions between 'local' and 'foreign' Jews; but that came to an end with the Russian revolution of 1917. Though the whole of the Emirate of Bukhara then became part of the Soviet Union, popular anti-semitism and attendant pogroms continued very much as before—and the trickle of emigration proceeded.

Jerusalem became home to a large number of Bukharan and Mashadi émigrés. Its Bukharan Quarter, founded in 1892, soon became the world centre of a community which jealously strove to preserve its own separate identity.

Many Mashadis too moved to Jerusalem where they opened two synagogues. Others moved south to Teheran. The first Mashadis reached London at around the turn of the century, including a dealer in oriental carpets who arrived from Jerusalem, via Constantinople.

In 1914, on the outbreak of the First World War, Jews from Meshed with their Russian-sounding names were treated with suspicion by the Turkish authorities in Jerusalem. They were given the choice of taking up Ottoman citizenship or departing. Those who refused to accept Turkish nationality were deported. They were sent to Cairo, then under British control—as also were British-protected Jews from Syria and elsewhere. Some of them eventually moved on to London; and the story of this very special community is continued in the chapter on London in Part Three of this book.

Small Jewish communities were still in existence in Samarkand, Bukhara and Tashkent when one of the authors visited the region in 1981. Well over two hundred men then attended the Rosh Hashanah service in Tashkent's sole remaining synagogue, though none of the younger men or children could take time off on a 'normal' working day.

Most of Afghanistan's estimated five thousand Jews left in 1951. It was reported that only two hundred or so, including some originally from Bukhara, were still in Kabul and Herat at the time of the Soviet invasion of 1976.

60   Bride and Bridegroom from Bukhara

Egypt

The love-hate relationship of the Jewish people with Egypt is as old as the Jewish tradition itself. The first book of the Bible relates how Abraham travelled to Egypt in his great epoch-making voyage of discovery, in his search to establish a new religious identity. Later, it was from Egypt that Moses led the mixed multitude to Sinai to receive the Torah, and thence to the Promised Land where the Jewish nation was forged.

King Manasseh of Judah (698-643 B.C.E.) was an obedient vassal of mighty Assyria, then at the peak of its power. Part of his army may have accompanied that of King Ashurbanipal in his invasion of Egypt; and it is thought that, after the conquest, Jewish soldiers remained in Egypt to guard the border town of Elephantine (near modern Aswan) for the Assyrians. When Egyptians later regained control of their country, they also employed a colony of mercenary Jewish soldiers at Elephantine to protect their southern border against the Nubians. Again, under Persian rule from 525 B.C.E., there was a large Jewish garrison at Elephantine; and the chapter on Babylon in Part One of this book contains an account of King Darius II's instruction to his garrison in the year 419 B.C.E., concerning the correct way to celebrate Passover.

Elephantine (Yeb, in Aramaic) was not only a military outpost, but also a trading centre through which goods from Nubia, such as ivory, passed on their way to Egypt. A Jewish civilian colony existed there alongside the garrison. It must have been wealthy to have been able to build the magnificent temple described in surviving fragments of ancient documents.

The form of Judaism practised in Yeb was tinged with idolatry, as was that of King Manasseh himself; for two goddesses were worshipped in the temple alongside the one true God of Israel—and this is the reason that scholars think the temple was built during Manasseh's reign, or soon after. It was finally destroyed by priests of the Egyptian god Khnub in 411 B.C.E., at a time when Persian influence in the region was fast waning.

Numbers of Jews, including the prophet Jeremiah, fled to Egypt in 587 B.C.E., after the conquest of Jerusalem by the Babylonians. We read in the Bible of Jeremiah's railing against the Jews of Egypt for their idolatrous ways—could he have had the Yeb temple in mind? And there is a Christian tradition, not echoed in Jewish sources, that the prophet was stoned to death in Egypt by fellow countrymen, exasperated beyond reason by his continuous scolding.

Egypt was conquered by Alexander the Great in the year 332 B.C.E. His successors, the Ptolemies, encouraged Jews to settle there and form a middle class on whose loyalty they could rely. Jews responded with alacrity, establishing themselves first in Alexandria and the surrounding districts, and later in the rest of the country. They worked as farmers, tradesmen and government officials; and served prominently in the army, the police, and in banking and financial administration. By the first century C.E., Jews were in the majority in Alexandria itself, and formed about twelve per cent of the total population of the country.

Though treated with tolerance and allowed to flourish unchecked, Jews as a group were not granted full citizenship as were the Greeks. Though some individuals did attain the status of free citizens, most had to be content with the guaranteed right to observe their own ancestral laws. Jews increasingly adopted Greek ways and the Greek language in preference to their original Aramaic and Hebrew. The Bible was translated into Greek; and it was that translation, the Septuagint, that was read out in the synagogues.

The Great Synagogue of Alexandria was so vast that a system of flags had to be used there to elicit the proper responses from worshippers, many of whom were sitting so far away from the Reader that they were unable to hear him.

A second temple was built in Egypt by a group of refugees from Judah, led by a former High Priest, during the Maccabean revolt in the middle of the second century B.C.E. This was at Leontopolis, near Heliopolis; and it lasted for over two hundred years before it was closed down by the Romans.

Relations between the Greeks and the Jews deteriorated with time until, by the end of the Ptolemaic period, there was much ill-will and strife between them.

The Roman conquerors of Egypt increasingly favoured the Greeks to the Jews, who were subjected to discrimination and restrictions. Constant struggles between the communities resulted in many appeals to Rome for justice—usually granted in favour of the Greeks. Jewish property was looted and synagogues desecrated by Greeks; and Jews sometimes reacted violently, once attempting to burn the Greeks assembled in their own amphitheatre.

The rivalry was settled once and for all in the year 115 C.E. when the Jews of Egypt and Cyrenaica (in modern Libya) revolted against Roman rule. The precise causes of the revolt are obscure; but local Greek hostility to the Jews must have played a part, as well as the messianic pretensions of Lucuas of Cyrene, its leader.

The rebellion was crushed by the Romans with habitual savagery. Much of Alexandria was destroyed, together with its Great Synagogue; and the resulting massacre put a virtual end to the Jewish community. Jewish property was confiscated wholesale and all Jewish courts were suspended, thus terminating organised communal life as it had previously existed.

Though there is little hard evidence, there can be no doubt that some Jews continued to live in Egypt during the Christian period. Christian anti-semitism, added to that of the Greeks, must have made life very difficult for them. The Orthodox Church reacted badly to Jewish support for the Arian heresy; and it branded the Jews as 'hated enemies of the Church' as a result. There was certainly a pogrom in the year 415, when a decree was issued expelling all Jews from Alexandria. But very little is known about what actually happened, except that some Jewish life survived.

The Arab conquest of Egypt in 640 brought relief to the Jews; and, though records are scanty, it is clear that they were tolerated and even favoured by the early Arab rulers and only occasionally subjected to persecution. We

61 The Ben Ezra Synagogue of Cairo
The synagogue was built in 882 on the remains of a Coptic church sold to the Jews. It is the site of the famous Geniza (store for discarded documents) which was discovered in the 19th century, and which has provided scholars with much invaluable information on the Geonic period of Jewish history.

know that they traded with their brethren in Kairouan (in modern Tunisia) and were in close contact with the Babylonian Academies to which they referred their religious problems. Indeed, the fact that Sa'adia Gaon (born in 882) was summoned from Egypt to head the leading Babylonian religious academy may well be indicative of the standards of learning and the status of the Egyptian Jews of his day.

Many Jews from Mesopotamia and a few from Palestine and Syria also settled in Egypt—which again suggests that conditions there were good. The Baghdadi Jews had their own separate synagogues; and there was occasional tension between them and the others who followed the Palestinian tradition. The cycle of readings from the Torah, for example, took three years to complete in the Palestinian synagogues, and only one year in the Babylonian ones.

Despite some bad times caused by the 'mad' Caliph al-Hakim, the Jews fared well under the Fatimid dynasty which conquered Egypt in 969. Their condition was reported in glowing terms by Benjamin of Tudela in 1171, by which time their number had risen to between twelve thousand and twenty thousand souls.

Maimonides, whose family had fled from persecution in Spain, finally settled in Cairo, where he became Court Physician and the head of its Jewish community. The Rambam, who always refused to earn his living from the Torah, had to work hard for his daily bread. Some inkling of the everyday life of this luminary of the age can be gleaned from the following extract from one of his letters:

I dwell at Mizr (Fostat, or Old Cairo) and the Sultan resides at Kahira (New Cairo). These places are two Sabbath-day's journey (about three miles) from each other.

I am obliged to visit him every day, early in the morning. And when he or any of his children, or any of the inmates of his harem are ill, I dare not quit Kahira but must stay in the palace for most of the day... Even if nothing unusual happens, I do not return to Mizr until the afternoon.

Then, almost dying with hunger, I find my antechambers filled with people—Jews and Gentiles, nobles and commoners, judges and bailiffs, friends and foes ...I dismount from my animal, wash my hands ...partake of the only meal I take in twenty four hours.

Then I go forth to attend to my patients ... I converse with and prescribe to them while lying down for sheer fatigue; and when night falls, I am so exhausted that I can scarcely speak. ....Consequently no Israelite can have any private interview with me except on the Sabbath.

On that day ...the majority of members (of the congregation) come to me after the morning service, when I instruct them as to their proceedings during the whole week. We study together a little until noon, when they depart. Some of them return and read with me after the afternoon service until evening prayers ....

I have here related to you only a part of what you would see if you were to visit me.

A long period of harsh discrimination and frequent persecution started under the Mamluks, who took over in the middle of the thirteenth century. Egypt itself became progressively poorer; and its Jewish population declined with it. This lasted until 1517, when Egypt was incorporated into the Ottoman Empire.

As described in the chapter on the Ottoman Empire in Part One of this book, the Turks favoured the Jews and used their services widely —especially in financial administration, which in Egypt was entirely in Jewish hands. Egypt however was far from Constantinople and, in time, its Turkish governors often came close to open rebellion against the Sultan in asserting their own despotic authority. Impelled by greed, they squeezed their Jewish finance ministers mercilessly; and many were executed when no more money could be extorted from them. Matters grew progressively worse for the Jewish community, which again declined in numbers, in educational standards and in wealth.

Egypt, like other places in the Ottoman Empire, had welcomed Jewish refugees from Spain to its shores. The Spaniards, generally superior in education and other accomplishments to the indigenous Arabic-speaking Jews and those of North African origin, at first formed their own separate community. There were disputes between the three groups; but eventually they all merged into a single community.

62 **Moses Maimonides (1135-1204)**
The 'Rambam' — Rabbi Moshe ben
Maimon. State of Israel banknote, 1986.

Napoleon's invasion of 1798 brought a new dimension to Egyptian life; for Napoleon arrived in Egypt with French scholars and scientists, and with plans to modernise the country by building hospitals, schools, libraries, printing presses and factories. Though French rule lasted for only three years, it resulted in Egypt's becoming a focus of European interest and rivalry in the Near East.

Shortly after the Ottomans, in alliance with the British, regained control of the country from the French, an Albanian contingent of the Turkish army of occupation rebelled against the Sultan and installed one of its own generals as ruler of Egypt. He was promptly assassinated; and command passed to Muhammad Ali, another Albanian officer. The Sultan eventually confirmed Muhammad Ali as Khedive (Viceroy) of Egypt, thus conceding sanction for him to rule the country as an autonomous province of the Ottoman Empire. Muhammad Ali's dynasty ended with Fuad, who remained as titular king for one year after his father, King Farouk, was compelled to abdicate in 1952.

Muhammad Ali reorganised the country and effected many basic administrative reforms. He revived agriculture by planting large tracts of land in the Nile delta with cotton and corn—it should be remembered that fertile Egypt was once the granary of the Roman Empire. But his attempts to industrialise the country were not so successful.

The American Civil War (1861-5) quadrupled the price of Egyptian cotton and created a short-lived boom. The opening of the Suez Canal in 1869 also brought new wealth. Alexandria, then the commercial capital of Egypt, attracted settlers from all over Europe and the Ottoman Empire. Its population grew to one hundred and fifty thousand by the middle of the nineteenth century; and a full third of that total were foreigners.

Mounting public debt and political tension resulted in repeated British and French interference in Egyptian affairs. In 1882, after rioting had broken out in the cities, a British army occupied Egypt to restore order, protect the Suez Canal and other investments and ensure the repayment of foreign debts. From that time on, the country was effectively ruled in

63 Prayer timetable
This board, giving the times of the various services, comes from the Sha'ar Ha-Shamayim Synagogue of Cairo. The times shown are, of course, incorrect.

the Khedive's name by a British Consul-General.

The government and administration were reformed, with British 'advisors' attached to every Egyptian ministry. For the first time in Egyptian history, the country's Jews were granted full equality with all other citizens, under the law. Egypt was finally declared a British Protectorate in 1914 on the outbreak of the First World War.

A new constitution was imposed by the British in 1922, when the Khedive was transformed into a King and a Parliament was established. Political power was then shared uneasily between the King, the Parliament and the British. That continued, more or less, until the Egyptian Revolution of 1952 deposed the King and finally freed Egypt from the last vestiges of European rule.

Muhammad Ali's reforms had brought new hope to the members of the decayed and oppressed Jewish community. From that time on, their lives were protected by law and they were no longer subjected to arbitrary ill-treatment—though they were still discriminated against. Their property too was protected by law, even if excessively heavy taxes were sometimes imposed on them by the government.

Egypt's Jews shared in the revival of the country. They also benefited from the new horizons revealed by the large-scale immigration of other Jews, attracted by the opportunities presented by a booming economy. The newcomers arrived mostly from Italy, the Balkans, Austria-Hungary and from other places around the Mediterranean coastline.

The size of the Jewish community grew from about five thousand in 1800 to twenty-five thousand in 1897, and to sixty thousand in 1917. There were sixty-five thousand Jews in Egypt in 1947, mostly living in Cairo and Alexandria.

In educational and cultural terms, the re-awakening of the community came gradually with the effects of exposure to European ways and education. With the coming of better education, the occupations of moneychanging and petty trading, habitual during the long period of their oppression, no longer sufficed. Many Jews entered the professions towards the end of the nineteenth century.

The community also developed in commercial importance. It included prominent financiers and bankers, as well as those who had made their way in industry and business—particularly in sugar, cotton, building and the railways. Some Jews acquired great wealth and owned large tracts of land. And, as a result, several Jewish names became household words in Egypt. Eventually, leading Jews were able to play a full part and mingle freely in the highest circles of Alexandrian society

The system of Capitulations, described in the chapter on the Ottoman Empire in Part One of this book, also applied in Egypt which was nominally a part of the Empire. Once registered as a foreign subject, a person was fully protected by his consul and could not be molested in any way by local Turkish officials. Indeed, he could be brought to justice only in the consular court of his protecting country.

Foreign Jews naturally sought the protection of their countries of origin in preference to becoming subject to local law; and numerous Jews not entitled to such status managed in some way or another to persuade or bribe foreign consuls to accept them under their wing — particularly those of Austria-Hungary and the Italian principalities. A separate Ashkenazi community, for example, was established under the protection of the Austro-Hungarian consul. Consequently there was hardly a prominent Jewish family in Egypt which did not contain any European nationals or at least foreign-protected subjects.

Unlike many other Jewish communities of the Ottoman Empire, there were no institutions of higher religious learning in Egypt during this period. Consequently its Chief Rabbis and dayanim (judges of religious law), including several distinguished scholars, had to be imported from Jewish centres abroad. Many complaints were voiced about the ignorance of Hebrew and religious matters prevailing in the community at large.

The lay leadership was shared between the wealthiest families; and this sometimes resulted in bitter quarrels. There were also some painful conflicts between different sections of the community — for example between Ashkenazim and Sephardim. However the community as a whole maintained well-developed and efficient hospitals, schools and other charitable institutions. It always acted generously to those in need, often being called upon to assist refugees from persecution abroad who increasingly sought and found refuge in Egypt.

Jews began to take an active part in Egyptian public life during the first decades of the twentieth century. One was appointed a government minister and others as members of Parliament. Education was widespread in the community; and its economic situation was excellent. There were several Jewish periodicals in circulation, written in Arabic, Ladino and French. There was also an active Zionist movement.

64 The Eliayu Ha-Navi Synagogue of Alexandria

65 Joseph and Renée Gubbay
Photographed in 1932 in Buenos Aires
where they were then living. The couple
met and married in Cairo. Joseph's family
was of Baghdadi origin and came to Cairo
via Calcutta and Aleppo. Renée's family,
the Farhis, was of Spanish origin and came
to Cairo via Italy and Damascus. Her
father was educated in Beirut and London.
The couple finally settled in Manchester.
Cosmopolitan Egypt, with its strong
European influences, attracted many Jews
from all over the Near East.

The records contain conflicting accounts of the relations between Jews and their Mohammedan neighbours. On the whole, the Jews of the nineteenth century maintained a low profile, behaving with great caution and avoiding open displays of wealth which might excite the envy of the Egyptians. British writers appear to have taken pleasure in describing the contempt and hatred with which they say the Jews were regarded by the Moslems; and certainly several wealthy Jews did leave Cairo for Alexandria in 1882, fearing trouble that never actually developed.

However, personal accounts of Jews who lived in Egypt in the twentieth century mostly refer only to the kindness and tolerance of individual Egyptians, and to the harmonious relations they maintained with their Mohammedan neighbours. In many cases they sympathised to some extent with Egyptian nationalism, even though they had themselves suffered as a result of its manifestations. With some exceptions, neither the members of the educated Egyptian middle class nor their simpler brethren were ever swayed by the extreme fanaticism displayed in so many other countries of the Middle East. And though war with Israel did evoke some ugly reactions from Egypt's rulers and the mobs they whipped up, even those blots were mild compared to what was experienced by Jews elsewhere.

The first Egyptian anti-Jewish riot of modern times took place in 1945, when the Jewish quarter of Cairo was targeted by the mob; but that was a tame affair by any standards. 1947 ushered in the beginning of the end for the Jewish community, which increasingly came under attack as Egypt's leaders committed the country to armed struggle against the State of Israel established in the following year. Crisis followed crisis, with more and more Jews departing after each—often stripped of their possessions and with nothing to show for a lifetime's work. The Suez crisis of 1956 was a particularly bad time. The Six Day War with Israel of 1967, which resulted in a humiliating defeat for the Egyptian army, proved to be the last straw. After that, what was left of the community rapidly dwindled to one or two hundred survivors. The story of those who left is continued in Part Three of this book.

From 1978 to the date of publication of this book, Egypt has been the only Arab country at peace with Israel, and the only one to have accepted an Israeli ambassador in its capital city. However, of its own formerly flourishing Jewish community, only a few elderly people now remain. The community's hospitals and schools have long since ceased to exist. Its historic monuments are badly neglected and its splendid synagogues deserted. Can this really be the end of the four thousand year old relationship of the Jewish people with the Land of Egypt?

Turkey Rhodes and the Balkans

66 Jewish women in Turkey
A 19th century print.

The Ottoman Turks, an Islamic warrior tribe originally from the steppes of Central Asia, caused near panic in Christian Europe after Turkish armies finally conquered Constantinople in 1453 and then slowly but relentlessly marched up through the Balkans to the very gates of Vienna. Though unsuccessful in their siege of 1529, the Turks remained a potent threat until 1683, when their final attempt to capture Vienna ended in a decisive defeat at the hands of the Christians.

The Turks, comparatively few in number, were faced with the formidable task of stabilising and governing the vast empire created by the brilliance of their armies. In the Balkans they took over cities and a countryside partly emptied by the ravages of war, as well as a resentful and potentially untrustworthy Christian population.

The existing Jewish communities of the lands conquered by the Turks in Asia and in Europe had for centuries suffered only humiliation, harassment and persecution at the hands of their former Christian rulers. The Turks changed all that. They trusted the Jews and valued the contribution they could make to the economic development of their Empire. Within the bounds of Islamic law, they treated them with fairness and justice. The Jews responded with gratitude and loyalty. In 1440 the Rabbi of Adrianople issued a circular letter to the Jews of Germany, Austria and Hungary, inviting them to come and settle under Turkish rule, where life was 'agreeable, peaceful and happy'; and some moved to Turkey as a result.

The chapter on the Ottoman Empire in Part One of this book describes in general how the Turks welcomed the expelled Spanish Jews to their newly conquered lands, favoured them and encouraged them to settle in self-governing communities. Several of the chapters in Part Two are devoted to details of Jewish life in the more important Islamic North African and Middle Eastern provinces of the Empire.

Turkey itself, the Balkans and the islands of the Eastern Mediterranean became the heartland of Spanish-speaking Sephardi Jewry after the Expulsion from Spain. Iberian Sephardim in those Ottoman provinces retained much of their inherited Spanish culture to the end, and long after the immigrants to Arabic-speaking ones had lost theirs.

Brief descriptions are given below of just a few of their leading communities.

CONSTANTINOPLE (ISTANBUL)

Constantinople, the fabulous capital city of the Christian Byzantine Empire, fell to the armies of the Ottoman Sultan Mehmed II (1451-81) in the year 1453. After three days of frantic looting of what once was one of the richest cities in the world, the Sultan—known from that time on as Mehmed the Conqueror—finally moved to restore peace.

One of his first acts was to order the former inhabitants who had fled during the siege to return under a guarantee of safety. The Conqueror specifically included the Jews in this decree; and there is a tradition that his proclamation included the following words:

May the man who is for me be supported by his God. Let him come up to Constantinople, the seat of my royal throne. Let him live in the best of the land under his own vine and under his own fig tree—with silver and with gold, with wealth and with cattle. Let him dwell in the land, trade in it and take possession of it.

It matters little whether or not those words are accurate; for the Sultan's tolerance was amply demonstrated by his actions. Jews were attracted to Constantinople from all parts of the Empire and beyond. And when Mehmed II conquered a new town containing a sizeable Jewish community, he often transferred it to his capital city.

Yacoub, a Jew, became the Conqueror's financial adviser. So well did Yacoub please his royal master that he, his entire family and their descendants, were granted exemption from paying taxes; and that privilege

67 Mehmed the Conqueror (1432-1481)
Sultan Mehmed II conquered
Constantinople in 1453.

68 Moses Hamon (1490 –1554)
Moses Hamon was personal physician, friend and adviser to Sultan Suleiman the Magnificent. He always used his considerable influence on behalf of his fellow Jews. A 17th century print.

was maintained by three subsequent generations of sultans.

Moses Capsali was appointed the first Haham Bashi, or Chief Rabbi, of Constantinople; and, in the Council of State, he was accorded higher precedence than the Greek Christian Patriarch. The Jews of Constantinople, close to the Sultan and his seat of power, occupied a very special position among the Jewish communities of the Ottoman Empire. The Haham Bashi was the political as well as the religious head of them all. It was his job to collect the taxes levied on the Jewish millet, or nation, and to represent its interests at court. In later times, when the office of Haham Bashi had lapsed, Jews had to depend for representation on influential individuals close to the Sultan; and disasters occurred when none could any longer be found to speak for them.

Sultan Bayazid II continued his father's policy. He welcomed many thousands of Spanish Jews expelled from Spain in 1492 and spoke disparagingly of King Ferdinand, who had impoverished his own country to Turkey's benefit. He declared that Ferdinand had committed an act of folly and that Spain's loss of its Jews would be his own gain. The Sultan is reported to have sent officers throughout his Empire with orders that Jewish refugees were to be greeted cordially on arrival and granted the right of domicile.

Joseph Hamon, from Granada, became the Sultan's trusted courtier and adviser. Joseph, who was appointed physician to the royal household shortly after arriving in Constantinople, served both Sultan Bayazid and his son, Sultan Selim I. His considerable influence was frequently used on behalf of the Jews; and after his death, the position passed in turn to his son, Moses, and then to his grandson.

The Jews of Constantinople and elsewhere did their utmost to succour their unfortunate Spanish brethren, most of whom had arrived destitute. Moses Capsali personally visited the separate congregations of the capital, compelling each member to donate a suitable amount. Some synagogues even sold their sacred ornaments to raise money to redeem from slavery Spanish refugees captured by pirates and those held to ransom by unscrupulous ships' captains.

With the arrival of Portuguese Marranos from 1497 onwards, Constantinople's mosaic of Jewish communities was complete. The oldest congregation was that of the original Byzantine Jews, the Romaniots. Then came the Ashkenazi settlers from Germany and elsewhere. Last to arrive were the Italians, the Spaniards and the Portuguese. Each group settled down to form a community based on its place of origin—country, province or city; and it was very many years before those divisions broke down and the culturally superior Sephardim absorbed most of the others. In the meantime, the rivalry between them was such that no Haham Bashi could be appointed and the office lapsed.

Each community was self-governing and jealously guarded its own independence. It was responsible for the assessment and collection of taxes on its individual members and for passing them on to the Turkish government. Each had its own rabbi and secular leadership, its own schools and charities. By the middle of the sixteenth century, there were from thirty to forty such congregations in the capital, with a total membership of about fifty thousand. All were represented on a single umbrella organisation which dealt with common problems.

Sultan Suleiman the Magnificent (1520-66) and his son Sultan Selim II (1566-1574) both had close Jewish friends and advisers; and their reigns were happy ones for the Jews of Constantinople and the Empire. Moses

PLATE XI

Above left
Jewish merchant from Algeria
A 19th century etching.

Above centre
Jewish Bookseller
19th century etching (Algeria).

Above right
Jewish Women of Constantinople
From Camille Rogier's 'La Turquie', Paris 19th century.

Left
Jewish Woman of Tangier
in traditional dress
This drawing of 1878 shows the woman wearing the keswa el kbira.

A fine example of 19th century primitive art from Gibraltar.

PLATE XII

Two Ketubot (Marriage Contracts)

This document from Tangier, dated 1891 , relates to the marriage of Solomn Levy to Mazal Tov Levy. It lists seven generations of the bridegroom's male ancestors, all scholars and rabbis.

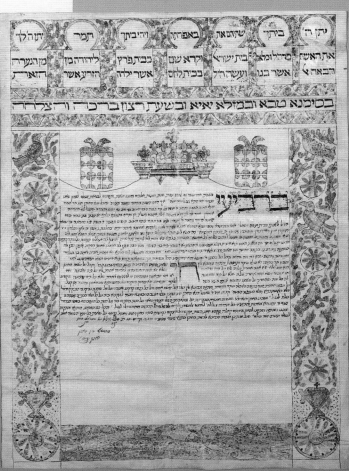

69 Sultan Suleiman the Magnificent (1520-1566)

Engraving by Knolle published in 1603.

Hamon, the court physician, was especially influential with Suleiman. He constantly used his influence on behalf of Turkish Jewry, and especially for communities in distress. In 1530, Moses managed to persuade the Sultan to issue a decree forbidding his subjects to accuse Jews of the crime of ritual murder.

The intellectual and cultural stimulus provided by the influx of Iberian Sephardim ensured that, in the sixteenth century, Constantinople became one of the leading centres of the Jewish world. Many famous Spanish rabbis settled in the city, where they set up institutions of learning to augment those already there. Some brought their libraries of rare manuscripts with them. From Spain and Italy came masters of the new art of printing. Freed at last from the vexations of Church interference, they were able to produce Hebrew works of high quality; and those were the first books ever to be printed in the Ottoman Empire.

Wealthy Sephardi merchants, industrialists and bankers also made their mark on the life of the capital, with its trade and commerce largely in their hands. Don Joseph Nasi, created Duke of Naxos, acquired great influence at court and became a leading diplomat. It was he who prompted the Sultan to intervene with the Pope on behalf of the oppressed Marranos of Ancona. He obtained permission to rebuild Tiberias in the Holy Land and to establish a haven there for persecuted Jews. The Sultan also intervened with the rulers of Venice and with King Henri II of France to rescue the fortune of the fabulously wealthy former Marrano, Dõna Gracia Mendes, Joseph Nasi's mother-in-law, who settled in Constantinople in 1553 and acted with so much generosity to the city's synagogues, schools and institutions of higher learning that she became known as the 'guardian angel' of the Marranos.

It was only when Murad III ascended the throne in 1574 that the first shadows fell across the mostly prosperous and self-confident Jewish community of Constantinople. Murad started by issuing a series of decrees with the object of limiting Jews from dressing ostentatiously in public and holding lavish parties. Then, provoked by a report that a Jewish woman had been seen on the streets of the capital wearing a very valuable necklace, he impulsively decreed the mass-slaughter of all the Jews of the Empire. The Sultan's mother, the Grand Vizier and Solomon Ashkenazi, a prominent Jewish courtier and diplomat, acted promptly to persuade the Sultan to cancel his order. But though Jews still continued to wield influence at court, their confidence was very badly shaken; and the rabbis imposed even more drastic restrictions than the Sultan's on what fine clothes and jewellery (none!) women could wear out of doors.

The glory of the Jewish community of Constantinople eventually began to fade as the Sultans loosened their grip on government, corruption and nepotism flourished, lawlessness increased and Turkey itself declined in wealth and influence.

By 1636 there was no longer a Jewish leader who could command the Sultan's favour; and as a consequence, a highly respected delegate from Salonika was arrested and unjustly executed. Woven cloth for army uniforms was delivered to the capital each year from Salonika as a form of community tax. Its receipt and acceptance often prompted a round of extortion and even blackmail against those bringing it; and on that occasion, the usual bribes proved insufficient when the cloth was declared to be of inferior quality.

However, the community still led all the others in the Ottoman Empire and continued to act with the greatest possible generosity to the oppressed Jews of Christian Europe.

The Chmelnicki massacres of 1648 in Poland and the Ukraine resulted in a multitude of Jews being captured and enslaved. A contemporary chronicler wrote that the Jews of Constantinople competed with themselves to perform the sacred duty of redeeming the captives, travelling as far as Italy and Amsterdam to raise the necessary funds. He also recounted that a group of Jews taken by Tatars and loudly lamenting their fate were consoled by their captors by being told not to despair, for they would soon be taken to Constantinople, where their brethren could be counted on to pay handsomely for their liberation.

Constantinople's Jewish community also served as a centre for channelling funds to the Holy Land. In the eighteenth century it imposed a special tax on its own members and on those of all other communities in the Ottoman Empire to pay the debts of the Jews of Jerusalem.

As the wealth and influence of the community declined, so too did its level of education and Hebrew knowledge. The rabbis responded by writing and publishing books in Spanish and Ladino, including the highly popular Me-am Lo'ez by Jacob Culli. Individual Jews were increasingly restricted in their dress, being made to appear in distinctive and modest attire in public. With no leader in a position to bend the Sultan's ear, they became more exposed to the tyranny and arbitrary exactions of greedy government officials; but they were not actually persecuted as in Christian Europe. The story of Shabbetai Zvi's appearance in Constantinople as the Messianic King of the Jews is described in Part One of this book; and it is a most remarkable tribute to Turkish tolerance that the widespread support he received in his bid to seize the Sultan's crown did not result in the ill-treatment of Turkish Jewry.

In 1826 the Sultan ordered his corps of Janissaries, who had effectively ruled the country in his name, to assemble at Meydani, the site of the old Hippodrome. At his command, they were massacred to the last man. Those leaders of Constantinople's Jewish community, allied to the Janissaries, fell from power at the same time; and some were executed. That was at a time when the fortunes of the Jews as a whole had reached their lowest point and most had been reduced to a state of poverty and ignorance.

In the series of reforms that followed, as the Sultan and his successors attempted to regain the reigns of government, the office of Haham Bashi was restored and the special poll tax on Jews was abolished. Jews, again allowed to dress in a similar manner to Mohammedans, became officials, consuls, judges and military doctors in a genuine attempt to remove their disabilities.

70 **The Haham of Smyrna**
From "Les Costumes Populaires de la Turkie", published in 1873.

71 **Three Jewish girls at a fancy-dress party**
Istanbul, 1925.

Bitter dissent broke out within the community as the first Jewish secular schools were opened in Constantinople, and instruction in the French language was introduced. The contribution of the Alliance Israélite Universelle to the emancipation of the Jews of the Ottoman Empire is described in more detail in Part One of this book. The Jewish population of Constantinople, swelled by a wave of refugees from Russia, increased to about one hundred thousand in the early years of the twentieth century.

The convulsion of the Balkan wars, followed by the First World War of 1914–18 and the end of the Ottoman Empire, brought renewed hardship to the Jews of the capital, many of whom emigrated to seek a better life overseas.

The establishment of a secular Turkish Republic by Kemal Atatürk in 1923 caused the end of Jewish autonomy. Jews could no longer control their own marriages and divorces. They could not impose their own taxes to maintain the synagogues and charitable institutions. Their schools were secularised, with the teaching of religion strictly forbidden; and Turkish replaced French as the language of instruction. The community dwindled even further in 1942 after many were ruined by the imposition of an unfair and harsh capital levy.

The situation was much eased in 1949, when the remaining Jewish community of at least fifty thousand was again allowed a measure of autonomy in its internal affairs. By then, Jews were freely attending government schools and universities and were well represented in commerce, the professions, and even in Parliament.

Spurred by unease at the rising tide of Islamic revivalism, seemingly kept in check only by the power of the army, more than half the community emigrated, mainly to Israel. Its present size is between ten and twenty thousand. Its members, loyal to their city and country, live in freedom.

SALONIKA

The Jewish community of Salonika was founded by Jews from Alexandria and enjoyed local autonomy under Roman rule. Its members, engaged in international trade, lived close to the port. The New Testament relates that Paul visited Salonika for three weeks and preached in its synagogue.

The Byzantine Emperors and later Christian rulers treated the Jews of Salonika as harshly as they did Jews everywhere. The community survived; but whether or not it was continuous throughout the period is not known for certain. Benjamin of Tudela visited the city in 1169, when he reported that about five hundred Jews were living there.

The community appeared prosperous, with most of its merchants engaged in the silk trade, when the city was sold to Venice by its governor in 1423. The heavy taxes then imposed on its Jews prompted them to send a delegation to Venice to plead for mitigation. Despite discrimination and the heavy taxation, by then Salonika had already attracted refugees from Hungary and Germany.

A new era dawned in 1430 when the Ottoman Sultan Murad II conquered the town. For the first time in many centuries, the Jews were accorded equal rights with other non-Islamic inhabitants and treated justly. Sultan Mehmed II, the conqueror of Constantinople, favoured Jews and encouraged them to settle in the almost deserted town by granting special privileges to certain families. As a result, Jews expelled from Bavaria and Hungary came to join their brethren already in Salonika where, mostly engaged in gold and silver mining, they established a small Ashkenazi community alongside the existing Greek one.

After their expulsion from Spain in 1492, many thousands of Spanish Jews found permanent sanctuary in Salonika. They were soon joined by a flood of other refugees from Portugal, Provence, Sicily and the Kingdom of Naples. There was also a steady trickle of Portuguese Marrano settlers during the course of the next two to three hundred years, all seeking to return to Judaism.

Though originally a poor and insanitary place with narrow streets and ravaged by a succession of devastating plagues and fires, Salonika attracted a larger number of Jewish refugees than any other town in the Ottoman Empire, except perhaps Constantinople. But in contrast to the capital, Jews soon formed the majority of its population. They controlled most of the commerce and industry; and they engaged in almost every occupation from the most menial to the elevated. Work ceased in the port on Jewish Sabbaths and holydays. Spanish was the language spoken by all Jews, including the Ashkenazim. Dress, manners and customs followed those of Castile and Aragon. And after much of Salonika was rebuilt, following the great fire of 1545, even its appearance came to resemble that of a Spanish city.

The oldest established Jewish community, with two synagogues, was that of the Greek-speaking Romaniots. Next came the Ashkenazim from Germany and Hungary. The Spanish Sephardim established the five communities of Castile, Aragon, Catalonia, The Expulsion and Majorca; and those from Portugal, the three congregations of Lisbon, Evora and Portugal. Jews from Sicily had their own synagogue; and those of Italy grouped themselves together under the names of Apulia, Otranto, Estruc, Calabria and Italia. A large number of Jews from Provence, enticed by a letter from compatriots already in Salonika urging them to settle in the city

...where you will live in peace and freedom ... and where even the poorest are given the opportunity to earn a modest living ...

swelled the ranks of the Provençal congregation.

As elsewhere in the Ottoman Empire, each small community was entirely self-governing. Its members lived close together as a separate nation in exile, administered their own laws and jealously guarded the particular customs brought with them. They combined together for the primary purpose of assigning to each a fair share of the government taxes which had to be paid by the Jews of the city as a whole; but each was responsible for taxing its own members and for the sometimes difficult task of collecting that tax. They also combined together to support joint enterprises like the splendid Talmud Torah, which was the pride of the entire community.

Unfortunately all was not sweetness and light. Bitter quarrels plagued the separate communities, compelling many of them to split into yet more groups, despite a general ordinance by all the rabbis and lay leaders forbidding such behaviour. At times only outside threats seemed to unite them — such as when, acting together, they would send a delegation to Constantinople to ask the most prominent Jew at court to intercede on their behalf against unjust treatment from local officials.

Salonika's wealth was based on the twin foundations of trade and industry. Its port, being strategically situated, enabled its Sephardi merchants to trade with their brethren to be found all round the Mediterranean coastline. Even more vital for the port's prosperity was the fact that it had been developed by Venice as the main outlet for its extensive trade with the Balkans. To quote from J. Néhama's article in the book 'The Western Sephardim',

The merchants of Salonika established their own representatives ... in every important port of the Adriatic. From Ragusa (Dubrovnik), Salonika received caravans of cereal, untanned hides, wax, honey... Ancona sent fine textiles in exchange for wheat, cattle, leather ...It (Salonika) acted as a pump, sucking in the riches of the Balkans and flooding the peninsula with every manner of manufactured goods ...

By far the most important industry was that of weaving and dyeing textiles, first introduced by the Sicilian Jews. The production of textiles was a major occupation; and it is said that there were few households in

72 **The Haham Bashi (Chief Rabbi) of Salonika**
This photograph is dated 1873.

which the clacking of looms could not be heard. Even the Talmud Torah had a textile workshop attached, the profits of which were used to defray some of its expenses. From the latter part of the sixteenth century, Salonika's taxes were paid in the form of woven cloth, taken each year to Constantinople to be used for the manufacture of uniforms for the Sultan's Janissaries. The annual transportation, examination and acceptance of this cloth could on occasion be fraught with peril for the community; and one particular instance is described in the preceding section on Constantinople.

The sixteenth century was Salonika's Golden Age for Jewish scholarship and intellectual attainment. The distinguished Spanish rabbis who settled in the town, sometimes with entire libraries of rare manuscripts, helped to create what became the leading centre of Jewish learning in the Balkans and the Mediterranean. The galaxy of famous names of the period includes Isaac Adarbi, Solomon Alkabetz, Moses Almosnino, Jacob ibn Habib and his son Levi, Joseph Caro and Samuel de Medina. Knowledge of Hebrew was widespread; and Hebrew was the language of instruction in the numerous schools and yeshivot to which pupils came to study from far and near. Salonika, also home to an influential community of kabbalistic scholars, was visited by both Solomon Molcho and Shabbetai Zvi. Nor was secular learning neglected. The Iberian Sephardim, with their knowledge of Spanish, Latin and Arabic, maintained contact with the outside world and engaged in all kinds of literary and musical activity.

The Talmud Torah, which was founded in 1520 and survived for well over four hundred years, was the particular pride of the community. To quote Isaac Adarbi,

...even those inhabiting distant lands have their eyes and hearts turned towards it.

It was the most important community centre in the town, the place where all grand meetings were held. It housed the elementary schools which provided every poor child with a set of new clothes each Hanukah. It also contained institutions of higher Jewish learning, a fine permanent library and a lending library. Its secular college included Latin, Arabic, philosphy, astronomy, natural sciences and medicine in its curriculum; and for a time, the famous physician Amatus Lusitanus taught there.

The happy relationship between the early Ottoman sultans and their Jewish subjects was not always reflected at local level, especially in places far from the capital — like Salonika. Government officials were often corrupt and cruel. Greedy to divert Jewish wealth into their own pockets, they readily used the weapons of unjust imprisonment and confiscation to extort huge bribes.

Restrictions and humiliations on non-Moslems, suggested by Islamic law but more usually disregarded, could be enforced at the whim of local governors. They caused increasing difficulty as the years passed. The Sultan's crack corps of Janissaries, generally above any law, were also a major source of trouble for the Jews; and regular tribute had to be set aside to avert the worst of their excesses. As early as 1568, the Jews of Salonika were threatened with mass-expulsion; and that decree was rescinded only

73 **An elderly Jewish couple from Salonika**
A late 19th century photograph.

after their leader Moses Almosnino appealed to Joseph Nasi in Constantinople to intercede with Sultan Selim II.

Such behaviour grew ever worse during the long decline of the Ottoman Empire, when lawlessness increased seemingly without limit. The prosperity of Salonika's Jews decreased with that of the Empire as a whole; and as the stimulus provided by the Spanish refugees waned with time, educational standards also declined.

The initial cultural superiority of the Spaniards was such that they assimilated the Greek-speaking Jews and the Italians. Only the German Ashkenazim stubbornly maintained their own special traditions to the end. After the debacle caused by the false messiah Shabbetai Zvi's conversion to Islam in 1666, described in Part One of this book, all other congregations united into a single community under the leadership of the three most distinguished rabbis of the day. That system of rule by a committee of three rabbis survived until 1880, when a single Haham, or Chief Rabbi, was appointed in its stead.

The Turkish reforms instituted in the middle of the nineteenth century, described in the preceding section on Constantinople, had their effect in slowly reviving Salonika's Jewish community — which by then had declined into poverty, ignorance and apathy. By the beginning of the twentieth century, Salonika had once again become a prosperous centre of Balkan trade. The Bank of Salonika had been founded, a new port built and the city connected to the rest of Europe with a railway. Members of the Jewish community, then about ninety thousand strong, took a leading part in this restoration of commercial activity.

If anything, the struggle between the rabbinic establishment and those progressives who started new schools, teaching secular subjects and the French language, was even more bitter in Salonika than in the capital. In the end though, with the help of the Alliance schools, the outlook of the Jewish community was slowly transformed. Again facing towards Western Europe and increasingly prosperous, it enjoyed a cultural rebirth. Many of its young people attended universities abroad and then came home to join the professions. There was also a simultaneous revival of religious learning, still taught together with secular subjects in the traditional Sephardi manner. Interest was born in Ladino culture, previously disregarded.

Many Jews enthusiastically supported the Young Turks in their revolt against Sultan Abdul Hamid II in 1908. In Constantinople, Western-educated Haim Nahum was appointed Haham Bashi with the help of the Young Turks, who did all they could to demonstrate their sympathy towards the Jews. Under their regime, Zionist organisations were able to come out into the open for the first time. However, one thing went badly wrong. For the first time, Jews like all other citizens became liable for conscription to the Turkish army; and rather than accept this, many thousands of young men emigrated, mostly to the United States of America. The same thing happened all over the Balkans. The dissolution of the Balkan Sephardi Jewish communities had started.

The Balkan wars, followed by the First World War of 1914-18, completed the break-up of the Ottoman Empire. Salonika fell to Greece in 1912; and though King George promised equal rights for all minorities, the Greek government worked hard to transform Salonika from a great cosmopolitan trading centre to a Greek city. In 1918 circumstances were so arranged that the seventy thousand Jews, who had lost their homes when the heart of the town was devastated by a great fire, were prevented from returning to live near the centre of the city. Many Jews left for Palestine, France, Italy, England and the United States, The exchange of populations between

74 Rabbi Haim Nahum (1872-1960)
Rabbi Nahum served as Haham Bashi
(Chief Rabbi) of the Ottoman Empire
between 1908 and 1920. He was appointed
Chief Rabbi of Cairo in 1925.

**75 Members of the Zionist federation
of Edirne**
This photograph was taken in 1916, at a
time when open Zionist activity was
permitted in Turkey.

Greece and Turkey in 1922 completed the process, when a hundred
thousand Greeks from Asia Minor were moved to Salonika.

With the coming to power of the Greeks, Salonika was again under
Christian rule. The declaration of Sunday as a compulsory day of rest in
1922 interfered with the tradition of centuries in which the whole town
rested on the Jewish Sabbath; and more Jews emigrated. Between the two
World Wars, anti-semitic incidents proliferated and there was a nasty
pogrom in 1933. The Jewish population continued to dwindle.

About fifty thousand Jews were left in Salonika when the victorious
German army entered the city in 1942. The details of their fate and those
of the other Jews of Greece are too painful to relate here. It closely followed
that of Jewish communities all over Europe, with alternate moments of
desperate hope followed by despair. All Jews were deported to the
extermination camps of Northern Europe where, with few exceptions, they
perished.

Only a pathetic handful of survivors returned to Salonika after the war;
and the present community consists of recent immigrants.

OTHER BALKAN COMMUNITIES

Space permits no more than a brief mention of just a few of the twelve other major Balkan communities, with a total population of over one hundred thousand at the beginning of the twentieth century.

Though the settlement of Jews in Belgrade (Beograd) dates from the Byzantine era, that in most other places was the direct result of the expulsions from the Iberian Peninsula, France and Italy.

Closely associated with Salonika, and to a large extent dependent on it for trade and religious support, was the Greek-speaking community of Janina in Macedonia, and those of the Dalmatian ports of Dubrovnik (Ragusa) and Split (Spalato) — each an Italian-speaking city state. (Dubrovnik owed allegiance to Turkey, and Split was a protectorate of Venice.)

Dubrovnik in particular was an important transit point for Jewish and Marrano refugees from the Iberian Peninsula; and there are records of shiploads of Sephardim arriving there en-route for the Ottoman Empire. The preceding section on Salonika contains details of Dubrovnik's trade with that largely Jewish port.

Sarajevo in Bosnia was the last staging post for camel traffic within the Ottoman Empire. Goods carried by camel were transferred to horses or mules in the town before continuing on their journey north. It was an important trading centre, with its formerly Christian population having been converted to Islam following the Turkish conquest.

Sarajevo's Jewish community was established in 1577 and grew slowly. Its members followed a balanced variety of occupations — from labourers and craftsmen to pedlars and substantial international traders. They were well integrated into local life and supplied Bosnia with most of its doctors. Ashkenazi settlers from the North came later and built their own synagogue.

Sarajevo eventually became a centre of Jewish learning. Its Jewish population, of over ten thousand at the beginning of the twentieth century, also supported a vigorous cultural life and a thriving Jewish press, partly Ladino. The religious secondary school established in 1928 did much to raise educational standards in general. Two of its graduates came to London just before the Second World War, where they completed their studies and then served the Spanish and Portuguese Jewish Community of London in the capacity of Haham and Senior Hazan respectively.

The whole community was deported to Croatian concentration camps and to Auschwitz during the Second World War. Those few who escaped to join the partisans managed to survive. So also did some men who, having been conscripted into the Yugoslav army, became ordinary prisoners of war.

Most emigrated to Israel after the war. The large Sephardi synagogue is now a theatre; and the old Sephardi synagogue has become a Jewish museum, where the names of the murdered members of the community are recorded in a great memorial book suspended from the ceiling in the centre of its main hall. Only a small number of Jews now remain in Sarajevo.

76   Dubrovnik (Ragusa)

RHODES

Jews had lived on Rhodes since the days of the Roman Empire. Benjamin of Tudela visited the island in 1166 and recorded that its Jewish community then numbered five hundred.

The first Sephardim arrived from Tarragona, Spain, in 1280 to seek refuge under the Saracens who ruled the island.

Under the Crusader Knights of St. John of Jerusalem, who conquered Rhodes in 1307, the Jews appeared to have lived reasonably well despite some restrictions and constant attempts by the Greek Christian population to undermine their position. They faithfully helped the Knights to defend Rhodes against Turkish attack in 1480, when a large part of the Jewish quarter was destroyed in the siege. For this they earned the thanks of the Knights, whose Grand Master Pierre d'Aubusson awarded them one hundred ducats to build and embellish a new synagogue to replace the one demolished by the bombardment.

After a devastating earthquake in 1499, the town was rebuilt, together with the impressive walls, gates and fortifications admired by tourists today.

Great hardship followed the war and the earthquake, forcing some Jews to leave. In 1487 a traveller, Rabbi Obadiah de Bertinoro, found only twenty-two Jewish families left. Nevertheless, he lavishly praised their education, culture and bearing. He declared that there were no more beautiful women in all the world than the Jewish women of Rhodes. In this, he was echoing a Christian pilgrim from Cologne, who had stopped in Rhodes on his way to the Holy Land and also praised the beauty of its Jewish women.

In 1502 Grand Master d'Aubusson was elevated to the rank of Cardinal. No doubt influenced by the wave of intolerance spreading from Spain, he decreed that all Jewish children should be converted to Christianity. The adults had just forty days in which to convert or be deported to Nice. The only alternatives were torture, slavery or death. No Jew was allowed to leave for the Ottoman Empire.

The Jews of Cos, which also belonged to the Knights, were given the same choices and were deported to Nice. Those of Rhodes were saved from deportation by the timely death of the Cardinal; but some were tortured to death and most of the remainder forcibly converted to Christianity. Even Jewish passengers on ships captured by the piratical Knights were seized and brought back to Rhodes as slaves.

When the Turks next attacked the island in 1522, its converted Jews actively helped Sultan Suleiman the Magnificent to take the town and expel the Knights. One forced convert, a doctor, provided the Turks with a map of the town. Both he and the valet to the Knights' Chancellor, another reluctant Christian, were sentenced to death for spying; and the doctor was hacked to small pieces for his treachery. A large number of former Jews helped the Turks by filling in part of the moat with sandbags.

The island's Jews greatly rejoiced at Suleiman's victory — especially as many of their compatriots returned to Rhodes in the wake of the Turkish

77 **Sultan Suleiman the Magnificent (1520-1566)**
The greatest of the Ottoman Sultans.

78 A Turkish Hodja

army. Those previously compelled to accept the Cross promptly returned to their ancestral faith.

Suleiman, anxious to establish a loyal element within the population, encouraged Jewish immigration by offering certain exceptional privileges. These included a monopoly to exploit the sulphur mines, tax exemption for ten years, free housing and cheap kasher meat, as well as the right of self-government enjoyed by all the other Jewish communities in his empire. Jews from Turkey took advantage of Suleiman's invitation to come to Rhodes; but the bulk of the immigrants consisted of Jewish refugees from Spain. Rhodes also became known as a place to which Marranos came in order to return to the faith of their ancestors before moving on elsewhere. The Sephardim dominated the community and completely assimilated the original Greek-speaking Romaniot Jews within fifteen years of their arrival.

The Jewish community of Rhodes generally shared in the ups and downs of others in the Ottoman Empire. Though harassed occasionally by the constant hostility of the Greek Christians, only kept in check by the Turkish governors, its members lived in peace and relative contentment until Hitler's Holocaust. There were however some nasty moments — such as the revival of the blood libel by the Christians in 1840, which prompted the personal intervention of the Sultan and the issuing of his firman dismissing the charges.

Greek Christian antagonism, represented by at least forty instances of blood-libel accusations in the Dodecanese Islands, left a deep impression on their Jews. Isaac Levy, in his book 'Jewish Rhodes: A Lost Culture', recorded the following custom from his childhood:

On seeing a hodja (Moslem religious leader), the Jewish children kissed his hand for good luck. Conversely, they spat on the ground at the sight of a papas (Greek priest) in order to ward off bad luck.

Despite much bickering and many internal quarrels, the people took great pride in their rabbis and scholars, both local and imported from abroad. Especially in its earlier days, Rhodes was a centre of Jewish learning for the area. Nor was general education neglected until Rhodes, like the rest of the Ottoman Empire in the nineteenth century, gradually declined into a trough of ignorance and poverty.

Throughout the period of Ottoman and later Italian occupation, the Jews of Rhodes lived in their own relatively secure and self-contained community. Bound together by unquestioning devotion to their religious faith, they developed their own particular brand of Sephardi culture which permeated all aspects of daily living — from food and music to social customs and superstitions. Former residents, whether rich or poor, speak nostalgically of a smiling past, coloured by memories of fragrant flowers and cascading vines.

Secular French education, introduced with the help of the Alliance Israélite Universelle against the strenuous opposition of the religious establishment, did much to widen the horizons of the people from the beginning of the twentieth century onwards. The sons of the rich studied abroad and returned to good jobs on the island. The poor, lacking those opportunities, emigrated in large numbers to South America, the United States, the Belgian Congo and Rhodesia.

The Italians occupied the island in 1912 and remained until 1944. They brought peace and, with larger exposure to European influences, a measure of prosperity. Under their rule, the fortunes of the Jews revived once again. Several hundred immigrants came to Rhodes from the Jewish communities of Turkey, Bulgaria and Greece, devastated by war.

A rabbinic college, teaching a variety of secular subjects alongside the religious ones, was opened in 1928 with the permission of the Italian governor. Its purpose was to train rabbis, hazanim and teachers for the Jewish communities of the Middle East, Turkey and the Balkans; and over four hundred of its graduates returned to serve their communities in those capacities. King Victor Emmanuel III knighted Chief Rabbi Rueben Israel on one of his visits to the island. The story is told that the sovereign showed his respect for the rabbi by raising him from the kneeling position and kissing his hand — an unique gesture.

A new and fervently fascist governor was installed in 1936. He closed the college and began to implement stern anti-semitic measures. More Jews left — this time for Palestine, Tangier, the Belgian Congo and Rhodesia. The situation eased when the fascist was replaced as governor by the humane Admiral Campione. He was able to protect the Jews from excesses, even under German occupation, until the Gestapo arrived two years later.

Though informed by spies on the island of the precise date of the transports, the British armed forces declined to intervene to prevent the mass deportation of the Jews of Rhodes. Forty to fifty of them claimed Turkish nationality and were spared. The remaining seventeen hundred were taken to death camps in Poland, from which only one hundred and fifty returned.

A few survivors came back to Rhodes after the war, hoping to rebuild their lives on their beloved island and re-create some of the richness and warmth of the former community. Quoting again from Isaac Levy's book,

What the shattered souls of the Nazi death camps found on their return was a war-ravaged Juderia whose houses and streets belonged to strangers. They sought in vain for familiar faces; the warmth of memories became a constant reminder of tragedy.

Sadly, most of them departed, haunted by the past; and very few Jews remain on the island.

The Maghreb

The area of North Africa from the borders of Egypt to the Atlantic Ocean, and bounded by the Sahara desert in the south, is known to Arab historians as the Maghreb. From west to east, it comprises the modern states of Morocco, Algeria, Tunisia and Libya — which itself includes Tripolitania and Cyrenaica.

The origin of its Berber inhabitants is disputed by scholars. Berber legends, echoed by Jewish, early Christian and Mohammedan sources, relate that they came from the Land of Canaan at the time of Joshua. It may be that Berber origins became confused with those of the Phoenicians who arrived early in the region and who spoke Punic, a Semitic language closely related to Hebrew. But there is no real evidence one way or the other.

The city of Carthage, close to modern Tunis, was founded by Phoenicians in the ninth century B.C.E. For the next six hundred years, until Carthage was conquered by the Romans and its site ploughed over and sprinkled with salt, the Phoenicians extended their influence over the entire Maghreb. By the sixth century B.C.E., knowledge of the Punic language had spread from the Mediterranean coastline to the fringes of the Sahara.

Lack of surviving records prevents any reliable account of when Jews first arrived in Africa. Again, all we have is a variety of legends. One relates that Israelite merchants travelled to the main Phoenician gold market of Morocco in the time of King Solomon. The tradition in several Jewish communities, including that of Djerba in Tunisia, was that they were established during the Babylonian exile in the sixth century B.C.E. This is accepted by a few scholars, supported by the supposed existence of Hebrew-speaking Jewish communities in the Maghreb long after Aramaic had displaced Hebrew as the spoken language of the Land of Israel.

The first hard evidence of Jews in the Maghreb is in 312 B.C.E. when King Ptolemy Lagi of Egypt, seeking to strengthen his grip on territory close to his western border, settled Jews in the cities of Cyrenaica. There was further Jewish settlement in the same area in 145 B.C.E., after which Libya must have formed a simple extension of the Egyptian diaspora.

Jews were already living in Tunisia when waves of refugees arrived from Palestine, Egypt and Cyrenaica between 70 and 118 C.E. It was reported by Yosephon that:

Vespasian gave his son Titus the country of Africa and he settled thirty thousand Jews in Carthage, besides those he established in other places.

At the far end of the Maghreb, Hebrew inscriptions on second century C.E. tombstones are the first evidence of Jewish settlement in Morocco.

The Roman conquest of Africa from the Carthaginians had mixed results for its Jewish communities. In the east, the Jews of Cyrenaica revolted against Rome and were brutally suppressed in 118 C.E. Most of the survivors either fled westwards to Tunisia or else sought refuge with the Berber tribes of the interior. Few Jews appear to have lived in Cyrenaica for hundreds of years after that event.

Elsewhere in the Maghreb, Jewish life flourished under the Romans. As explained in Part One of this book, Judaism was a licit religion in the Roman Empire. Jews could become Roman citizens and, in what now seems an extraordinary degree of tolerance, they alone of the peoples of the Empire were exempted from all civic and religious duties which would conflict with the practice of their faith. From the second century on, the wealthy mercantile communities of Algeria, Tunisia and Libya controlled much of the region's internal trade and also supplied Rome with large quantities of food.

Africa, at that time, was one of the most fertile Roman provinces bordering the Mediterranean. The Atlas mountains were still covered in primaeval forest and the coastal plains served as the granaries of Rome and Southern Europe.

Religious life must have been vigorous and well organised, for Jewish communities enjoyed a large degree of local autonomy under the Romans. They controlled their own finances, courts and schools. They built richly decorated synagogues, as can still be seen in fragmentary remains near Tunis. As reported by St. Augustine, the Christian bishop of Tripoli did not hesitate to consult a Jewish scholar in a difficulty over one of Jerome's faulty translations from the Hebrew Bible, or to accept his ruling.

Links with the rabbis of the Holy Land were maintained. Rabbi Akiva journeyed to the Maghreb; and it seems that Rabbi Hillel (third century C.E.) knew the countryside near Tunis at first hand. There must also have been frequent interchange of correspondence between the two places.

Babylon, at that time, was in a part of the world hostile to Rome; so there can have been little or no communication with its rabbis. In terms of the definition adopted for the purposes of this book therefore, the original Jews of the Maghreb did not form part of the Babylonian/Sephardi tradition.

As elsewhere in the Roman Empire, groups of converts and semi-converts were attached to each Jewish community and even seem to have had a say in their government. Judaism was an attractive faith in the last days of paganism before the triumph of Christianity, and its influence was wide spread. Jewish concepts and beliefs permeated African society, spreading even to groups unconnected with Jews. The early Church Fathers railed against this Jewish influence, which extended to their own following, and did their best to combat it. Tertullian, the leading Christian intellectual of the third century, complained bitterly of Berbers' observing the Jewish Sabbath, festivals and fasts, and keeping the dietary laws.

Conditions changed for the worse in the fourth century when Christianity became the official religion of the Roman Empire. From that time on, Jews were increasingly discriminated against and denied civil rights.

Matters improved under the rule of the Vandal invaders, who arrived from Spain in the year 406. The Vandals were Arian and not Orthodox Christians; and they restored Jewish religious freedom. But the better times were brought to an end by the Byzantine Emperors who finally defeated the Vandals and drove them out of Africa. The Byzantine Greeks interfered closely in Jewish life and abolished all remaining vestiges of autonomy — even in matters of family law, such as marriage and divorce. They censored Bibles and other books used in the synagogues; and forbad marriage between Jews and Christians on pain of death.

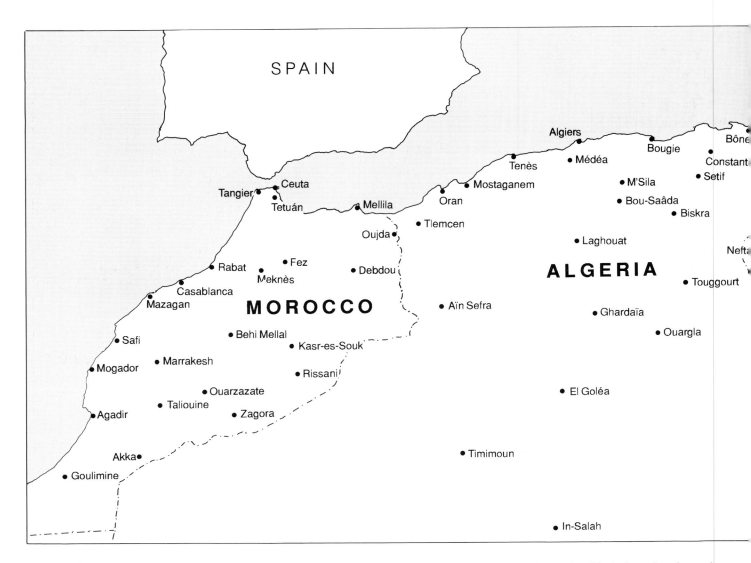

As oppression increased, the Jews retreated from the Christian–dominated towns of the coastline and sheltered with the Berber tribes of the interior, constantly at war with the Byzantines. Jewish influence on the Berbers was strong; and both peoples appear to have absorbed much from each other.

The Byzantines proved no match for the Arabs who, following the death of their Prophet Muhammad, swept though the ancient world in a vast swathe of conquest. Cyrenaica and Tripolitania fell in 642; and the Byzantines were expelled from North Africa five years later. However the Berber tribes of the interior were a different proposition. The fortunes of war alternately favoured one side and then the other for many years before resistance was finally overcome and most Berbers accepted Islam.

It was post-conquest Arab historians who first stated that several important Berber tribes were Jewish at the time of the conquest. These tribes, mentioned by name and including some nomadic ones, led Berber resistance to the Arab invasion. This view, pointing to the conclusion that some North African Jews today are of Berber descent, was accepted uncritically by subsequent historians.

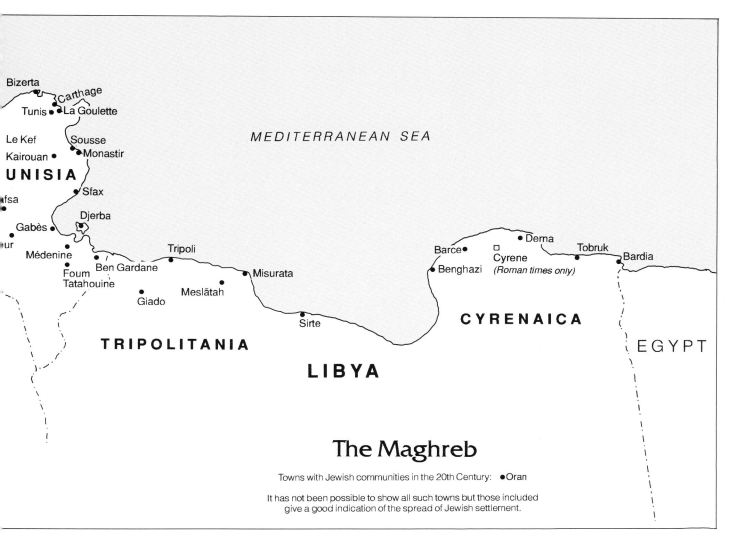

The Maghreb

Towns with Jewish communities in the 20th Century: ●Oran

It has not been possible to show all such towns but those included
give a good indication of the spread of Jewish settlement.

However the meticulous scholar H.W.Hirschberg, in his book 'A History of the Jews in North Africa', has added a strong cautionary note for, as he says, no trace of this theory appeared in Jewish writings until the fifteenth century. Nor is there is evidence of Jews ever having used the Berber language; and no Berber words entered the Jewish dialects of the region.

Hirschberg points out that such large-scale conversion cannot have occurred in the Byzantine period without coming to the attention of the Church — which it did not. During the period between the defeat of the Byzantines and the consolidation of Islam in the Maghreb, its Jewish communities were in close touch with Babylon and Palestine. Hirschberg argues, very reasonably, that mass conversions would surely have caused many halachic (religious/legal) problems — yet there is no mention of any at all in surviving rabbinic responsa.

Nevertheless, Hirschberg does not dismiss the theory out of hand on the grounds that the sheer volume of reference is too large to be disregarded and that the Arab historians had no reason to invent such a story. Perhaps all that can safely be concluded is that Jews did live amongst the Berbers and that there was strong mutual influence. It is possible that large groups of Berbers were close to Judaism — and even that some became Jews eventually — but there is no proof.

Ibn Khaldun and other Mohammedan historians wrote that the final resistance to the Arabs was led by Jewish Berber tribes, the most powerful of which were the Nefusa and the Jerawa. The defeat of Queen Kahena of the Jerawa — the main Berber leader — became the prime objective of the Arab commander, Hassan.

Hassan led his forces towards the Jerawa heartland in the Aurès mountains (straddling the border of modern Algeria and Tunisia). He was defeated there by the Jewish queen and forced to retreat to Tripolitania. It seems that Kahena, then the undisputed leader of the Maghreb, governed her kingdom with great cruelty. The nomadic warriors under her command devastated the countryside in a scorched-earth policy designed to discourage the Arabs from returning. This was bitterly resented by the settled Berbers, who defected to the Arabs in increasing numbers. When Hassan came a second time, he was rewarded with success. Kahena was slain and her severed head delivered to the Caliph. The Arabs subsequently blamed her for the permanent decline in the fertility of the region.

The Jerawa and other defeated Berbers were treated well by the Arabs, converted to Islam and incorporated into their armies. And, in the end, it was Berber tribesmen and not Arabs who subdued most of the Maghreb in the name of Islam. The Christian Berbers soon disappeared. Many Jews survived and remained loyal to their faith.

New Jewish settlers from the East followed in the wake of the conquering Arab armies. They rebuilt ruined Jewish life along the Mediterranean coastline and set up their own centres of learning alongside the new Islamic universities. By the ninth century, there were already well-organised Jewish communities in Kairouan, Constantine, Tlemcen and Fez.

The incorporation of the Maghreb into the world of Islam, followed in the year 711 by the Arab conquest of Spain, suddenly exposed its Jews to powerful influences from the other end of the Middle East. Contact was established and maintained with Sura and Pumbeditha, the great Jewish academies of Babylonia. Their famous Geonim imposed their authority from one end of the Islamic world to the other; and they corresponded frequently with the rabbis of North Africa and Spain. Jews, who had fled to Africa from Christian Visigothic persecution in Spain, returned home. Jewish scholars moved freely to and fro throughout the entire region. It was thus because of the Islamic conquests that, for the first time, many of North Africa's Jews entered into the Babylonian/Sephardi tradition.

This was not the case for the smaller and more isolated Jewish communities of the deep interior. They continued with their own individual brand of religion and life-style, much influenced by their Berber neighbours and largely unaffected by rulings from Baghdad or from the centres of Jewish scholarship springing up in the cities of the Maghreb. And some of those communities survived, largely untouched by the outside, until the middle of the twentieth century.

79 Jewish village of Ait Mahamad in the Atlas Mountains, Morocco. This photograph was taken in the 1950s.

Kairouan, in modern Tunisia, was the leading city of the Maghreb for the first four hundred years of Mohammedan rule. Arab historians described the splendour of the place, with its sumptuous mosques, palaces, villas and suburbs. Jews flocked there from all over the North Africa as well as from Spain, Italy and Sicily. It was the commercial and intellectual centre of Africa, home to many famous rabbis and scholars. Its academies taught and studied in the Babylonian tradition; though there was some tension when, at the beginning of the eleventh century, one of them went over to relying on the opinions of the Palestinian rabbis in preference to those of Baghdad. The city as a whole prospered exceedingly towards the end of the period. Surviving records mention the extravagant tastes of its Jews, who loved music and particularly appreciated rich Persian brocades and costly perfumes.

Nor were duties to less fortunate fellow-Jews neglected. The holy task of redeeming Jewish captives, enslaved by Arab pirates, became an ever-increasing burden in the years of Kairouan's eventual decline. Nissim, a rabbi held in high regard by the Babylonian Geonim, told how a simple butcher displayed great merit by his own charitable act of redemption. It seems that he spotted a young girl amongst a crowd of captives. The girl, weeping bitterly, said that she was Jewish and feared for her religion in slavery. The butcher ransomed her at great cost, took her home and betrothed her to his own son. A young man unexpectedly appeared at the wedding feast and claimed that he had betrothed the girl before her capture. On realising what had happened, the pious butcher immediately annulled the wedding contract. Instead, he had the girl married to her former intended.

Kairouan was sacked by a wave of Bedouin invaders from Egypt in the middle of the eleventh century and never regained its former status. Its Jews scattered far and wide; and those few who remained were expelled a hundred years later, when the city was declared holy to Islam. None returned until the French protectorate of Tunisia was established in 1881. In fact, the havoc wrought to city and countryside by this and by subsequent waves of highly destructive Arab nomads was responsible for the permanent decline of that area of the Maghreb to the east of Tunis.

Fez, in Morocco, was the leading centre of Jewish intellectual and commercial activity at the western end of the Maghreb. The story is told that its Emir fell in love with a Jewish girl, who denied his suit. In the year 860, driven to desperate measures, the Emir forced his way into the house and raped the girl in her bath. That caused a popular uprising, with a mob of Mohammedans and Jews, led by an Islamic Sheikh, pursuing and killing the Emir. Order was only restored in Fez after the intervention of forces loyal to the Governor of the region. The story, whether true or not, is a remarkable indication of the position in local society occupied by Fez's Jews at that time.

The rabbis of Fez were in contact with the Geonim of Baghdad as well as with their colleagues in Palestine, Kairouan and Spain. Their most famous scholar — Rabbi Isaac ben Jacob, known as Alfasi (1013-1103) — wrote the first really authoritative Code of Jewish Law, the one used as a reference by most subsequent codifiers. There was frequent interchange of scholars between Spain and Fez; and Jewish learning in the city long remained at a very high level, though Alfasi himself left for Cordova in Spain in his old age.

There is no simple way to describe the conditions in which the Jews of the Maghreb lived during the period from the Arab conquest to the coming of the Europeans over a thousand years later. For much of the time, the area was fragmented into a mosaic of small and mutually hostile states, each pursuing the selfish interests of the particular tribal dynasty at its helm. To complicate the picture, coastal towns coveted by European powers were seized and occupied by them for long periods. Rulers were for ever supplanting other rulers; and boundaries were fluid, not corresponding with the modern borders imposed by Europeans. Thus, while Jews were enjoying peace and prosperity under one particular king, they might simultaneously have been suffering badly at the hands of another not far away.

Jewish and other accounts are contradictory when describing the state of various Jewish communities. Some authors wrote mostly of prominent Jewish merchants, courtiers and diplomats in the service of their Moham-medan masters, living grand lives in which wealth and learning went hand in hand. Others preferred to concentrate on experiences of humiliation and degradation, which they claim were rarely experienced elsewhere in the world.

André Chouraqui, in his book 'Between East and West: A History of the Jews of North Africa' adopted the latter viewpoint —

Virtual outcasts of inferior status, the Jews became the victims of every crisis... an easy prey for a population constantly embroiled in inter-tribal and inter-dynastic warfare. Usually unarmed, they were at the mercy of the mob eager for rape and pillage. Every

80 Shrine of Rabbi Abraham the Miracle Worker.
A 1989 photograph. The shrine of Rabbi Abraham in Azemour, Morocco, is still constantly visited by believers seeking miraculous cures.

Veneration of the tombs of saintly rabbis was always a feature of Jewish religious life in the Maghreb. An example occurred in the 1930s when a crippled youth from Manchester suddenly made a radical and medically inexplicable recovery after visiting the tomb of Ribbi Yahya in Mazagan, accompanied by a friend of the authors. He promptly changed his name to incorporate Yahya in it, thus acknowledging the source of his recovery.

change of regime, every famine or epidemic, every incident however small was likely to mark an outburst of gory uprising against the Jews. Such tragedies were so frequent that it is impossible to list them...'

The truth — or rather, a more balanced picture — would probably show that until the coming of the Almohads in the twelfth century, the lives of Jews in the Maghreb were probably not very much less satisfactory than those of the rest of the population.

Enlightened Berber rulers certainly valued their Jewish communities and protected them for as long as they were useful — or for as long as they were able to do so. Jewish traders, with their extensive contacts in Europe, brought much appreciated prosperity; and a wealthy Jewish community was a prized source of revenue for a Mohammedan king. Skilled Jewish physicians tended his health. Jewish financiers directed his economy and farmed his taxes. Jews also frequently served the Berber kings on embassies overseas — even if, for the sake of appearances, they sometimes had to be described as mere interpreters.

The Jews had no place in the tangled web of Berber tribal loyalties; and so, usually, could look only to the ruler for support and protection. Of course, when a king arbitrarily turned against his Jews, when he became too weak to shield them or when he was succeeded by a less sympathetic ruler, they could fall victim to the jealousy and spite of a fanatical Moham medan mob; and that certainly occurred with increasing frequency after the twelfth century.

But, apart from during the Almohad period, Jews were to be found at all levels of society except in the very highest echelons of government — and even there, exceptions did occur. Some were well-established economically; and their leading scholars, in contact with Babylon, Spain and Palestine, enjoyed a vigorous intellectual and religious life. As a permanent minority, Jews suffered more than other inhabitants from the chronic instability and warfare of the region — but not excessively more. Even enforcement of humiliating taxes and restrictions in dress, prescribed by Islamic law, appear to have been accepted as a matter of course, provoking neither comment nor complaint.

A century of most extreme hardship and tribulation started in 1145 when the Almohads — a puritanical Berber tribe from the High Atlas mountains — swept through Mohammedan Spain and the Maghreb, and for a time united the whole area under a particularly fanatical brand of Islamic rule. It was a black period for its Jews, an unmitigated catastrophe. From Morocco to Tunisia, surviving accounts tell only of martyrdom, forced conversion to Islam, massacre and mass destruction. Many Jews fled from Morocco to Christian Spain, where they were well received. In Algeria, the community of Tlemcen was utterly destroyed. In Tunisia, those not killed or converted to Islam fled overseas or into the deep interior. Only in Tripolitania, where few Jews lived, is there no record of forced conversion or loss of life.

Some Jews fled south to join the established communities of the Saharan border region. There they sheltered under the protection of nomadic Berber tribes, who had never been conquered by the Almohads and were not interested in religious intolerance. In time, they thrived on the developing Saharan trade.

Religious persecution slackened as the Almohads weakened and were succeeded by less fanatical dynasties of rulers. Jews who had been forced to embrace the Crescent returned openly to their true faith. Trade revived in the main cities of the Maghreb. Jewish merchants, spearheaded by many from the island of Majorca, began to return from across the sea and helped the survivors to rebuild their shattered communities. Though an Arab historian, writing in 1224, was probably correct in asserting that there was not a single synagogue in the Maghreb, communities of Jews certainly did exist in Fez, Tunis, Algiers, Bougie and Djerba at about that time.

Eventually, Jewish life in Africa returned to a shadow of that existing before the catastrophe. But once kindled among the ignorant Mohammedan masses, the fire of religious intolerance was never completely extinguished and sporadic outbursts of violence frequently recurred. The ruin inflicted by the Almohads was permanent in that the former state of well-being was never fully restored.

A ferocious pogrom was launched against the Jewish Quarter of Seville in the year 1391. That heralded a whole century of massacre, forced conversion and persecution of the Jews of Spain, culminating in their total expulsion in 1492.

Conditions in Morocco were unfavourable for Jewish settlement in 1391 because of economic malaise and Mohammedan persecution. Consequently, most of the early refugees from Spain and Majorca headed for Algeria, where they were well received by its rulers.

Tradition ascribes the arrival of the first refugees in Algiers to a miracle; and indeed their friendly reception by the princes of the region does seem something like a miracle. The first ship reached Algiers with a famous rabbi (Simon ben Zemach Duran) on board. The rabbi went ashore with a delegation and so greatly impressed the Mohammedan ruler that he and his followers were admitted to Algiers and given their own quarter in which to live, work and practise their faith in freedom. They were also granted valuable tax concessions not available to the local Jews. That first ship was followed by many others, until several communities of Spanish Jews were established along the Mediterranean coastline.

Much later, in the seventeenth and eighteenth centuries, Jews from Leghorn (Livorno) also settled along the coastline of the Maghreb, particularly in Algiers. They were successful merchants, who brought wealth to the country. One of their main activities involved acting as agents for European governments in the ransoming of Christians captured by the Barbary pirates.

In Tunisia, the initial harmony between the indigenous Jews and the later immigrants from Livorno, known as Gornim, deteriorated for a time into something approaching open hostility. The Gornim wore European clothes and hats, whilst the local Jews were compelled to dress in the distinctive garb specified by local Islamic law. Indeed, the objection of the Bey to

81 Jewish woman from the Valley of Ziz in Morocco
This photograph dates from about 1950.

Gornim under foreign protection wearing hats caused several serious incidents with European powers, including one in which the British Mediterranean fleet set sail to avenge an insult to a British subject of Gibraltar origin.

Few Jews headed for Algeria after their expulsion from Spain in 1492, most preferring to make their way to Morocco where they were warmly welcomed by the Sultan. Unfortunately, bands of Bedouin robbers set upon the unarmed columns of refugees on their way to Fez from the coast and stripped many of their possessions. On their arrival, being so numerous, they were obliged to camp in the open fields outside the city walls. There, about twenty thousand of them are said to have died of cholera and starvation; and in sheer despair, some even returned to Spain.

Though the authorities remained friendly, the hardship endured by the refugees was intense. Rabbi Judah Hayyat's account of his own suffering

82 Ponta Delgada Synagogue
This synagogue is on the island of Saõ
Miguel in the Azores. Opened in 1836, it
was the first on Portuguese territory since
the Inquisition. The above photograph was
taken in 1968 and shows the synagogue's
two caretakers.

includes the following passage, the flavour of which is echoed in many other descriptions:

...I went to the great city of Fez. There was famine ... we ate the grass of the field. Every day I worked a mill at the house of some Arabs, with both my arms, for a small, extremely thin slice of bread, not fit even for dogs. And because of the great cold of the autumn, and because we had no covering against the cold, nor houses to lodge in, we made ditches in the dung ... and put our bodies therein ...

Though some Spanish Jews moved on to Italy, Turkey and Palestine, and a few even returned to Spain, the majority settled down in towns with existing Jewish communities, both along the coast and in the interior. Morocco later became a haven for Marranos escaping from the Inquisition. They arrived from Spain and Portugal, Madeira, the Canary Islands, the Azores and even from the Americas. Once in Morocco, they attended special centres in Fez, Meknes, Tetuán and Marrakesh for reconversion to Judaism.

The Maghreb, to which the first Spanish refugees made their way in 1391, was divided into the petty kingdoms known in Europe as the Barbary States. They were mostly in confusion and often near to anarchy. The Kingdom of Tlemcen, for example, changed rulers violently no fewer than six times in just twenty-two years. Many of its people were so poor that, to quote Chief Rabbi Barfat of Algiers,

They have not sufficient bread nor water. They sleep on the ground and use their daywear for night covering. Their clothes are patch upon patch and most of them walk about barefooted.

Books were so scarce that seldom were even ordinary Bibles available for teaching purposes; and texts had to be written on blackboards. Few communities could afford to maintain a rabbi or a decent Scroll of the Law for synagogue readings.

Many rabbis themselves were not far removed from the ignorance of the masses. The Talmud was unknown to most of them; and they had to make do with Maimonides's Code as their only source of reference. Even then, they often made errors in their rulings; and it was not unknown for tricky matters to be referred to Islamic courts for decision.

Though fervently pious, for many Jews that piety was based on the unquestioning faith of ignorance rather than on that of knowledge. They lived within an elaborately developed framework of superstition and magic, which differed little from that of their Mohammedan neighbours — and indeed owed as little to the religion of Moses as it did to that of Muhammad. Even in the peculiarly North African custom of venerating saints, never accepted by mainstream Judaism, distinctions were blurred; and both Jews and Mohammedans could sometimes be seen worshipping at the same shrine. This kind of religious life, tempered in time by a little more learning, continued in those isolated communities of the Maghreb that remained untouched by Spanish-Jewish or European influence until their extinction in the middle of the twentieth century.

To this situation, the Spanish refugees brought their superior culture, commercial ability and learning. They were at first resented by the older residents, not least for the preferential treatment accorded to them by the Berber princes; and it took a great deal of tact by the Spanish rabbis to overcome initial reservations.

The newcomers formed separate communities wherever they settled, administering their own affairs and maintaining the manners and customs of Spain. In time they overtook the 'native' Jews in numbers and gradually absorbed those who lived alongside them. They acquired considerable wealth through commerce and rose to positions of influence in the courts of the Mohammedan rulers. Their higher culture and intellectual abilities helped to raise their African brethren from the sorry condition into which they had fallen.

In short, the contribution of the Spanish refugees, and especially that of their famous rabbis, to the spiritual and economic uplift of North African Jewry was fundamental and far-reaching. Only in the deep interior of the country, and other isolated places, did their influence not penetrate; and only there did conditions remain very much the same until our own days.

The Turks occupied the whole of the Maghreb, except for Morocco, during the sixty years that followed their conquest of Egypt in 1517. They were assisted in this by an irregular navy of Turkish pirates, or Corsairs, which kept Spanish predatory ambition at bay. Far from Constantinople, the new Ottoman provinces were governed by the chiefs of the Janissaries (the elite army corps) and the Corsairs, under the titular control of the Sultan's representative.

Trade with Europe, in which Jewish merchants had a prominent role, continued to flourish. But the importance and prosperity of the Maghreb as a whole began to decline after the development of the sea route to India and substantial trading links with the New World. The region drifted steadily downwards into obscurity and poverty; and the bulk of its Jewish population followed in the same path. European travellers of the early nineteenth century wrote detailed descriptions of the degradation and poverty in which most of the Jews were then living.

Of course, wealthy Jewish families with European connections continued to render indispensable services to the Islamic rulers, and were valued and protected by them in return. The Turkish Dey (Ruler, elected by the local chiefs of the army and navy) of Algiers intervened with the French Consul in 1827 in an attempt to persuade the French government to settle a long overdue debt of millions of francs to the Jewish firm of Bacri and Busnach. During that interview, the Dey lost his temper and struck the Consul with his fly whisk. That conveniently unforgivable insult led directly to the French occupation of Algeria in 1830.

Algeria
Tunisia
Libya
and
Morocco

ALGERIA

In 1830, the Jews of Algeria welcomed the soldiers of the French army with wild enthusiasm. They had no regret for the passing of Turkish rule and looked forward eagerly to enjoying the liberty, fraternity and equality proclaimed by the new colonists. And in that expectation, they were only partly to be disappointed.

The Jews were at first treated as an autonomous nation under French rule; and they were represented as such on all the new administrative bodies. Many legal anomalies arose later, as the community rapidly proceeded towards its goal of full emancipation. Jews were treated almost as Frenchmen in some parts of the country, whilst in others they remained subject to rabbinic jurisdiction — especially in matters of personal and family status. It was not until the adoption of the Crémieux Decree of 1870 — signed by Adolphe Crémieux, Minister of Justice, and a veteran champion of Jewish rights — that the Jews of Algeria became full French citizens; and even then, the Decree was applied only in the departments of Algiers, Oran and Constantine, and not in the south of the country.

French education played a major part in the Jewish community's speedy adaption to European ways; and this stood its members in good stead when they finally departed for France after Algeria gained its independence in 1962.

Judaism was, to some extent, left behind in this sudden translation from one world to another. The traditional Talmud Torah, teaching by rote and with little real understanding, evoked small sympathy and even less enthusiasm in the minds of the new Europeans. The Alliance Israélite's attempts to introduce Jewish history, grammar and meaningful religious knowledge to the teaching of Judaism had little success, especially as it could not penetrate the secular French government schools. Consequently, many Algerian Jews came to relegate the faith of their ancestors to a backward and irrelevant past, while others were content to pay only lip-service to it. The rate of assimilation was very high; and it remained so until the community's end.

One effect of the Crémieux Decree was to create a powerful new Jewish electorate in Algeria. That, and abundant evidence of the general economic and social progress of the community, prompted many outbursts of virulent anti-semitism from some of the French settlers who had brought the popular poison with them from home. Numerous ugly incidents occurred; but the good sense and moderation of the majority, as well as the stance of the Mohammedans in remaining aloof, led to a considerable easing of tension in the opening years of the twentieth century.

Hitler's rise to power in Germany, compounded by sympathetic echoes of his doctrines in France, caused a renewal of many of the worst manifestations of anti-Jewish hatred in the 1930s. After France's capitulation to Germany in 1940, Marshal Pétain's Vichy government abrogated the Crémieux Decree, disenfranchising Algerian Jewry and causing much misery in the process.

Incredibly, the French administration, set up by the Allies after their

83 A Jewish woman from Algiers in traditional costume

84 The Corrida
This anti-semitic cartoon from an Oran newspaper of 1897 shows one of the leaders of the anti-semitic campaign as the matador confronting the bull - Simon El Kanoui, President of the Consistoire, and one of the first Jews to wear European dress.

85 . The Anti-Semitic party at the Polls
An extract from the list of candidates for Oran's municipal election of 1897, published in a local newspaper. All openly declared themselves to be against the common enemy - the Jew!

landings in North Africa in 1942, attempted to perpetuate Pétain's policy; and General Giraud actually abrogated the Crémieux Decree all over again the following year. It took representations by American-Jewish interests, by General de Gaulle's Free French Committee in London, by President Roosevelt and even by Algerian nationalist leaders to nullify this frankly anti-Jewish policy.

The Jewish community as a whole stood aside from the bitter struggle in which an independent Algeria was forged. They felt great loyalty to France, to whom they owed much; but they could not betray their land and its Mohammedan inhabitants in whose midst they had lived for so many centuries. However Algerian nationalists sacked the Great Synagogue of Algiers and desecrated the Jewish cemetery of Oran in 1962. At the same time, several Jewish leaders were murdered and some were kidnapped. That was the signal for departure; and only a few thousand remained to witness Algerian independence soon after.

TUNISIA

Of all the Jewish communities of the Maghreb, that of Tunisia enjoyed by far the best conditions of life during the first part of the nineteenth century. Tunisia had formerly welcomed Jews fleeing from persecution in neighbouring countries; and that policy of active benevolence was continued by its rulers, who repeatedly appointed many Jews to positions of importance in the administration. Ahmad Bey (1830-56) so favoured Jews that he was derisively called 'The Bey of the Jews' by some of his Mohammedan subjects.

Successive Beys of Tunis, wishing to free themselves from Turkish control, had developed close ties with France as well as lesser ones with Italy and other European countries. Their influence stimulated the introduction of liberal ideas into government. On the individual level, the resident foreign consuls often intervened to right injustices committed against members of minority groups.

In 1856 Muhammad Bey — builder of an exquisite palace to house the twelve hundred women of his harem — abolished all special taxes on Jews. That was a truly radical departure; for the religiously inspired taxes were a principal means of enforcing the second-class status of Jews in Islamic society.

This idyl was abruptly checked by the arrest and trial of Batto Sfez — a Jew who, after a quarrel with a Mohammedan, was charged with uttering blasphemy against Islam. The result of the trial was a foregone conclusion; for even on such uncorroborated evidence, the oath of a Jew could not count against that of a Mohammedan in an Islamic court. Despite heavy bribes, many protests and the intervention of the French Consul, the Bey confirmed the sentence of death and Batto Sfez lost his head.

After that shocking episode, the strongest pressure was put on the Bey to grant Tunisia a European-style constitution. But nothing happened until a French naval squadron arrived at the Tunisian port of La Goulette in

1857. The Bey then suddenly changed his mind and proclaimed the 'Pacte Fondamental'.

In its general provisions, the Pact attempted to close the door on Tunisia's feudal past. Its grand declarations provided a firm basis for the establishment of a modern state, in which all subjects of the Bey were to be secure and equal before the law, irrespective of race or religion. Jews were specifically guaranteed freedom to practise their religion; and provision was made for the appointment of a Jewish judge to the bench of any criminal court trying a Jew.

Four years later, laws were enacted for the implementation of this new dispensation, in which secular affairs were to be separated from the religious. These were all inspired by French idealism and were drafted under French guidance. During his visit to Tunis, Napoleon III was formally presented with the manuscript copy by Muhammad al-Sadiq Bey.

It seems though that the mass of the people was ill-prepared for the radical change to their age-old traditions. Enraged by the loss of Islamic privileges and the imposition of heavy taxes, they blamed the Jews for the reforms. Discontent flared into open rebellion against the Bey; and the Pact was withdrawn after order was finally restored. However, Jews were not penalised as a result of the popular reaction. They retained their exemption from special taxes and the victims of mob violence were compensated.

86   A family of Tunisian Jews
Engraving, 1842.

87 **A Hebrew class at La Goulette, Tunisia, 1922.**

Fearful for the future, many Jews sought the protection of foreign consuls during the difficult period following Batto Sfez's trial and execution; and several hundred of them actually managed to acquire the status of protected subjects of European powers.

The French never attempted to make Tunisia a part of France, as they had Algeria. Nevertheless, a French Protectorate was established over the country in 1883 and powerful French influence was directed towards reinforcing those liberal tendencies already displayed by most of its Beys.

The Alliance Israélite Universelle moved in with the French. Its blend of secular education with Jewish religion, history and culture was a counter to the purely secular education given in the French government schools increasingly favoured by the Jewish middle classes. Perhaps because of this, the extreme pattern of rapid assimilation experienced in Algeria was not repeated in Tunisia where Jewish religious identity remained significant.

It became possible after 1910 for Jews to obtain French citizenship under certain conditions. Over seven thousand Jews in all managed to obtain French nationality during the period of the Protectorate. In time, they and their descendants came to comprise one-third of the total Jewish population. The remaining two-thirds looked to the Bey and his government for fair play and protection, and continued to exercise a degree of autonomy in the traditional manner. On the whole, they lived in peace with the rest of the population, rapidly and enthusiastically adapting to European ways.

A German army occupied Tunisia in 1942. It immediately started to implement plans for its Jews similar to those already being put into effect in Nazi-dominated Europe. Fortunately, the Germans were driven from the country by Allied forces after only a few months and before their evil schemes could be fully implemented. Tunisia's Jews were saved from disaster — though there was humiliation and pillage, arbitrary execution and individual deportation to European concentration camps.

After the Second World War, Tunisia's Jewish population — partly French and partly Tunisian by nationality — found itself poised uneasily between loyalty to France and to the new Tunisian nationalism. On the eve of independence, the Jewish middle class was highly educated and occupied a good position in society. Some of its members were on friendly terms with the nationalist politicians; and one was even included in the first independent government.

Standing aside from the more extreme attitudes of other Arab governments, Tunisia at first adopted a moderate stance in respect to opposition to the State of Israel. All the same, some Jews hastened to leave the country after independence; and as incident followed incident, more and more departed. Some particularly alarming anti-Jewish manifestations, including the desecration of Tunis's Great Synagogue, occurred on the outbreak of the Six Day War of 1967 between Israel and Egypt. That prompted the community to embark on the wave of emigration that brought it finally to its end. From the establishment of Israel in 1948 until 1970, it is estimated that about forty thousand Jews left for Israel, an equal number for France and about a thousand for Canada and elsewhere.

LIBYA

Most Jews left Tripoli in 1510, when the city was captured by the Spaniards. Christian rule lasted for just over forty years, with Tripoli in the hands of the piratical Knights of Malta for the latter half of that period.

Tripoli was conquered by the Turks in 1551. At first ruled by a Pasha appointed by the Ottoman Sultan, real control gradually passed to the Dey, commander of the Janissaries. Successive Deys, eager to assert independence from Ottoman control, concluded treaties with European powers which allowed their Consuls some influence in local affairs.

Jews must have begun to return to Tripoli with the establishment of Turkish rule. They seem scarcely to have recovered from the Almohad persecutions, for their knowledge of Judaism was scanty. Their ignorance caused Rabbi Simon Labi, a Spanish rabbi, to interrupt his journey from Fez to the Land of Israel. As quoted from Hayim Azulai in Hirschberg's 'A History of the Jews of North Africa',

When he came to Tripoli, he saw that they knew neither law nor judgement, nor even prayer and blessings in their proper form. And he said in his heart that it was fitting for him to bring them closer to the Torah and to teach them Torah and the fear of the Lord; and that this was better than going to the Land of Israel. And so he did, and he almost succeeded in turning them into proper Jews ... according to a tradition current in Tripoli, he laid the foundations for the local community ...

Rabbi Simon Labi was an all-round scholar and mystic, also well versed in astronomy and the natural sciences. He served as personal physician to Yahya Pasha, the governor of Tripoli; and it seems that he was revered by the leading Islamic government officials.

The community was strengthened in the seventeenth century by the arrival of settlers from Leghorn (Livorno), known as Gornim. These were international traders, ship owners and money changers, who brought wealth to the country and to the local Jews. So too did those Marranos who also found their way to Tripoli.

With the Sultan's full approval, Ahmad Karamanli Pasha took power in 1711 and ruled Tripoli as a semi-independent state. His dynasty continued until 1835, when Tripoli became an ordinary province of the Ottoman Empire, administered by officials sent from Constantinople and periodically replaced. Only then was government control extended from the coastal region to the interior of the country, previously ruled by Berber tribal chiefs.

The fortunes of Tripoli's Jews fluctuated in sympathy with those of the country as a whole. The Jews always supported the legal government against foreign invaders and local usurpers. Bad times alternated with good times. By the early years of the nineteenth century, the United States Consul in Tunis, himself a Jew, was able to report that the Jews had greater influence in Tripoli than in the other Barbary States. Two thousand Jews, out of a total population of twenty thousand, then lived in Tripoli; and a Jew was sent by its Pasha to handle peace negotiations with the United States.

The Jewish community prospered under direct Turkish rule, when many restrictions against it were abolished. The resident European consuls also exerted a beneficial influence by interfering, and exerting pressure on Constantinople, in cases of injustice. European travellers of the nineteenth century reported favourably on the condition of the Jews of Tripolitania, despite isolated instances of Mohammedan intolerance.

Italy copied France in attempting to infiltrate its culture into a region on which it had designs. The first Italian government school in Tripoli was established by a Jew in 1876. This was immediately popular with middle class Jews, who formed the majority of its pupils. The Italians were followed by the Alliance Israélite Universelle, which founded its own French-speaking schools. This movement towards Europeanisation was opposed by the traditionalists and the underprivileged, who saw the adoption of European ways as a threat to their ancient way of life.

Italy conquered Tripolitania, Cyrenaica and Fezzan in 1911; but it took several years more to subdue the Berber tribes of the interior. Because of Italian attempts to placate the Mohammedans, Jews at first thought they had been better off under Turkish rule — even though they were fully emancipated by the Italians. However, Italy pumped money into the country to encourage its development; and the Jews co-operated wholeheartedly in many Italian commercial, cultural and educational enterprises. By 1931, the

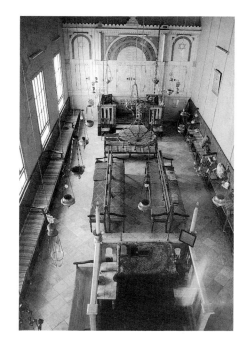

88 The Ben Simon Synagogue of Mazagan (El Jadida) in Morocco, still in use.
Photograph taken in 1981.

Jewish population had increased to about twenty one thousand, of which fifteen thousand lived in Tripoli and over two thousand in Benghazi.

Anti-Jewish laws, put into effect in Italy in 1938 by Mussolini's fascist government, were not applied to Libya until 1942, the middle of the Second World War — and then with little enthusiasm. Nevertheless, the British army was welcomed as a liberator by the Jews when it arrived.

The Germans and Italians took their revenge when the British were later forced to withdraw from Cyrenaica. Its Jews were deported to concentration camps in the south of the country, where over five hundred died of starvation and disease.

Jewish communal life revived after the end of the war; but it was never to be the same again. Anti-Jewish riots broke out in Tripoli in 1945; and when the British army of occupation did not intervene, they spread throughout the country. One hundred and thirty five people were killed, many were injured and much property was looted or destroyed. The Jews then organised and armed in self-defence. When rioters assembled again, after the declaration of the State of Israel in 1948, they met with strenuous resistance. It is estimated that there were then just under thirty thousand Jews living in Tripolitania and about five thousand in Cyrenaica.

All but six thousand of the Jewish community had left by the time the Kingdom of Libya, comprising Tripolitania, Cyrenaica and Fezzan, obtained its independence in 1952; and those who remained included wealthy merchants with close ties to Italy. Some went to Italy; but the overwhelming majority emigrated to Israel. Further riots, which broke out during the Six Day War of 1967 between Egypt and Israel, caused the rest to flee. Fewer than one hundred Jews now remain in Libya.

MOROCCO

Morocco, always managing to repulse the aggressive designs of the Turkish rulers of neighbouring Algeria, never became part of the Ottoman Empire. Eager for friends and allies to counter constant Turkish pressure, its rulers developed commercial and diplomatic ties — and even treaties — with Spain and Portugal, with Britain, France and the Netherlands. Those powers, eager to obtain a foothold in the lucrative African trade, and port facilities on the route to India, established their own consuls in Morocco. Treaty rights enabled the European consuls to extend their protection to their local agents and employees, usually Jews; and the consuls were never slow to intervene with the authorities on behalf of their proteges.

Not only did the leading Jewish merchants enjoy a virtual monopoly of overseas trade, but it was they who largely handled relations with the European powers. Jews negotiated treaties on Morocco's behalf with the Christian countries of Europe and even, in 1787, with the United States of America. Enterprising Jewish merchants served as foreign consular officials in Morocco, and as Moroccan ambassadors abroad. Samuel Palache, for example, greatly helped the infant Jewish community of Amsterdam during his residence there from 1609 onwards.

89 Rabbi Aharon Butbul
The rabbi is shown praying in his synagogue in Fez, Morocco, in 1926.

Learned Jews also acted as personal physicians and advisers to several of Morocco's rulers and sometimes occupied important positions. There was thus established a small but wealthy upper class of Jewish merchants, with close links to the Court and to the European powers under whose protection they often sheltered. These Jews were indispensable to the Sultans and, with the growth of European trade, they became increasingly influential.

The remaining Jews, like their Mohammedan fellow subjects, were poor, and sometimes desperately poor. Surviving Jewish sources tell of the many misfortunes they endured over the years and of the occasional disasters that befell them. European Christian observers wrote of the degradation to which the Jewish masses were subjected and of the filthy, insanitary conditions of the mellahs (ghettos) in which they lived.

It is hard to tell whether or not the lot of the Jews really was very substantially worse than that of their fellows. As a minority, they probably did attract rather more than a fair share of the woes shared by the population as a whole — but, though some of the accounts of the humiliations they endured are horrific, it is not easy to form a truly balanced view.

Two dynasties of Sharifs (descendants of the Prophet Muhammad) enjoyed power in Morocco from 1553 to 1912. They were assisted by Jewish advisers, financiers and armourers in first establishing their sway over the country. This was consolidated in 1578 by the Battle of the Three Kings, when a large Portuguese army was defeated by Abd el Malik. Thousands of Christian prisoners were ransomed by the descendants of Jewish refugees from Spain and Portugal, who treated them well and eventually enabled them to return home in exchange for large quantities of gold.

However, the Sharifs were rarely able to maintain control over the entire country. Anarchy generally prevailed away from their seats of power — with Berber and Arab tribal chiefs and the heads of fanatical Islamic sects (Marabouts) doing very much as they chose. Added to this, conflict between rival members of the Sharifian clans ensured that, for part of the period, there was also chaos at the centre.

The death of Sultan Mulay Ismail in 1727 signalled a thirty year long period of anarchy, which exhausted the country's resources and impoverished the Jewish communities of the interior. Many of its Jews then migrated to the towns, where they transformed their mellahs (Jewish Quarters) into slums. Even principal towns of the interior, such as Fez, were progressively abandoned for Safi, Rabat and other ports — closer to their wealthier brethren and to the European consuls.

The most cruel of the subsequent rulers was Mulay al Yazid, who came to power in 1790 with a grudge against the Jews of Tetuán who had refused to finance his rebellion against his father. Almost his first act was to give the Jewish community of Tetuán over to his army, with a free hand to pillage, rape and murder. Other Jewish communities then suffered a similar fate; and Jewish notables who had served his father well were strung up by the heels at the gates of Meknes, there to suffer a lingering death. In Meknes, the local Mohammedans rebelled against this barbarity and managed to save many Jews; whilst in Rabat, the Mohammedan governor sheltered his Jews from the worst excesses. In Marrakesh, not only was the Jewish quarter sacked and its inhabitants massacred or enslaved, but the eyes of three hundred leading Mohammedan citizens were also put out and several thousand more were murdered in their mosque.

Conditions for the Jews of Morocco fluctuated during the nineteenth century, with wealthy Jews playing an increasingly prominent part in diplomatic affairs, with some Jews migrating from surrounding countries and the masses continuing to endure the hardship, poverty and humiliation of their everyday lives.

Jews, as the supposed agents of European powers, began to incur the

90 Picnic in the Diplomatic Woods
This photograph was taken in about 1910
in Tangier, Morocco.

resentment of the Berber masses. When extra humiliations were heaped
upon them, and injustice was followed by further injustice, Sir Moses
Montefiore interceded with Sultan Mulay Muhammad. In 1864 the Sultan
received the seventy-nine year old English baronet with much honour in
Marrakesh where, in an impressive ceremony, he promised much but
performed almost nothing.

The American and European Consuls protested vigorously when it
became clear that the Sultan had gone back on his word and that Sir Moses's
mission had failed to alleviate Jewish suffering; and they took more and
more Jews under their protection. The Alliance Israélite Universelle, which
opened its first school in Tetuán in 1862, was the only ray of hope in that
dark period.

In 1912 Tangier was declared an international zone. A Spanish protectorate was established over Tetuán and the northern part of the country,
in all about five per cent of the area of Morocco; and a French protectorate
was proclaimed over the rest. The treaty was heralded by a frightful pogrom
in Fez, where one-third of the Jewish quarter was burned down, sixty Jews
killed and many others injured or raped. It took twenty years for the French
to pacify the entire country and bring it firmly under their control.

Though freed by the French from the worst of their humiliations and
disabilities, those Moroccan Jews not under foreign protection continued

91 **A Jewish family from Tetuán, Spanish Morocco**
The photograph was taken in about 1920.

to be fully subject to the authority of the Sultan. Thus, under Islamic law, they could never aspire to equal rights with the Sultan's Mohammedan subjects. Though internal personal matters between Jews were judged in rabbinic courts, and criminal cases in French courts, all civil suits involving Mohammedans and Jews came under Islamic jurisdiction — where evidence given by a Jew was of little account against that of a Mohammedan, and where Jewish redress against Mohammedans was very limited.

Where they could, the Jews adapted to European culture with enthusiasm. Children of the wealthy were educated in French secular schools and received their religious education at home. The strong rabbinic tradition in Morocco, coupled with social pressure, prevented the mass assimilation experienced in neighbouring Algeria. The Alliance schools did splendid work in bringing a modicum of modern secular education to the underprivileged masses. They were however opposed by some rabbis, who accurately foresaw the danger that too quick and superficial a change might bring in its wake.

The Jewish community developed rapidly under Western influence. It ended as a third force in the land, poised uneasily between the French colonists, who never accepted them as equals, and the Mohammedans whom they had outstripped in the race for modernity.

The French Vichy regime of 1940 interned all 'foreign' Jews, of whom there were many in Morocco. The 'local' Jews were given only half the food rations of their Mohammedan neighbours, had their access to schooling severely restricted, and were forced to live in the mellahs where disease arising from the gross overcrowding took heavy toll. Former conditions were restored after 1943, when General de Gaulle's Free French Committee assumed the reigns of government.

Anti-Jewish riots became almost commonplace after the establishment of the State of Israel in 1948. Though perpetrators were brought to justice by the authorities, sixty seven thousand Jews had emigrated to Israel by the time Morocco achieved its own independence in 1956.

On his return from exile to lead the newly independent nation, Sultan Muhammad V declared Morocco's Jews to be citizens with equal rights. Jews were also included in the first government and in the administration. But it was not long before emigration to Israel was forbidden. Increasing obstacles were placed before Jews wishing to leave the country for any reason at all; and Jews were eventually dismissed from government and official positions. Another forty seven thousand Jews managed, in one way or another, to leave for Israel during that period.

Sultan Hassan II, on his accession to the throne in 1961, reversed his father's policy. Jews were once again legally allowed to emigrate, even to Israel; and many were given important posts in the country.

92 Circumcision in Morocco
Rabbi Massas, Chief Rabbi of Jaffa, is here shown sitting in Elijah's Chair and holding the infant.

93 Talmud Torah
A traditional Talmud Torah class in Morocco.

Despite the Sultan's benevolent attitude to his Jewish subjects and his repeated attempts to protect them, politically inspired anti-Jewish agitation grew. This reached its peak on the outbreak of the Six Day War between Egypt and Israel in 1967. Most of the remaining Jewish community then departed for Israel; though this time, the wealthy and educated also left, making for France and Canada. Many of them travelled through a transit camp established in Gibraltar with the tacit consent of the British government.

By 1970, only an estimated thirty five thousand Jews remained in Morocco, protected by the King and living in tolerable conditions.

94   The Jewish cemetary of Tetuán, Spanish Morocco
The photograph, showing mourning Jewish women, dates from the early twentieth century.

160 TÉTUAN. - LE CIMETIÈRE JUIF. LES TOMBES.   L. L.

France

France, on Spain's northern border, might have provided at least a temporary haven for the persecuted Jews of the Iberian Peninsula had not its Catholic King already expelled all Jews from his domain in 1394, and had not his successors formally maintained that ban — with some minor exceptions — until the eve of the French Revolution at the end of the eighteenth century.

Provence was not incorporated into the French Kingdom until 1481; and Spanish Jews had fled there from Mohammedan persecution as early as the twelfth century. Those Sephardim stimulated the intellectual life of Provence, broadening the scope of its previously Ashkenazi culture by the introduction of interest in philosophy, literature and the natural sciences. Study of Kabbalah also took deep root in Provence, as did that of the Halachic Codes favoured by Sephardi scholars. The Jewish communities of Spain and Provence remained in close touch until both were expelled from their respective countries within a few years of each other.

King Louis XI of France was eager to participate in the lucrative trade with the New World, dominated by Spain and Portugal. In the year 1474, he tempted foreign merchants — mostly Spaniards — to settle in Bordeaux by offering them special privileges. Many took advantage of the King's offer, including New Christians from Spain. Some were secret Jews; and the publisher of this book is himself directly descended from one of the Marrano families who came to France at that time. Others were genuine converts to Christianity, escaping from the attentions of the Inquisition.

After the forced conversion of Portugal's Jews, and the introduction of the Inquisition into that country in 1536, pressure to escape to a better life abroad intensified. French records include a number of applications from Portuguese merchants who wished to regularise their residence in France.

In 1550 it was noted that

Among the said Portuguese, known as New Christians, there has arisen a great desire, which grows day by day, to take up residence in our kingdom.

Finally, responding to a petition from twenty eight New Christians of Bordeaux, King Henri II issued a collective certificate of naturalisation, called Letters Patent, authorising the Portuguese New Christians to enter France with their families, servants and goods, and to 'live wherever they desire'.

Those Letters Patent were confirmed by King Henri III in 1574 in a document described as

A guarantee granted by the King to the Spaniards and Portuguese of the city of Bordeaux

and it contained a highly significant phrase forbidding 'any inquiry whatsoever' into their lives. It seems therefore that royal policy was to welcome Portuguese New Christians into the kingdom and, providing they behaved with discretion, to turn a blind eye to their private beliefs and practices. When in 1614 King Louis XIII ordered all Jews, disguised or otherwise, to leave his kingdom, the New Christians of Bordeaux alone were not molested, nor were their rights seriously challenged. By the end of the eighteenth century, the community had grown to number about one thousand people and was served by six synagogues.

Many, and probably the majority, of the early settlers assimilated into the general population. But some did preserve their Jewish identity in the secrecy of their own homes; and it was they who laid the foundation for the later establishment of the flourishing Portuguese (Jewish) 'Nations' of South-West France.

Communities of Portuguese New Christians also began to form close to the French border — at St. Jean-de-Luz, Biarritz, and in and around the flourishing port of Bayonne. In 1632 the Agent of the Inquisition at Pamplona complained despairingly that 'troops of Portuguese' were passing into France with all their wealth.

The two-hundred strong community of St. Jean-de-Luz had paid handsomely for the protection of the Comte de Gramont. It received a nasty shock however in 1619 when a sixty-year old lady, newly arrived from Portugal, attended mass at the local church. She was seen concealing the host in her handkerchief instead of swallowing it. Denounced by the scandalised priest, she was arrested and imprisoned on a charge of sacrilege. The unfortunate woman was plucked from her prison cell by an angry mob, thrust into a barrel filled with tar and straw, and burned alive. The community rapidly dispersed; and it was many years before the Portuguese began to return to the town.

It was towards the middle of the seventeenth century that organised communities of Marranos began to emerge, if not always into the open, then at least into the pages of surviving historical records. Gérard Nahon described the Marranos of South-West France in some detail in 'The Western Sephardim'; and much of what follows here is derived from his account.

Paradoxically it is the Inquisition which provided a wealth of information on several of the groups. It infiltrated spies into their midst; and those spies reported in great detail, naming names and even relating the words of some of the prayers recited in the secret synagogues.

The other major source of information and a very powerful influence on the emerging communities was the Jewish Community of Amsterdam. This did much by means of advice, expertise and funds to smooth the path of the Marranos back to the Jewish faith. South-West France became an important staging post for New Christians travelling to Amsterdam from Spain and Portugal in order to return to Judaism; and the closest ties were maintained with what became the parent community.

Marrano settlement in France spread up from the Spanish frontier as far as the English Channel. Towns such as Nantes, La Rochelle, Rouen and Le Havre, as well as Toulouse, Montpellier and Marseilles in the south, all contained groups of Marranos; but except for Nantes and Rouen, these were not large enough to develop into formal Jewish communities. There was even a tiny synagogue in Paris in 1662, led by a court perfumer and by the physician to Marie de Medicis, who had been granted the exceptional privilege of being able to practice his Judaism without concealment.

The community of Bayonne, which eventually grew to a peak of about

95 Omer board, Bayonne
The board, dating from the 18th century, was used in the synagogue to mark each of the 49 days between Pesah (Passover) and Pentecost (Shavuot).

two thousand five hundred souls, with no fewer than thirteen synagogues, incurred the particular wrath of the Inquisition. To that organisation, a visit to Bayonne was a sure sign of the vile crime of Judaism; and it was probably right for, as soon as Bayonne appointed its first Rabbi in 1670, it became the leading Marrano community of France.

The city magistrates of Bayonne never wavered in their hostility to the Portuguese and caused continual trouble to the community throughout its history. They absolutely forbad the Portuguese to live in the town itself; and so the Marranos settled instead in the suburb of St. Esprit. There they lived under the protection of the local church's canons, who even permitted them to bury their dead with Jewish rites in their own cemetery until a Marrano burial ground was established.

The three satellite villages of Peyrehorade, Labastide-Clairence and Bidache also had their own Marrano communities, each with its own cemetery. Of these, Bidache alone was not subject to the King's rule. There, in the seventeenth century, the word 'Jew' was actually used in two official documents instead of 'Portuguese' the usual term of disguise.

The Marranos continued to behave as New Christians for many years. They submitted their children for baptism and entered them in the parish records. They married first in Church before conducting the Jewish wedding ceremony at home. However open their secret became, Jews were not allowed to practise their religion openly in France until the eve of the French Revolution.

Bayonne became the first town in which the presence of Jews was tacitly acknowledged by the authorities. Its synagogue attracted sightseers as early as 1679, when a French lady visited it and reported that she had witnessed 'nothing remarkable in it'. An expulsion order of 1694, directed against Jews recently arrived from Martinique, required them to move to

that suburb of Bayonne where the King has permitted them to dwell

— the first time that the presence of Jews in France was unambiguously acknowledged, if not yet accepted.

Portuguese Jews were threatened with expulsion several times during the following century; but on each occasion the decrees were revoked and new Letters Patent obtained after the payment of large sums of money. The fiction was still being maintained as late as 1776, with Jews officially described as New Christians in the royal taxation ledgers.

The Portuguese 'Nations' of Bayonne and Bordeaux became more firmly established, more prosperous and more confident as the eighteenth century progressed. They governed themselves firmly under laws confirmed by royal approval and sometimes modified by royal command. They employed all the staff necessary to run their affairs, religious and secular, including resident Agents to represent their vital interests in Paris. They ran the main synagogues, the religious schools and the cemeteries.

In Bayonne, for example, the Nation was ruled by three Parnassim (Syndics), elected by a 'Junta' of thirteen of its wealthier members. Only occasionally was a General Assembly of the Nation convened to dictate

ESSAI

SUR

LA RÉGÉNÉRATION

PHYSIQUE, MORALE ET POLITIQUE

DES JUIFS;

Ouvrage couronné par la Société royale des
Sciences et des Arts de Metz, le 23 Août 1788,
Par M. Grégoire, Curé du Diocese de Metz, actuelle-
ment de la même Société.

*Dedisti nos tanquam oves occarum, et in gentibus
dispersisti nos. Psal. 43.*

96 Essay
From l'Abbé Grégoire's highly influential
article of 1789 on the regeneration of
France's Jews.

97 Lettres Patente
An extract from the decree of 1790
granting full citizenship to the Portuguese
Jews, the first in Europe to be so
emancipated. This led directly to the end
of the special status of the 'Nations' for a
further decree in 1791 stated that those
individuals who took the civic oath would
be considered to have renounced all their
former privileges.

major policy. The Parnassim were all-powerful, the role of the Rabbis being restricted to the affairs of their ministry — for they were all New Christians, and officially no Rabbi could exist in France. They imposed and collected the taxes, both for the royal treasury and for their own community. They organised the charities and looked after the poor — paying their rent, retaining a doctor to look after them and arranging supplies of food. When the number of poor grew too numerous for the Nation to support, the Parnassim did not hesitate to obtain a royal order expelling the surplus. Rare murmurs of discontent with this authoritarian rule were promptly stifled by the Parnassim, who wielded the dread power of excommunication to enforce discipline.

The Nations maintained close contact with Amsterdam, with London, with Curaçao and with other Jewish centres abroad. They were visited regularly by emissaries from the Land of Israel on fund-raising expeditions. The trading activities of the Marrano diaspora are described in more detail in the chapters on the Marranos and on Amsterdam elsewhere in this book. The Portuguese of France shared fully in all this enterprise. In religious as well as in commercial and social matters, they drew heavily on their brethren in the wider Sephardi world for help and advice. Amsterdam, of course, always remained the primary source of inspiration and authority.

Small numbers of Ashkenazi Jews had also lived reasonably undisturbed in Lorraine, on the German border with France, since the sixteenth century though they could not openly practise their religion, nor could they shelter under the guise of Christians. A small community also collected in Paris — but they had no rights there whatsoever. The number of Ashkenazim grew as France acquired more of Lorraine and neighbouring Alsace. When France finally took over the whole of Lorraine in 1766, French thinkers became interested in the status of the Jews and the question of how they could be made more useful to society. The King responded by finally abolishing the humiliating 'body tax' on Jews, which had likened them to cattle, and by asking a Minister of State to formulate proposals for reform. The Ashkenazim and Sephardim met to draw up proposals; but matters did not proceed because of the Revolution which soon overtook them all.

The Portuguese Nations of the South-West were justly criticised by their Ashkenazi brethren for being reluctant to assist in their struggle for emancipation. This is understandable; for the Sephardim, whilst welcoming the prospect of civil rights for all Jews, were naturally unwilling to lose the advanced political privileges they already enjoyed and which enabled them to live in reasonably secure, self-governing communities. Nor did they relish the prospect of being swamped by the Ashkenazim, five or six times more numerous, and thus losing their identity.

Indeed, in the subsequent elections to the States General, the Ashkenazim were excluded totally. But the Nations claimed and were conceded the right to participate as separate bodies.

It was however a hollow victory. The Nations lost their political rights when the Assemblée Nationale granted full citizenship to all French Jews in 1791, specifying at the same time that Jews would simultaneously lose

98 Abraham Furtado (1756-1817)
The son of Marrano parents from Portugal, Abraham was born in London, where he returned to Judaism. He became a municipal councillor in Bordeaux just before the Revolution. Abraham Furtado was President of the Assembly of Jewish notables convened by Napoleon and served as Secretary to the Paris Sanhedrin of 1807.

99 Napoleon's Sanhedrin
The Sanhedrin was summoned by Napoleon to re-define the principles of Judaism. This lithograph is dated 1868.

all special privileges previously granted. The individual members of the Nations had finally attained the coveted status of French citizens — the first Jews in Europe to have achieved emancipation. But the Nations themselves lost all their powers in the process and became redundant. They were promptly dissolved and simple charitable organisations set up in their place.

Sephardi personalities played a leading part in the deliberations of the Grand Sanhedrin, summoned by Napoleon to re-define the principles of Judaism and the place of believing Jews in modern society. Still jealous of their special identity, they did however finally veto proposals to unite the minhagim of the Ashkenazim and Sephardim into a single common liturgy.

The French legislators had defined the status of the country's Jewish population with clarity and relentless logic. To the Jews as a separate nation in exile, with its own peculiar identity, nothing but uncompromising hostility was conceded. To individuals, on the other hand, who differed from their fellow Frenchmen only in their belief in the religion of Moses, all was granted. They could become citizens, equal in all respects to other Frenchmen.

Having survived the ups and downs of Napoleon's Jewish policy, the Jews of France — both Sephardim and Ashkenazin — settled down to their new status as 'French citizens of the Israelite persuasion' with gratitude, and seemingly without protest. Maintaining the lowest possible profile, they assimilated fast into French life. Not even the phenomenon of modern racial (as opposed to the old religious) anti-semitism — which was born and nurtured in nineteenth-century France, and not in Germany as is often supposed — was sufficient to deflect them from the rapid process of losing their separate identity and disappearing into the population at large.

Widespread neglect of Jewish education resulted, as elsewhere, in a slackening of religious commitment; and, under the new French dispensation, no other commitment was legitimate for its citizens.

Though never numbering more than four or five thousand at most, a few of the descendants of the former Marrano communities attained prominent positions in French life — and not just in their traditional pursuits of commerce and banking, but also in politics, literature and the arts. However, the Sephardi community as a whole had faded to relative insignificance by the end of the nineteenth century.

Though the position of Jews in nineteenth-century France was far better than that of most other Jewish communities in Europe, its integration into society at large was still beset with problems. The rapid rise of racial anti-semitism, illustrated by the impact of the Dreyfus case on the whole French nation, made the Jews feel that their position was peculiarly vulnerable. Reports of blood-libel accusations in the East, taken up avidly by the French press, were interpreted as reflecting directly on France's Jews.

To its great credit, during the nineteenth century, the Jewish community of France emerged as the champion of oppressed Jews throughout the world. Following the French occupation of Algeria in 1830, that country's Jewish population was given every encouragement and assistance to acquire full French citizenship and — equally important — sufficient French education and culture to enable its members to progress as quickly as possible to the same status as that enjoyed by the Jews of France itself.

It was Jules Carvallo, a Sephardi Jew from Bordeaux, who first proposed the establishment of an international Jewish congress to work for the emancipation of oppressed Jews everywhere, and to provide moral and material support for what he called their 'regeneration'.

The Mortara affair of 1858 — described in the section on Sir Moses Montefiore in the chapter on England in Part Two of this book — provided the final stimulus which led in 1860 to the formation of the Alliance Israélite Universelle. This was founded by a number of prominent French Jews including Carvallo. It was headed by Adolphe Crémieux, a veteran politician with high reputation as a champion of Jewish rights. Crémieux had already done much for the Jews of Algeria; and in 1870, as the responsible minister, he was to sign the Crémieux Decree, making them all French citizens. In the company of Sir Moses Montefiore, Crémieux had also intervened in person with the Ottoman Sultan in their successful bid to rescue the Jews of Damascus, unjustly accused of the blood-libel.

The Alliance Israélite Universelle's aims were set out with high idealism in its initial manifesto. Quoting from Aron Rodrigue's book 'French Jews, Turkish Jews',

If you believe that a great number of your co-religionists, overcome by twenty centuries of misery, of insults and prohibitions, can recover their dignity as men, win the dignity of citizens, if you believe one should moralize those who have been corrupted and not condemn them, enlighten those who have been blinded, and not abandon them, raise those who have been exhausted and not rest by pitying them ... If you believe in all these things, Jews of the world, come and hear our appeal ... the work is a great one ...

100 The degradation of Captain Dreyfus, 1895
Captain Dreyfus is shown here being reduced to the ranks in a public ceremony following his conviction on a false charge of treason. The long struggle to establish his innocence deeply divided the whole of French society and aroused much open anti-semitic feeling.

101 Dreyfus
A contemporary cartoon, 1895.

The achievement of the Alliance, with its system of schools, in doing so much to liberate the Jews of North Africa, Turkey and the Middle East is fully described in the chapter on the Ottoman Empire in Part One of this book.

The early years of the twentieth century saw a renewal of Sephardi life in France, first through an influx of immigrants from the Ottoman Empire, particularly the Balkans, and then from North Africa. The network of Alliance schools taught so many Sephardim of North Africa and the Near East the French language and the rudiments of French culture, that it was only natural that some would look first to France in their search for economic opportunity. Indeed so pervasive was the French education transmitted by the Alliance schools that the father of one of the authors, from Aleppo in Syria, was able to declare with sincerity that he felt he had finally come 'home' on first setting foot in Paris.

The old Spanish and Portuguese connection was remembered and used to advantage during the Second World War of 1939-45, when a number of Jews of Sephardi origin were granted Spanish or Portuguese passports by sympathetic consuls; and those passports saved them from the deportation and almost certain death that was the fate of so many others.

The formation of the State of Israel caused other North African Jews to seek refuge in France; and those were joined by most of Algeria's Jews when that country achieved its independence from France in 1960. Jewish life in France was transformed, with Sephardi Jews spread out all over the country and not just in the main towns. Though the official French Jewish community continued to be led by the old Ashkenazi families of distinction, the newer North African element strained to supplant them. The rabbinate, including the office of Grand Rabbi, is now dominated by Sephardim who form a large majority of the country's Jewish population of over seven hundred thousand.

With the arrival in France of the Sephardim from Algeria, Tunisia and Morocco came the beginning of a subtle change in the self-perception of its Jewish community. Many of the North African immigrants were middle class French citizens, already steeped in French culture but retaining awareness of their identity — and not without pride in their origins. Unlike the Ashkenazim they encountered in France, they saw little value in the traditional French-Jewish posture of discretion and self-effacement. As quoted in Simon Sibelman's chapter on France in 'The Survey of Jewish Affairs' (Blackwell 1990),

The Sephardim demonstrated none of the complexes about positive Jewish identity which frequently characterised the Ashkenazi community. Dr Huber Dayan, a Sephardi leader, noted that on holydays or Shabbat when he walked through the streets with a Tallit on his shoulders, Ashkenazi Jews would shamefacedly suggest that he refrain from such outward displays of Jewishness ...

General de Gaulle's famous press conference of 1967, in which he described Jews as domineering and elitist, was a kind of turning point; and when they had recovered from the shock, the Sephardim began slowly to respond with a pride and assertiveness quite alien to French Jewry.

102 Adolphe Crémieux (1796 - 1880)
Isaac Adolphe Crémieux, from an old
Comtat family, was a prominent lawyer
and politician who championed Jewish
rights in France and all over the world.

In 1840 he accompanied Sir Moses
Montefiore in a successful mission to
rescue the Jews of Damascus who had been
falsely accused of the blood-libel.

As Minister of Justice, he signed the
Décret Crémiex in 1870 which granted
French citizenship to the Jews of Algeria.
He served on the Central Consistory and
also as President of the Alliance Israélite
Universelle.

Two factors contributed to the gradual development of this new attitude.
The first was the growing anti-Israel and pro-Arab policies of successive
French governments, visibly 'soft' on Arab terrorism even within the
borders of France. And the second was the wave of open anti-semitism,
sometimes not even barely disguised as anti-Zionism, which gripped the
French media — including the most respected newspapers. This anti-semitism, only feebly discouraged by the government, also manifested itself in
crude acts of violence against the Jewish community. Synagogues were
bombed and cemeteries desecrated. In a monumental gaffe, Prime Minister
Raymond Barre referred to the victims of one outrage as 'one Jew and three
innocent Frenchmen'.

The question was asked — should French Jews continue to maintain their
traditional low profile and remain passive in the face of such threats to
themselves and to their brethren in Israel; and were they really no more
than 'Frenchmen of the Israelite persuasion'?

This challenge to the habitual stance of the Jewish community reached
its peak in 1981, during the last year of Valery Giscard d'Estaing's
presidency, when the Jews organised an active campaign to prevent his
re-election. Such political action by a minority community was unprecedented in France's recent history; and it was reported that Giscard d'Estaing
himself blamed his defeat partly on the massive Jewish vote mobilised
against him.

Under President Francois Mitterand's more sympathetic regime, for the
first time since the Revolution, France's Jews have asserted the right to be
different from other Frenchmen — and what is more, to glory in that
difference in a new spirit of cultural democracy. Suddenly, the word 'Jew'
was no longer to be uttered hesitantly and with shame, but to be proclaimed
with self-confidence and pride.

Even before the political awakening just described, France had already
experienced a remarkable flowering of Jewish intellectual and literary life
which continues unabated today. A large group of Jewish thinkers and
writers contributed to a detailed probing of the problems posed by the
assertion of separate Jewish identity within French culture; and some
attempted to employ the criteria of ethics and morality to define 'Jewishness'
outside a religious context.

Starting with André Schwartz-Bart and Elie Wiesel in the 1950s, over a
score of talented Jewish novelists produced a steady stream of work of the
highest quality; and that stream had become a flood by the 1980s. Much
of this deals with the crisis of identity experienced by its authors. And even
though the Jewish predicament may not even be mentioned as such in some
books, the actual themes and the symbols employed in them are all
traditionally Jewish.

The situation in France regarding Jewish religious observance is, to some
extent, contradictory and obscure. Jewish education at all levels, from
elementary day schools to yeshivot, flourishes as never before; and for the
first time, Jewish subjects can be studied at several universities. Groups of
Sephardim, some influenced by Ashkenazi rabbis, are turning to Judaism

103 Jewish girl from Morocco
A mid 20th Century photograph.

with uncharacteristic fervour. At the same time, assimilation is rife — with an out-marriage rate of over forty per cent — and many children of former North African Jews leave the community with a speed and indifference truly sad to observe.

The Jewish community of France, now said to be approaching three-quarters of a million in size, is the fourth largest in the world. It is very much to be hoped that the ferment taking place within it — the expansion of Jewish education, the new pride and assertiveness, the firm support for Israel, the intellectual vigour and the literary output — will be sufficient to prevent a return to that timidity and torpor which gripped France's Jews in the not too distant past.

Amsterdam

The movement of small groups of Portuguese New Christians, first to Antwerp and then on to the trading centres of Northern Germany, was described in Part One of this book. Driven by fear of the Inquisition, many simply sought new and more tranquil lives for themselves and their children. Others yearned to return openly to the faith of their fathers, even if by then they could remember few of its practices.

The first official record of a Marrano in Amsterdam is dated 1595, but at least one family was already in the city before then. It was in December 1601 that a group of ten adults and four boys from Portugal landed at the port of Emden in Germany. There they were befriended by Uriel Ha-Levy, an Ashkenazi rabbi, who sent them on to Amsterdam. Uriel and his family followed the refugees and rented a house in Joncker Street. The Marranos were circumcised by Uriel's son — among the nine hundred and thirty one circumcisions performed during his lifetime — and taught the fundamentals of Judaism.

The tiny community had to behave with care, for its legal position was highly ambiguous. Though the arrival of the Jews seems to have been cautiously welcomed by the civic authorities, who hoped they would bring benefit to the city, the admission of openly professing Jews was strongly opposed by the Elders of the Dutch Reformed Church. The Union of Utrecht of 1579 had guaranteed freedom of conscience in the Protestant Dutch provinces; and so protection of the lives and property of the Jews was assured. But they were not recognised as full citizens and could not work in any trade organised into a Christian guild.

The crisis came in 1603, during the course of the second Kal Nidre service ever to be held in Amsterdam. The house in Joncker Street was raided and Rabbi Uriel arrested. The record of his interrogations before the magistrates contains details of his claim to have served as Rabbi of Emden for about thirty years before coming to Amsterdam 'with the knowledge and consent of the Burgomasters'. Uriel briefed the magistrates on many details of Jewish observance and admitted that he had conducted Jewish religious services in his house as well as serving as shochet (ritual slaughterer) on a weekly basis.

104 **Trial record**
An extract from the Municipal Archives, Amsterdam, of the record of the interrogations by magistrates of Rabbi Uriel Ha-Levi in 1603.

The Jews must have decided to become even more discreet in their worship after Uriel's release from prison, for they moved their meeting place to the much quieter district of Vloonburg on the outskirts of the town. The first Jewish congregation of Amsterdam was formally established in 1604. It was however refused permission to acquire land for a cemetery; and its dead had to be buried in the village of Groet, near Alkmaar.

More Marranos arrived; and by 1614 the community numbered over two hundred, divided into three separate congregations. Samuel Palache, who as Moroccan ambassador to the Netherlands was able to live openly as a practising Jew, did much to help the newcomers settle in the city. That same year, land for a cemetery was bought at Ouderkerk and the community's first proper synagogue was opened with the knowledge and probably with the permission of the Burgomasters.

The Protestant Church did not easily give up its opposition to what it regarded as the scandal of open Jewish worship. Only four years before, complaints from its Elders had resulted in the temporary closure of the largest of the three Jewish houses of prayer. In 1620, Jewish acquisition of land adjacent to the synagogue for the building of classrooms prompted an anguished appeal by the Elders to the Burgomasters of Amsterdam, complaining that the Jews were once more

openly exercising their rites contrary to the ban issued by their worships the Burgomasters

and further that

the children of Hauseken Langebroek ... have married Jews and are reckoned among them.

Three years later the Elders resolved to collect evidence

of examples of Jews blaspheming the Christian religion and the Lord Christ

— but again to no avail, for the Burgomasters failed to respond and continued to extend their protection to the Jews.

By 1630 the community had grown to one thousand strong and the three formerly rival congregations were acting together in loose federation on matters of mutual concern. They finally merged in 1639 to form the Kahal Kadosh Talmud Torah (Holy Congregation of the Study of the Torah) and the biggest of the three synagogues was enlarged to serve their joint needs. This became so attractive a local curiosity that the Protestant Elders felt compelled to issue a formal statement strongly discouraging their members from visiting to observe the Jews at prayer.

The community's final seal of approval came in 1642 when no lesser person than Prince Frederick Henry of Orange visited the synagogue with his son, his son's new bride and her mother — Queen Henrietta Maria of England (wife of King Charles I) — and listened to an address of welcome delivered by Rabbi Menasseh ben Israel. That was the first of many marks of favour by members of the House of Orange and of a responding loyalty by the Portuguese Jews which has lasted to this day.

The splendid Portuguese Synagogue, which still stands proudly in Amsterdam, was opened in 1675. Its architecture was copied in the Marrano diaspora in places as far apart as London and Curaçao. Its laws and network of charitable institutions were also widely imitated, as was its system of 'imposta' whereby its members paid a special income tax or 'finta' to support the community.

The Portuguese Jews of Amsterdam were governed by the 'Mahamad', a standing committee of seven wardens. The Mahamad had sweeping powers over the lives of the members. Its decisions were binding on all; and no verbal or written opposition was tolerated. No Sephardi Jew could, for example, take another Jew to court without the Mahamad's permission; nor could he print a book without prior approval. In 1656, Juan de Prado, Uriel da Costa and Baruch Spinoza were formally excommunicated by the Congregation which refused to tolerate any threat from within to the faith to which its members had so recently returned at such cost and in spite of all the horrors of the Inquisition.

The educational system established by the Portuguese Jews was the envy of the entire Jewish world as illustrated by the following extract from the report of Shabbetai Bass, an Ashkenazi who visited the city in the 1670's:

Since my arrival at the Amsterdam Community I have on several occasions visited the schools of the Sephardi Community (may their Rock preserve them) and there I saw many young children small as grasshoppers yet in my eyes as big as giants because of their great erudition in Bible, grammar, verse and poetry composition as well as in their clear spoken Hebrew. Happy are the eyes that beheld all this...

Adjacent to the Synagogue they have built six rooms for a school... in the first room they teach little children until they become conversant with the recital of prayers, from where they are transferred to the next class in which they learn the Pentateuch with musical cantillation. There they remain until they have mastered the complete Five Books of Moses. They then enter the third class where they continue to learn the Pentateuch until they are able to understand it and explain it in the vernacular. Every week they also learn Rashi's commentary on the Parashah. From here they are transferred to the fourth class where they study the Prophets and Hagiographa with musical cantillation, the pupil reading the verse in Hebrew and translating it into the vernacular. They then move to the fifth class where pupils are taught to learn and speak Halachah (Jewish Law) — in this class they speak no other language but Hebrew except for certain explanations of the Halachah. Here they also learn Hebrew Grammar thoroughly ...From here they proceed to the sixth class which is the Yeshivah of the Haham and head of the Bet Din (may his Rock preserve him). There they sit and study a single law each day with Rashi and Tosaphot, debating deeply the laws from the code of Maimonides, Tur and Bet Joseph as well as other codifiers ...

During the time that the students are at home, each householder engages an instructor to teach the children to write in the vernacular as well as in Hebrew and also revises his work with him. He teaches him poetry and verse and instructs him on how to conduct himself in an upright manner. Finally the pupil is taught any other subject he may require. These teachers are chosen and appointed by the congregation and are paid from communal funds called Talmud Torah, every one according to his capability, his needs and his qualifications, a fixed salary per year, hence no teacher needs to flatter a congregant and he is able to teach all his pupils whether rich or poor without discrimination ...

Amsterdam with its rabbis, scholars, physicians, poets and philosophers, was the intellectual centre of the Marrano diaspora. Rabbi Menasseh ben Israel established the city's first Hebrew printing press in 1637, and was soon followed by others eager to serve the community's thinkers and men of letters.

105 Rosh Hashanah in the Portuguese Synagogue of Amsterdam
One of the famous etchings by Picart to illustrate Jewish ceremonies. This one is dated 1723.

Amsterdam too became the principal staging post in the West for New Christians fleeing from the Iberian Peninsula. They underwent the rite of circumcision and studied the fundamentals of Judaism in the city before passing on to other destinations.

In Amsterdam as elsewhere, the proclamation of Shabbetai Zvi as Messiah in 1665 evoked a wave of extraordinary enthusiasm. Each letter from the East containing details of his activity was carried in triumph to the Portuguese synagogue where it was eagerly discussed by throngs of young men adorned in green silk sashes, the livery of the Messianic King. An account has already been given in Part One of this book of the effect of Menasseh ben Israel's messianic predictions and of their effect on Oliver Cromwell, which led directly to the tacit re-admission of the Jews to England.

The material condition of Amsterdam's Sephardi community fluctuated in sympathy with that of its host city. The first century or so of settlement, during which the Portuguese Jewish population rose to about three thousand (in 1743), was one of tremendous expansion. Dutch merchants travelled the world — from Europe to Africa, India, the East Indies, the West Indies, Brazil and South America — bringing great prosperity to their native land.

106 Rabbi Menasseh Ben Israel (1604-1657)
Menasseh sent this portrait of himself, by Salom Italia, to a colleague in 1643.

The Sephardim, with their close network of secret family connections among the New Christians of Portugal and Spain, Italy, France and the New World, participated to the full in the opportunities provided. A few became very wealthy indeed by trading in colonial commodities such as tobacco and diamonds. Others were increasingly drawn to the financial sphere, where they were able to provide what amounted to an international system of credit because of their widespread and trustworthy connections. Sephardim also became prominent on the stock exchange, owning some one-quarter of the East India Company's shares by the end of the seventeenth century. Others concentrated on home industries such as printing.

The decline of the Dutch share of world trade during the eighteenth century, and a series of economic disasters, had their effect on Amsterdam's Jews. Most were reduced to poverty. Following the French conquest of the Netherlands in 1794, two-thirds of the community was drawing poor relief; and the percentage of those on relief was still over half at the end of the century.

Though promised full emancipation by the supporters of the French Revolution, Sephardi Jews opposed the French and remained staunchly loyal to the House of Orange. Their rabbis feared — rightly as it turned out — that the granting of civil rights to Jews would damage the cohesion of the community. The French conquered the Netherlands in 1795 and established the Batavian republic under their protection. Jews were promptly granted full civil rights. This was followed by the Kingdom of Holland under Louis Napoleon.

The return of the House of Orange in 1814 was welcomed by the Portuguese Jews; but it did little to restore the economic prosperity of the country. Most Jews continued to live in comparative poverty, as did the majority of their fellow citizens. A trend towards assimilation among the upper class became established. Ironically, many descendants of former Marranos were converted to Christianity.

The size of the community, which had remained static during much of the eighteenth and nineteenth centuries, almost doubled during the first decades of the twentieth century. But it had declined again to fewer than four thousand by 1941.

Together with the city's very much larger Ashkenazi Jewish population, the Sephardim of Amsterdam were rounded up and deported to the Nazi extermination camps following the German invasion of Holland in 1941. Fewer than five hundred survived the war.

One of the authors visited the Portuguese Synagogue of Amsterdam exactly three hundred and fifty years after that second Kal Nidre service in Joncker Street, when the tiny and fearful congregation was rudely disturbed at prayer by the city's police and its rabbi was arrested. Sadly, the small band of worshippers huddled in the centre of the large, proud building was probably not very much greater in number than the original refugees assembled in 1603.

However in 1953, all the outer benches of the Synagogue were packed

107 Celebration of the Festival of Tabernacles
Another of Picart's famous 18th century prints of Jewish ceremonies. In this one, worshippers are shown in the Portuguese Synagogue of Amsterdam, each carrying a lulav (palm frond bound with willow and myrtle) and an etrog (citron) in solemn procession.

with Christians. It seems that during the German occupation of Holland in the Second World War of 1939-45 — despite the risk of Nazi punishment — they had started the custom of attending the Kal Nidre service as a brave gesture of sympathy for their Jewish fellow citizens.

In the intervening years, the Sephardim had become an accepted part of the city's life and culture. But the days in which the Portuguese children of Amsterdam could be described as

small as grasshoppers yet ... as large as giants because of their great erudition ...

had departed, probably never to return.

Italy

The first Jews of Italy came directly from the Land of Israel and remained in contact with it. So they and their descendants looked naturally to Palestine rather than to Babylon as the source of their religious customs. But more than just the barrier of the Alps divided them from the later Ashkenazim of Northern Europe — for culturally, much of Italy belonged to the Mediterranean world and not to the North. Also Italian Jews, active in trade with the East, remained in far closer contact with their brethren in Spain and the Islamic countries than did the Ashkenazim.

Consequently Italian Jewry developed its own independent tradition in liturgy, music and other matters, known as the Italian Rite. When Ashkenazim from the North and Sephardim from Spain and the Near East later arrived in the country, they set up separate Ashkenazi and Sephardi synagogues alongside the existing Italian ones. However the three groups mingled freely with each other and, in time, most differences tended to disappear. For example, Ashkenazim merged with the Italians in the north of Italy and adopted their rite, whilst in Florence it was the Sephardim who absorbed the others.

Jews have lived in Italy for over two thousand years. A few came as traders, and the remainder as slaves brought home by the triumphant Roman legions after Pompey's conquest of Jerusalem and the suppression of later Jewish revolts against Roman occupation. Most of the captives gained their freedom eventually and settled at first in Rome and the ports of Southern Italy and Sicily. They worked as artisans or in other humble occupations and were not prominent in Roman life.

Judaism was recognised as a 'licit' religion in the Roman Empire; and its followers were exempted by Julius Caesar from obligations, such as military service, that interfered with the practice of their faith. They were also excused from having to offer obligatory sacrifices to the Roman gods. Individual Jews were able to gain the privilege of Roman citizenship. St. Paul (from the city of Tarsus in Asia Minor), for example, wrote proudly in his letters of his dual loyalty, both as a Jew and as a Roman citizen.

Not even the heavy cost in blood and treasure of the Jewish revolts in Palestine, Alexandria and North Africa appears to have affected Rome's treatment of the Jews of Italy — though their position can hardly have been comfortable. And in the year 212, the Emperor Caracalla issued a decree enabling all freemen, including Jews, to become full Roman citizens.

It was the rise of Christianity that adversely affected the position of Jews in Italy and the Roman Empire. Their situation deteriorated sharply in the fourth century, and especially after Christianity became the state religion; for the Church then started to exact terrible revenge on members of the faith from which it had arisen and which had done much to stifle its birth.

After the final collapse of the Roman Empire, Italy gradually emerged as a patchwork of semi-independent states and principalities, dominated by its most powerful prince — the Pope. The well-being of Italy's Jews came to depend on the attitude towards them of each individual Pope. Under some Popes they lived in peace and with little interference; but others

108 The Florence Synagogue
The Sephardi rite is followed in this grand synagogue, opened in 1882.

subjected them to humiliating restrictions, made them live in ghettos and wear special signs on their clothes, and sometimes ordered their expulsion from city after city in turn.

Fortunately the anti-Jewish measures were never evenly applied, nor were they always rigorously enforced. In some places there is evidence of Jews being granted special privileges only a few years after their having in theory been expelled altogether. And those states not dependent on Papal approval — such as Venice and Florence — pursued their own interests and policy with little regard to the dictates of the Church.

Despite widely fluctuating fortunes therefore, Jews managed to maintain a continuous presence on the Italian peninsula from Roman times to our own. The community produced many distinguished rabbis and scholars, mystics, poets, men of letters and physicians. Its leading bankers and merchants often achieved considerable wealth and, in the process, also enriched the cities of their residence.

Refugees from Spain before the Expulsion of 1492, those who left in 1492 and the subsequent waves of Marranos from Portugal found a variety of conditions awaiting them in the city states that constituted the Italy of their day. In some places they were banned altogether. In others they were allowed to pause for a while before being sent on their way. Some rulers grudgingly tolerated their presence for the commercial benefit that flowed in their wake; and just a few of the more tolerant welcomed them and protected them from persecution by the Church.

Numerous complaints were made to the Inquisition during the course of the sixteenth century to the effect that there was scarcely a city of Italy in which New Christian fugitives from Spain could not be found. It seems that many made their fortunes in Italy before leaving for the Ottoman Empire, where they promptly reverted to Judaism.

Sicily and Sardinia both had Jewish communities which dated from Roman times. The islands, belonging to the Kings of Aragon, had also attracted thousands of Spanish Jews and Marranos seeking a more tolerable life. When the decree of expulsion of 1492 was also applied to them, there were over thirty five thousand Jews, mostly in humble occupations, living in Sicily alone. The introduction of an Inquisition, at roughly the same time, also caused many Marranos to leave.

Most sought temporary refuge across the water in the Kingdom of Naples, whose kings had since 1442 encouraged Jews to settle there, and especially in Naples itself. The most eminent of the Spanish refugees, Don Isaac Abrabanel, served as financial adviser to the Neapolitan Treasury.

The Jews of Southern Italy suffered very badly from the French invasion that followed the accession of King Alfonso II to the Neapolitan throne. Their fate was sealed later when Naples fell under Spanish rule. Apart from some two hundred wealthy families, who paid handsomely for the privilege, all Jews were expelled in 1510. New Christians were also driven out five years later; and Naples then remained free of Jews until the Bourbon kings took over in 1735.

Much of the lucrative trade between the Papal States and the East passed through the port of Ancona, where it was largely in the hands of Jews who maintained close connections with their brethren in Turkey and the Levant. Refugees from Spain, Sicily and Naples in turn were encouraged to settle in the town and contribute to its commercial prosperity.

The incorporation of Ancona into the Papal States made little difference at first. Pope Paul II continued the policy of the previous rulers by inviting foreign merchants from the Levant, regardless of their religion, to take up residence. In 1547 he extended that invitation to New Christians, or Marranos, at the same time promising to protect them from the Inquisition. When his successor, Pope Julius III, renewed the guarantee, some one hundred Marrano families settled in Ancona.

The next pope, Paul IV, abruptly reversed the policy of his predecessors. In 1555 he issued his Bull 'Cum nimis absurdum' which imposed harsh

109 **The title page of a Sephardi book** Printed in Mantua.

measures on Jews. It restricted them to one synagogue in each town, made them live in ghettos and wear special identifying marks on their clothes, forbad them to own real property and prevented them from following occupations other than dealing in second-hand goods and old clothes. Spurning a huge bribe offered by the Jews of Rome, the Pope applied this humiliating decree to Rome and to the Papal States, including Ancona.

Despite desperate attempts to buy him off, the Pope also acted against the Marranos of Ancona, ordering their arrest and the seizure of their property. He confiscated all debts due to the Marranos, as well as the merchandise of Turkish Jews in transit or on consignment. Prompted by his Jewish advisers, the Sultan made a strong representation to the Pope, threatening retaliation against Christians in his domains. As a result, those Marranos who could claim domicile in the Ottoman Empire were released from prison; but their property was not restored and many suffered grievous loss.

At their trial in Ancona, twenty six Marranos repented, were reconciled and sentenced to the galleys. Thirty others managed to bribe their way out of prison before sentence and slipped away. Others escaped to neighbouring cities, especially to Pesaro. Twenty four men and one woman, defiant to the end, were burned at the stake.

The Jews of Turkey retaliated by organising an economic boycott of Ancona and the Papal States. Though initially successful, this collapsed eventually because of pathetic appeals by the Jews of Ancona and the Papal States, who greatly feared reprisals. But as a result, many of Ancona's Christian merchants were bankrupted and the town itself never regained its former prosperity.

Genoa was one of the bad places. In 1492 permission was given for refugee ships from Spain to land, and for their passengers to remain on shore for just three days. Christian eye-witnesses reported being shocked by the scenes on the quayside as ardent friars, with a crucifix on one arm and loaves of bread in the other, wandered amongst the starving refugees, offering food and shelter in return for accepting the Cross. But even that limited concession was soon withdrawn because of fear of the plague that such ships sometimes brought with them. Later, some wealthy Jews were allowed to settle in the town, but they were few in number. The tiny Jewish community of Genoa endured several alarming reversals of fortune in the centuries that followed.

The Estes of Ferrara, in contrast, had long established a policy of sheltering persecuted Jews who could bring useful skills to their city, and of protecting them from Church molestation. In 1492 Duke Ercole I invited twenty one families of Spanish refugees to settle in Ferrara, promising to let them live under their own judges and to practise medicine and trade in freedom. He also granted them tax concessions. Realising the value of the Marranos, the Duke also encouraged them to come to Ferrara; and in 1553, in unprecedented disregard of the power of the Inquisition, he specifically allowed them to return to Judaism.

Other persecuted Jews from Milan, Naples and the Papal States also took

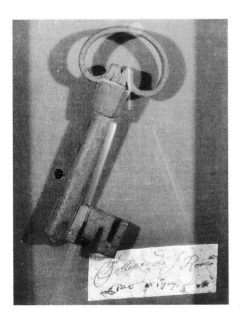

110　Proclamation of 1777
This proclamation details the taxes to be paid to the Jewish Community of Ferrara by visiting merchants, and the uses to which the monies would be applied. Its scope includes the neighbouring towns of Lugo and Cento, under the sway of Ferrara. Cento was the place of origin of the Disraeli family.

111　The Key to the Ghetto of Ferrara
This key to the San Romano Gate of the ghetto was presented by the Archbishop of Ferrara to Chief Rabbi Simone Sacerdoti in 1977.

refuge in Ferrara, as well as a small colony of German Jews who set up their own synagogue in 1532. By the middle of the sixteenth century, the city contained ten synagogues. Its flourishing Jewish community produced many outstanding personalities and became a beacon of Jewish learning and accomplishment. Conditions worsened inevitably in the following century, when Ferrara passed under Church rule and a ghetto was established.

Venice was another most important centre of Jewish life in the Italian Peninsula. Jews from Germany and the Levant had come to dwell in its vicinity in the twelfth century. In 1366 they were given permission to live in the city itself — though that lapsed after an interval of thirty eight years, after which the Jews were again obliged to live in Mestre on the mainland. A few Jewish merchants from Venice's colonies in the Levant did however maintain temporary footholds in the city.

Spanish Jews started to arrive shortly after the expulsion of 1492, when New Christians, or Marranos, also settled in Venice. The Marranos were promptly banished in 1497 just as soon as the scandalised Senate realised what was happening — but they soon re-appeared. There was a renewed influx of Marranos and Jews from 1509 onwards, when Jews were again allowed to live in Venice under a system of licences, renewable every ten years. Venice became the leading Marrano centre in Italy as more and more of the secret Jews of Portugal managed to make their escape.

The subsequent history of Venice's open and secret Jews is a bewildering succession of threats and favours. Many attempts were made to expel them; but those were always averted at the last moment by the payment of huge enforced loans. The usefulness of the Jews — and particularly of the Marranos — in the commerce with the East upon which the city's prosperity depended, was usually the deciding factor in determining Venetian policy; and the city's Marranos and former Marranos were generally protected by the authorities from too much interference by the Inquisition. Finally, merchants from Portugal and Spain were invited to settle freely and assured that no close inquiry would ever be made into their origins.

Popular anti-Jewish feeling fluctuated in Venice as attempt after attempt was made to rid the city of its Jews and its Marranos. German Jews, the least well regarded, were moved into a ghetto in 1516. They were followed by the much more useful Levantine Jews in 1541. Most favoured of all were the so-called Western Jews, the former Marranos, who were not confined to a ghetto until 1633. But even then, most Marranos continued to live outside its walls as insincere New Christians — thus inflaming the jealousy of their Christian competitors.

At its peak in 1655, the Jewish community of Venice numbered four thousand eight hundred people. Though not the most numerous of the three groups — Germans, Levantines and Ponentines (Westerners) — of which it was comprised, the former Marranos, or Ponentines, paid most of the taxes and had the largest representation on the community council. Their synagogue was the grandest and was the one used for important ceremonial occasions. Portuguese became a familiar language in the city. With its concentration of famous rabbis and mystics, of scholars, poets and physicians, of yeshivot and printing presses, for a time Venice became a leading centre of the Marrano diaspora.

The quality of Jewish life attained in the ghetto and in the city itself was not often surpassed in the diaspora; and this was astonishing considering the continual and very real threats of expulsion under which the Jews lived. One has only to glance at the rich and sometimes exquisite decoration and furnishings of the surviving synagogue buildings to get an idea of the standard of culture and the prosperity enjoyed by some of the Venetian Jews. Their intellectual life too was outstanding, as attested by the renown of so many of the community's leading figures.

112 Making the matzah
From the 16th century Venice Haggadah.

The Jewish population of Venice was greatly reduced in size and impoverished as the result of the ebbing prosperity of the Republic in the last stages of its ruinous war with Turkey. There were under two thousand left when the French conquered Venice in 1797; and even fewer remained after the political convulsions that followed.

Jews from Venice moved to Leghorn (Livorno) when times became difficult, tempted by the almost unprecedented freedom and prosperity enjoyed by the Jewish community there. It was in 1593 that Grand Duke Ferdinand I of Tuscany issued a charter designed to attract Marrano and other foreign merchants to settle in his free ports of Pisa and Leghorn. He promised that, within his domains, they would be free from molestation by the Inquisition, even if they had lived in the guise of Christians elsewhere; and both he and his successors certainly did their utmost to fulfil that pledge. Jews were never persecuted in Leghorn nor made to live in a closed ghetto, even during its many changes of ruler. For a very long time it was the only place in Italy where Judaism could be practised openly.

The Marranos who flocked to Leghorn came to dominate the port and helped to transform it into one of the leading commercial centres of Italy. Not only did they continue in the international trade for which they were originally invited, but they also contributed to industry and other pursuits. They pioneered the manufacture of soap and paper, the working of coral (highly prized then) and the weaving of silk. They also established a marine insurance business.

By 1645, there were more than two thousand Jews in Leghorn's total population of nine thousand; and by 1800, the number had risen to nearly seven thousand, mostly Sephardim. Both the port and its Jewish community declined in importance during the nineteenth century. The community lost its autonomy when Tuscany was incorporated into the French Empire in 1807. The decline accelerated after Leghorn became part of a united Italy and lost its status as a free port. The final remnants of the Sephardi community disappeared after the Second World War of 1939-45, when those of its survivors who had not already assimilated moved away.

Under the benevolent guidance of the Grand Dukes of Tuscany, the Sephardi community of Leghorn was almost completely self-governing. It passed and administered its own laws, civil and criminal; and even, by implication, had the power to grant Tuscan citizenship to outsiders. The Marranos imposed their own Spanish culture on all the Jews of the town, completely assimilating many Italian Jewish families such as the Montefiores, as well as immigrants from the Near East and from Northern Europe. They set up institutions of government and a network of charities based on former Spanish models.

Close contact was maintained with the Jews of Amsterdam and London as well as with the secret Jews of the Iberian Peninsula and elsewhere. As Leghorn was an entrepôt for trade between Europe and the Ottoman Empire, there was constant communication between its Jewish merchants and their brethren on the other side of the Christian/Islamic divide.

In its Golden Age, Leghorn was famous as a centre of Jewish learning

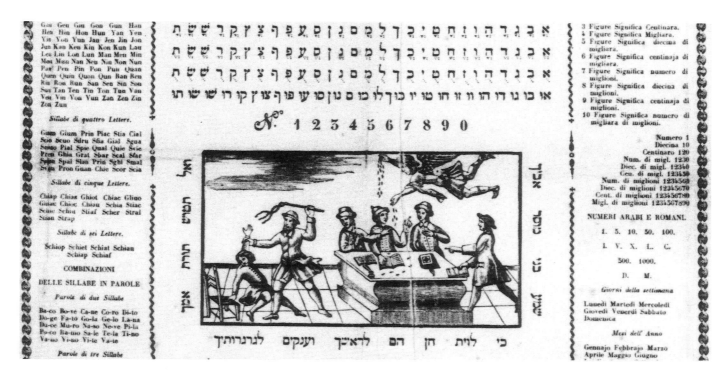

113 Detail from reading aid
This 19th century print from Livorno was published as an aid to learning letters and numbers. Both Hebrew and Roman letters are covered. The inset picture shows rewards for diligence and punishment for neglect. It is interesting to note that the original 18th century version only contained instruction in Hebrew.

— Torah and Kabbalah — equalling or surpassing that of Venice. Many Hebrew and Spanish books were printed on its presses; and its rabbis were widely consulted on a variety of matters. In true Sephardi manner, secular learning also flourished, with the community producing its own astronomers and scientists, poets and playwrights.

Though constantly warned by their rabbis to behave with discretion so as to avoid the envy of the populace, the Jews of Leghorn were often ostentatious and exuberant in their entertainments, both official and private. The wealthiest families rode in fine carriages and generally behaved in a proud and uninhibited manner highly unusual in Christian Europe at the time. Also unusual in the Christian world was the fact that the community was allowed to grow to its peak and then to fade away gently. It was not abruptly terminated by violent tragedy as was so often the case in so many places — and that was indeed a rare and well-merited blessing.

Italian Jews played a full part in the nineteenth-century struggle to unite Italy into a single country, in which for the first time they were to enjoy equal rights with all other citizens. Some fought with Garibaldi; and most identified completely with the aims of the Risorgimento. Partly because of this, and partly because of the tolerance with which they were treated by the Italian people, Jewish identity faltered as the years passed, with many Jews assimilating into Italian life.

Under the spur of Mussolini's pupil and ally, Adolph Hitler, the Italian fascist government did enact some cruel anti-Jewish legislation before and during the Second World War of 1939-45; and a small number of Italian Jews were imprisoned. But none of that came near to approaching the ferocity of the Nazis and their more willing accomplices elsewhere. It was only in the latter stages of the war, when Northern Italy was occupied by the Germans, that Jews were deported en-masse to the Nazi concentration camps; and even then, the few who managed to escape were sheltered by individual Italians, including priests and nuns.

After the war, those survivors with the strongest Jewish identity quit Italy, leaving the remainder to continue assimilating into Italian society. Their places were taken by new immigrants, comprising Ashkenazim from Northern and Eastern Europe, Italian-speaking Jews from Tripoli, Libya and Egypt, and other Sephardim fleeing from Syria, the Lebanon, Iraq and Iran. Milan, for example, is now home to a small but energetic community of Jews from Aleppo who still preserve a good deal of their distinctive culture, as well as to groups from Iraq and Iran.

Most of the ancient Italian communities have by now very much declined, if not completely withered away. Their former members moved to main cities such as Rome, Milan and Turin, where they reinforced the existing communities. There, with the help of the immigrants, Jewish communal life continues today with renewed vigour. All these centres maintain flourishing Jewish day schools. There is a rabbinic academy and a permanent Beth Din in Rome. Florence's Old Age Home is a model for the city as a whole. Elsewhere in Italy, the splendid historic buildings remain, but now mostly as monuments to a once glorious living tradition.

114   Scola Spagnola, Venice
A detail showing the Ark of the Spanish Synagogue. The interior of this splendid building was designed by Baldassarre Longhena in the 17th century.

England

Jews first arrived in England shortly after the Norman Conquest of 1066. They settled in many major cities, including London, York, Winchester, Lincoln, Canterbury and Oxford. They also lived in smaller towns; and a few families were even to be found in villages.

Jealously prevented by guild and other Christian restrictions from following most occupations, the leaders of the community earned their living by money-lending — the pejorative term used to describe financial operations in which Jews were involved. In fact, the Jews provided England with its first banking system. The major bankers had numerous family dependents and employed many other Jews in a variety of supporting roles, such as clerks, agents and servants.

Lower down the social scale, Jews worked as pawnbrokers, dealing also with the repair and sale of unredeemed pledges. English Jews certainly practised medicine openly as doctors; and there is evidence in Rabbinic Responsa to suggest that a few petty traders, selling goods from stalls in local markets, were also active. Apart from those occupations, it seems that the only others in which Jews were involved concerned the supply of essential services to their own communities — such as the provision of kasher food and wine.

Coming from Northern France, the community was wholly Ashkenazi in tradition. It contained several learned rabbis, who contributed to the Tosafot (Supplements to the Talmud and Rashi's Commentary on it). However London cannot have been isolated from the Sephardi world, for Abraham ibn Ezra — the famous Spanish scholar, poet, Bible commentator, astronomer and physician — visited the city in 1158 and remained there for almost three years. Ibn Ezra, who wrote two of his works in London, described England as a 'land of darkness and gloom'; and it is supposed that he arrived during a fog.

All Jews were expelled from England in 1290 by order of King Edward I, after which none returned openly for the next four hundred and sixty five years. Several tiny communities of Marranos did come into being from the reign of Queen Elizabeth I onwards; but on discovery by the authorities, they were promptly broken up and their members deported.

England had been preparing for profound religious and social change ever since John Wycliffe first translated the Bible from Latin into English in the 1380s. Possession of an English Bible remained a criminal offence until King Henry VIII, after his rift with the Pope in 1535, had the Bible freshly translated into English and prominently displayed in every church in the land for all to read.

It would be hard to exaggerate the startling effect of the Bible's impact on the Protestants of the sixteenth and seventeenth centuries, or the revolutionary result of its message. The Bible replaced the Pope as the ultimate spiritual authority; and the Old Testament, embodying the Jewish foundation of Christianity, was favoured to counter the claims of Rome and its Church. Hebrew replaced Greek as the prime object of study. The Bible was read everywhere and its contents eagerly discussed as the people of England identified with ancient Israel and those who had struggled against tyranny. The course of ancient Jewish history became common day-to-day knowledge. Children were given the Hebrew names of Old Testament heroes in preference to those of Christian saints. The Lord's Day (Sunday) became a copy of the Jewish Sabbath. And above all, the biblical prophesies of redemption were believed in their every detail.

The Puritan revolution led directly to the Civil War of 1642-49, at the end of which King Charles I was tried and executed for high treason and the English Commonwealth was established. It was during that period of conflict with the Pope and with Roman Catholic powers in Europe — principally Spain — that public perception of the Jews softened and the ground was prepared for the eventual tolerance on English soil of Jewish refugees from Catholic Spain.

Puritans and Jews held several important beliefs in common. They both venerated the Hebrew Bible, the Old Testament, accepting the literal truth of every detail of its prophesies. The Jews were urgently expecting their Messiah to lead them back to Jerusalem and inaugurate a New Age on earth; and the millennarian Puritans were awaiting with equal urgency the Second Coming of their Messiah, Christ, to establish his Kingdom of Saints on earth. Both groups accepted the prophesy that the Jews will be scattered to the ends of the earth, and the lost Ten Tribes will rejoin their brethren, before the return of the Jews to Zion heralds the advent of the Redeemer. But at that point expectations diverged sharply, with Puritans hoping that the Jews would then acknowledge Jesus and convert to Christianity as the last step before the Second Coming, whilst Jews hoped for just the opposite. The location of the Ten Tribes, the dispersion of the Jews to every known part of the world and their eventual return to Jerusalem, were thus of crucial interest to millennarian Christians as well as to Jews.

In 1644 Antonio de Montezimos, a Jewish traveller of Marrano stock, returned to Amsterdam from the New World. His story caused a sensation among the Jews of Amsterdam; and news of it soon spread to the Protestants, even coming to the ears of Oliver Cromwell in England. Antonio de Montezimos claimed to have stumbled across the lost tribe of Reuben in Ecuador in South America, after a hazardous journey through jungles, across rivers and over mountain ranges. Though 'scorched by the sun', the tribesmen were bearded, spoke Hebrew, practised circumcision, and greeted him by reciting the ancient Jewish affirmation of faith, the 'Shema'. So concerned were the leaders of Amsterdam's Jews to ensure that they were not being duped, that Montezimos was made to confirm the accuracy of his account on oath; and he voluntarily confirmed it again on his deathbed in Brazil some six years later.

Among those taken in by the plausible traveller was the celebrated Amsterdam rabbi, Menasseh ben Israel, a man respected by Jew and gentile alike for the breadth of his learning and for his knowledge of Kabbalah, the mystical tradition. Montezimos's discovery of Jews in America greatly excited Menasseh. It seemed to him that Jews were then living in every country of the world, save only for England. England suddenly become the key to the Redemption. Once the Jews were re-admitted to that country,

PLATE XV

Tablets of the Law

This picture, showing Moses and Aaron supporting the Ten Commandments, was painted in oils by Aron de Chavez in 1674 for the Spanish and Portuguese Synagogue in Creechurch Lane in the City of London. This was the first synagogue opened in England after Cromwell's tacit readmission of the Jews in 1656.

The Congregation's accounts contain the following entry (translated):
'For the canvas on which were painted the Commandments £1.17.6d. To Sr. H. Avilla for the gold £1.10., for his labour £3. To Aron de Chavez for the painting £5..'.

PLATE XVI

**Treasures from the
Spanish and Portuguese Jews'
Congregation, London**

Above left
18th century , silver Hanukah lamp.
Far left
19th century Torah cloak, embroidered in
silk.
Below left
18th century English silver and gilt bells
for a Scroll of the Law.

from which they had been expelled in 1290, they would certainly be scattered to every part of the earth, thus fulfilling the prophesy and enabling the Messiah to come.

The same idea had also occured to some Dutch and English Puritans. In 1649 Ebenezer and Joanna Cartwright, then living in Amsterdam, petitioned the English government to allow the Jews

again to be received and permitted to trade and dwell among you

and that

This nation of England with the inhabitants of the Netherlands shall be the first and readiest to transport Israel's sons and daughters in their ships to the land promised to their forefathers Abraham, Isaac and Jacob.

To devout Puritans the course was clear. Once Jews could be exposed to their own form of Christianity — so superior to the rank idolatry of the Roman Catholic version — their reservations would disappear, they would acknowledge Jesus as the Messiah and the Second Coming would take place. Though the ultimate motives were different, just for once Christian and Jewish ambitions converged.

Menasseh set to work with enthusiasm and high hope. He entered into correspondence with several prominent Englishmen, trying to persuade them to favour the prompt re-admission of the Jews to England. Very little is known of Menasseh's relationship with Oliver Cromwell at that stage; but in 1651 John Thurloe, secretary to Oliver St John, the English ambassador sent to the Hague to discuss an alliance with the Dutch, sought out the rabbi in Amsterdam. Cromwell — who had by then become Chairman of the Council of State governing England — then invited Menasseh to London; but the visit was prevented by the outbreak of war between Holland and England.

Cromwell made no secret of his visionary hopes regarding the Millennium and the prophesies relating to the return of the Jews to their Promised Land. He also had in mind the advantages his country would derive in the way of foreign intelligence and trade from the presence in its midst of a grateful community of cultivated Jews, with links to Spain and Portugal as well as with brethren all over the world.

By this time, a small Marrano community had again established itself in London. Indeed two of them had already rendered valuable service as 'intelligencers'. In 1654 Cromwell recommended to the Council of State a petition from a gentleman of rank then living in London as an outward Spanish Catholic, but in reality a secret Jew, that the Jews be admitted

to be dwellers here with the same equallness and conveniences which your inland subjects do enjoy

— but the petition was rejected. The supplicant however was naturalised by Cromwell and enabled to hold private Jewish prayer meetings at his house in Bishopsgate, London.

Cromwell again urged Menasseh to come to England and plead his case in person. The rabbi arrived in London in 1655. He was accommodated in

To GOD in memorye of his great deliueraunce from $\tilde{y}$ vnmatcheable powder Treason, 1605.

I heare and Laugh

I fee and Scorne

A deed of DARKENES

IN PERPETVAM PAPISTARVM INFAMIAM

November the fifte

In foueam quam foderunt

Fax

FAVX

PSALME 102 VER 18

PSALME 78 VER 7 8

This shallbe written for the generations to come and the people which shalbe created shall prayse the name of the LORD.

EVEN THE CHILDREN WO SHOVLD BE BORNE, WHO SHOVLD ARISE & DECLARE THEM TO THEIR CHILDREN THAT THEY MIGHT SETT THEIR HOPE IN GOD & NOT FORGET $\tilde{Y}$ WORKES OF GOD BVT KEEPE HIS COMANDEM.

115 The Gunpowder Plot
In this early 17th century print of Guy Fawkes and his attempt to blow up the Houses of Parliament, the horned figure of a Jew is seen with the Pope and the King of Spain in the group of conspirators. It is thought that this may have been prompted by the tiny, semi-secret community of Spanish Marranos in London at that time.

Whitehall, and entertained by Cromwell. He promptly petitioned the Lord Protector to admit the Jews to England on generous terms. The proposal caused a public outcry; and it soon became clear that centuries of prejudice could not easily be dispelled by newly acquired religious beliefs.

A special conference of judges, clergy and merchants was convened by the Council of State to decide the issue. The judges at once ruled that there was no legal impediment to the re-admission of the Jews; but the conference could not agree reasonable terms on which Jews might be permitted to reside in England. Cromwell intervened in person, speaking passionately in favour of Jewish settlement, and overcame many of the objections. In the end though, probably satisfied with the legal decision, he abruptly dismissed the conference without conclusion.

In March 1656 war broke out with Spain; and goods belonging to one of the Marranos, Antonio Rodrigues Robles, were seized as enemy property. Robles petitioned the Council of State for their restoration on the grounds that he was not a Spaniard, but a member of the Hebrew nation from Portugal, who had sought refuge in England. The Council restored Robles's

116 Jewish merchant with Indian tribal chiefs 1879
Julius Meyer, adopted into the Pawnee tribe with the name 'Curly Headed White Chief with One Tongue', is shown in this 1879 photograph with Red Cloud, Spotted Tail, Swift Bear and Sitting Bull. Until the early years of the 19th century, it was widely believed that the American Indians were descended from the Lost Ten Tribes of Israel.

property, thereby tacitly acknowledging that a Jew could live and trade in England.

In the same month, six heads of the most prominent of the twenty or so families of secret Jews then living in London as Catholics — regularly attending mass at the Portuguese Embassy — cast off their disguise and openly joined Menasseh in a more modest attempt to regularise their position. In a 'Humble Petition of the Hebrews at present residing in the City of London' to the Lord Protector, they thanked him for 'the manifold favours and protection' he had afforded them by enabling them to meet safely for prayer in the privacy of their own homes. They asked for a written assurance that this freedom would continue, and for permission to open a cemetery in which their dead could be buried with Jewish rites.

Cromwell referred this Address to the Council of State, which apparently decided that no written assurance should be given. Instead, it seems that Cromwell met the petitioners personally and gave a verbal guarantee of security under which they might open a synagogue for public prayer, acquire land for a burial place, trade as brokers on the Exchange, and enlarge

117 The Velho
The first Sephardi cemetery of London, founded in 1657. Shown in this photograph of 1875 are the Rev. David Aaron de Sola and the Rev. Abraham Pereira Mendes.

their community by bringing other Sephardi merchants of good standing to London.

Menasseh ben Israel was deeply disappointed by the compromise, which in no way fulfilled his glorious dream of an unrestricted flow of Jews to England leading to the coming of the Messiah. He had by then exhausted his funds, and turned to Cromwell for help. Cromwell gave him twenty five pounds for immediate expenses and a pension of one hundred pounds a year. After only two quarterly instalments had been paid, Menasseh returned to Holland with the body of his son who had died in London. Broken-hearted, he died soon afterwards.

In 1657 the Jews opened their first synagogue in a converted house in Creechurch Lane in the City of London, to be replaced forty four years later by the elegant building in Bevis Marks which is still in use. They also bought a plot of land in Stepney for burials. Their precarious privileges survived the death of Cromwell and the overthrow of the Protectorate. They were confirmed by King Charles II in 1664, and by him again ten years later. Jewish resettlement in England had started, even if at first very cautiously and very slowly.

The founders of the Spanish and Portuguese Jews' Congregation of London, who had so boldly cast off their protective cloak of Christianity and openly declared themselves to be Jews — some having themselves circumcised at the age of seventy — had great courage. They and their immediate descendants were people of vision for, during the course of their first hundred years, they set up the structures necessary to maintain the integrity of the community in a still hostile environment and to assist its members to live in England as practising Jews.

The Congregation framed a series of laws to govern the conduct of its members and levied what amounted to an income tax on them. It then set about the building of institutions, some of which survive to this day. First to be established was the Burial Society. Next came the Dower Society to provide dowries to fatherless brides. This was followed by a Boys' School, a Girls' School and a Learned Society. A special charity assisted poor boys to obtain apprenticeships or otherwise start work. A Board of Guardians cared for the destitute. A hospital with a special ward for maternity cases was endowed; and a ward for the aged was added later.

Nor were suffering Jews overseas neglected. Money was raised to redeem Jewish captives from the slave markets of the Mediterranean ports and to assist the needy in the holy cities of Jerusalem, Tiberias, Safed and Hebron.

An intermittent stream of Marrano refugees continued to reach London until the Inquisitions of Spain and Portugal were abolished in the early years of the nineteenth century. Most of them were helped and absorbed by the London community; but others were sent on their way with small grants of money to settle in the British colonies of America and the West Indies. Towards the end of the eighteenth century, the Congregation was also enlarged by a wave of immigration from Italy, North Africa and Gibraltar.

From the start, the leaders of London's Jews were wealthy, educated and

118 The Montefiore family
This pastel of 1797 by Jelgerhuis shows Joseph Elias Montefiore, his wife Rachel and their children.

119 The Jerusalem Infirmary
This caricature dated 1749 is of the Spanish and Portuguese Jews' Hospital in London and features many of the prominent members of the English Sephardi Community. They are all clean-shaven and wear English dress.

cultivated people who could associate with the best English society on more or less equal terms. They established themselves as shippers, brokers, financiers, bullion and gem merchants, army victuallers and commodity traders. Some even assisted in the starting of several of the City's financial institutions, including the Bank of England. But contrary to popular belief, the Sephardim were not all rich and educated. There were many humble craftsmen and artisans among them, as well as unskilled, unlettered poor.

The following statistics, taken from the Bevis Marks Records of the mid and late nineteenth century should dispose once and for all of the myth of the aristocratic nature of all London's Sephardim.

Percentages of bridegrooms working in different occupations

	1841–1850	1891–1900
Cigar makers	21.4	12.1
General Dealers (including hawkers)	22.1	3.9
Boot and Shoe trades	6.1	9.7
Tailoring and Clothing	4.6	9.7
Merchants	7.6	6.3
Commercial Travellers	3.2	3.9
Stock Exchange	–	3.9
Fruit Trades	0.7	4.3
Diamond Trades (merchant, polisher, cutter, or broker)	–	1.4
Feather Trades	0.7	2.4
Clerks	0.7	2.4
Butchers	2.4	1.0
Independent means of Gentlemen	5.3	0.4
Others	25.2	38.6

The former Marranos and their descendants also made a small but pleasing contribution to the life of their adopted country in other ways than business — mainly in medicine, letters and politics. A famous boxer, Daniel Mendoza, is also mentioned with pride in communal publications.

Benjamin Disraeli, the baptised son of a member of the Congregation, founded the Conservative Party and became Prime Minister of England. His father Isaac d'Israeli (1766-1848), a minor poet and literary critic, was chosen to be a Warden of the Congregation in 1813. But he declined to accept office and also refused to pay the fine of £40 which, according to the rules, was imposed in such cases. When the Synagogue attempted to enforce payment, d'Israeli resigned and had his children baptised as Christians. Jews were not allowed to become Members of Parliament until 1858; so had it not been for the quarrel, it is unlikely that Benjamin Disraeli would ever have become Prime Minister. Despite his conversion, he always took great pride in his origins and remained a well-wisher of the Jews. The Congregation still possesses the Register of Births in which Benjamin's name and the details of his circumcision are entered.

Moses Montefiore (1784-1885), whose family came from Leghorn

120 Benjamin Disraeli
In this picture, Queen Victoria is shown at Osborne in 1878, investing Benjamin Disraeli, Earl of Beaconsfield, with the Order of the Garter.

122 Sir Moses Montefiore (1784-1885)
Etching by Richard Dighton. 1818.

(Livorno) in Italy, was without doubt the most famous son of the Congregation. Retiring from the stock exchange at the age of thirty-seven, he devoted the rest of his long life to helping poor and oppressed Jews at home and abroad. He was knighted by Queen Victoria in 1837 and created a baronet in 1846 — an unique honour for a practising Jew at that time. His charitable endeavours in England were on a large scale. But even more important, he established himself as the outstanding Jewish leader of his generation by his journeys to Palestine, Morocco, Rome, Turkey and Russia. Those journeys, some undertaken in old age and in very hazardous conditions, caused him to became a hero to countless Jews all over the world. He visited the Holy Land seven times, where he endowed hospitals and almshouses as well as devising schemes to encourage agriculture.

The two journeys that most captured the popular imagination were those Sir Moses made in connection with the Damascus Affair and the Mortara Affair. Jews were being savagely persecuted in Damascus in 1840 after the revival there of the medieval libel that Jews had used the blood of a Christian for the making of their Passover wine. Sir Moses, accompanied by the French-Jewish leader Adolphe Crémieux and with the support of Lord Palmerston, obtained a firman from the Sultan of Turkey. This cancelled the charges against the Jews of Damascus and guaranteed protection to all the Sultan's Jewish subjects.

He was not so successful in the Mortara Affair. This concerned a Jewish child, secretly baptised by his nursemaid without his parents' knowledge and subsequently abducted by the Papal Guards to be brought up as a Christian. Many European sovereigns protested to the Pope, but to no avail.

123 Haham David Nieto (1654-1728)
In this mezzotint of 1705, the Haham of the Spanish and Portuguese Jews' Congregation, London is shown bare-headed, with a full-bottomed wig and a stiletto beard. He is wearing clerical robes with white bands.

Sir Moses went to Rome, but though courteously received by a Cardinal, who assured him that such a thing would not be allowed again, he was refused an audience with the Pope. The child remained under Catholic care and was eventually received into the priesthood by Pope Pious IX, who is said to have declared 'I have bought thee, my son, for the Church at a very high price'.

It was the failure of the English Sephardim in the field of Jewish learning and education that proved their ultimate undoing. The community always had to look overseas for its religious leadership, and it still does so today. Its Hahamim (rabbis) were imported from Amsterdam, Livorno and other great centres of Jewish scholarship; and were seldom recruited from within its own ranks. David Nieto from Livorno, appointed in 1701, came closest to the ideal Sephardi Haham, being described on his tombstone as:

Sublime theologian, profound sage, distinguished physician, famous astronomer, sweet

124 Ashkenazi-Sephardi wedding
A 19th century print of the wedding of
Marie Perugia to Leopold de Rothschild.
The Prince of Wales and members of the
Sassoon family were present at the
ceremony.

poet, elegant preacher, subtle logician, ingenious physicist, fluent rhetorician, pleasant
author, expert in languages, learned in history.

But men of that calibre proved almost impossible to find.

Setting aside the almost oriental exaggeration of the posthumous tribute
to Nieto, the contrast between the Sephardi and Ashkenazi conditions is
vividly illustrated by the fact that David Nieto died one year before the
birth of Moses Mendelssohn, creator of the movement for 'Enlightenment'
amongst Europe's Ashkenazim. That movement, it will be remembered,
encouraged Ashkenazi Jews to leave their ghettos for the first time and to
attempt to dress, behave and live as ordinary Europeans — a state the
Sephardim had already been enjoying for hundreds of years.

Denied the seedbed of home-grown Jewish learning, it is hardly surprising
that the Congregation declined with time, losing many members by
assimilation and through the schism that resulted in the founding of the
West London (Reform) Synagogue in 1841. The accession of a handful of
talented Ashkenazim, attracted by the decorum of the synagogue services
and by the English good manners of some of its members, helped but little;
and it was not until the twentieth century brought a flood of new Sephardi
immigrants to English shores that it gained a new lease of life.

PART THREE

SEPHARDI COMMUNITIES TODAY

Ψ

Sephardi Migrations of the Twentieth Century

The series of major political convulsions that shook Southern Europe, North Africa and the Middle East during the twentieth century precipitated the dispersion of Sephardim from the territories of the old Ottoman Empire, where they had lived for hundreds if not for thousands of years.

First came the Balkan Wars and the First World War of 1914-18, which resulted in the break-up of the Ottoman Empire. As disaster after disaster struck the Balkans and Turkey, the former heartland of Sephardi Jewry, many thousands of Jews fled to build new lives for themselves abroad, mostly in North and South America.

In the Second World War of 1939-45, entire Sephardi communities — such as those of Salonika and Rhodes — perished in Hitler's Holocaust. After the war, Bulgaria's fifty thousand Jews, who had escaped disaster, left for Israel rather than submit to the Russian-imposed communist regime. About the same number of Jews also left Turkey because of economic hardship and also because of the perceived precariousness of their position.

The establishment of the State of Israel in 1948, and the simultaneous rise of Arab nationalism, resulted in the destruction of all the ancient Sephardi communities of the Middle East. The gaining of independence by Algeria from France virtually emptied that country of Jews. Later, the triumph of Islamic fundamentalism in Iran caused many of its Jews to leave.

As the direct result of these mass migrations, the number of Sephardim in Israel increased to over half its total Jewish population. Large numbers of Sephardim settled in France; and the others spread themselves thinly, mostly in North and South America, in England, Spain and Italy, and also in more distant places.

The primary purpose of this book is to describe the origins of contemporary Sephardim. Many of the historic communities, including that of France, have already been covered in Part Two; and the English-speaking ones of New York, London and Gibraltar will be described more fully in later chapters. Other active groups in the Sephardi diaspora today are mentioned briefly below.

Modern Israel is the crucible in which Sephardim from all over the diaspora have gathered to forge new cultural patterns, based partly on their own varied backgrounds and partly on those already established in their rediscovered homeland. The story of their early difficulties and subsequent achievements, of their hopes and ambitions, is charged with interest; and an entire book would be required to do justice to this culmination of Sephardi history.

It is difficult to estimate numbers reliably, but there may be up to about one hundred and fifty thousand Sephardim in the United States of America. Apart from New York, described later, the largest concentration of Sephardi Jews is in Los Angeles, which is home to about fifteen thousand. Its several synagogues were each founded by groups of immigrants from Rhodes and the Balkans, Aleppo, India and Burma, Morocco and, most recent to arrive, Iran. There are about four thousand Sephardim — mostly from Turkey and Rhodes — in Seattle, the next largest community.

International Conference of Sephardi Jews
23rd. – 25th. Iyar 5695
26th. – 28th. May 1935

(In the Chair) Sir Francis A. Montefiore, Bart. (London); (Right) Grand Rabbin Dr. Nissim Ovadia (France), O. Camhy (Algeria), A. H. Navon (France), Rev. David Bueno de Mesquita (London), Grand Rabbin Sabattey Djaen (Roumania), David Vaz Nunes da Costa, David Beriro, Paul Goodman, F.R.Hist.S. (London), Prof. Moses Bensabat Amzalak (Portugal), Charles E. Sebag-Montefiore (London); (Left) Rabbi Shemtob Gaguin, Arthur de Casseres, Dr. Judah S. Benzecry (London), I. Nacamuli, Asher Benroy (Egypt), ⟶ ⟵ D. Jessurum Cardoso (Holland), David S. Sassoon, Dr. Lionel D. Barnett (London), Dr. J. Haim (Austria), M. I. Florentin (Manchester), Lazar Avramovitch (Yugo-Slavia); (Standing) Neville J. Laski, K.C., Denis D.G. Israel, Artom A. Romain, Michael Marchant (London).

125 International Conference of Sephardi Leaders at Bevis Marks, London in 1928

Smaller groups of Sephardim, but each usually large enough to run its own synagogue, can also be found in many other cities and towns in the United States. These include Atlanta, Boston, Chicago, Cincinnati, Detroit, Hartford, Indianapolis, Miami, Montgomery, New Brunswick, Philadelphia, Phoenix, Portland, Salem, San Francisco and Washington.

French-speaking Quebec and Montreal in Canada attracted many Jews from North Africa, Egypt and Lebanon in the 1960s. There are now well over ten thousand of them, mostly from North Africa, in Quebec. Montreal's Sephardi community of several thousand is more diverse and includes refugees from Algeria, Tangier, Egypt and the Lebanon. The city is also home to a thousand or so Iraqi Jews, many of whom would originally have preferred to have gone to the United States but are now well established in Canada. Toronto also has a Sephardi community, said to be about eight thousand strong, roughly half from Egypt and the remainder from North Africa.

Argentina, Spanish-speaking and with a Latin culture, was an easy

126 Stanley Street Synagogue, Montreal
The Congreation She'arit Israel was founded in 1768 by Jews from the West Indies, mainly originating in Spain and Portugal. Their first synagogue was erected in 1777. The Stanley Street Synagogue was built in 1887. It was demolished after the Second World War and replaced by one in a newer residential area of the city.

favourite for many Jews from the Balkans, Rhodes and Turkey seeking a better life overseas. It also attracted Sephardim from Syria in the early years of the twentieth century, some of whom made their fortunes there. The fourteen thousand or so Sephardim of Buenos Aires are divided into four separate communities, each corresponding to their countries of origin. By far the largest, with between seven and eight thousand members, is the originally Ladino-speaking congregation whose members came from Turkey, Rhodes and the Balkans. Next in size are the two Syrian congregations, one from Damascus and the other from Aleppo. The smallest, with only three hundred members, still jealously preserves its Moroccan heritage. Unfortunately, as in so many other places, the Sephardi community remains divided.

The Sephardi community of Brazil is slightly smaller than that of Argentina, but larger than that of Mexico. There are Sephardi synagogues in Mexico City and in the main towns of Brazil. As in Argentina, the communities of Brazil remain very much divided according to the origins of their members.

Smaller Sephardi communities also exist in other places in South and Central America, sometimes numbering no more than a few hundred and never exceeding a few thousand members. Of these, the largest are in Chile, Uruguay and Venezuela. At least one functioning Sephardi synagogue can also be found in Bolivia, Colombia, Costa Rica, Cuba, Guatemala, Panama, Paraguay, and Peru.

Though there was once a flourishing Sephardi community of between two and three thousand people in the Belgian Congo, this dispersed when the country gained its independence as Zaire and embarked on a period of prolonged civil war. The Sephardi community of Southern Rhodesia also dwindled during the process of its re-birth as Zimbabwe; but the community still survives today and looks to the Spanish and Portuguese Jews of London for advice and help. Unusual for black Africa, the country's Chief Justice is a Sephardi Jew. There are now small Sephardi congregations in Capetown and in Johannesburg, mainly composed of Jews from the newly independent states of Africa who moved south in their quest for security and peace.

There are several hundred Sephardim in Singapore and rather fewer in Hong Kong — but with active synagogues in both places. Singapore's first Prime Minister on attaining its independence was a Sephardi Jew. Manila in the Philippines has a synagogue with a mixed Ashkenazi and Sephardi membership — but which follows a largely Sephardi minhag.

Australia is home to several thousand Sephardim, mostly concentrated in Sydney and Melbourne. Many are immigrants from North Africa and India; but their number also includes descendants of Ladino-speaking Jews who immigrated to Perth and Adelaide in the early years of the twentieth century.

In Europe itself, the only contemporary Sephardi communities not already mentioned are the small ones of Spain, Portugal and Switzerland. All are comprised of former refugees, mostly from North Africa and Arab lands. The Geneva synagogue owes its foundation to wealthy Sephardim from

Arab countries and caters for a mixed Sephardi and Ashkenazi membership. Apart from the surviving Marranos, the only Sephardi congregation of Portugal is in Lisbon which has about five hundred members. Spain now has Sephardi communities in Madrid and Barcelona as well as smaller groups in Malaga, Seville, Marbella and Torremolinos. Their members include a few Sephardim from South America who sought a more tranquil life back in Europe.

127   Wedding of Victoria Chayo to Ezra Shammah, Paris 1934
.The fathers of the bride and groom were business partners from prominent merchant families of Aleppo. Ezra and Victoria settled in Manchester. Their several brothers and sisters lived for long periods in Beirut, Cairo, Istanbul, Tel Aviv, Kibbutz Ma'agam, Milan, London, Manchester, Bogota, Los Angeles, New York and Montreal — an illustration of the wide dispersion of the ancient Jewish communities of the Middle East.

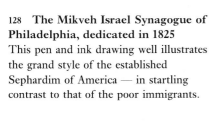

New York

The original Sephardi Congregation of New York — Shearit Israel (The Remnant of Israel) — had by the end of the nineteenth century become a little detached from its roots in the Sephardi diaspora. Its synagogue services were still being conducted strictly according to the Sephardi minhag; but many of its members were either of Ashkenazi descent or else of mixed origin. They saw themselves as an aristocratic elite, well integrated into upper-class America and far removed from the mass of poor Jewish immigrants starting to flock to New York.

The first three to four thousand of a new wave of immigration, destined to revitalise Sephardi life in the United States, arrived in the first decade of the twentieth century. Some came to attend the St. Louis Exhibition of 1904 and then remained. They either traded in oriental carpets or else were engaged in the manufacture of Turkish cigarettes. Others, much poorer and less well-educated, came from Aleppo in Syria, which had been in economic decline since the opening of the Suez Canal in 1869.

The Balkan wars, the First World War and the subsequent break-up of the Ottoman Empire caused more Sephardim to seek new lives in America. Their numbers were swelled by the great fires that devastated large areas of Constantinople, Smyrna and Salonika after the war.

The immigrants, poor and often destitute, were cared for by H.I.A.S. (Hebrew Immigrant Aid Society), which met the new arrivals, guaranteed that they would not become a charge on public funds and attempted to settle them. By 1926 it is estimated that about twenty five thousand Sephardim had reached New York. Some were sent on to Seattle, Rochester,

128 The Mikveh Israel Synagogue of Philadelphia, dedicated in 1825
This pen and ink drawing well illustrates the grand style of the established Sephardim of America — in startling contrast to that of the poor immigrants.

129 A seder at Ellis Island in the 1920s
Ellis Island, in New York's harbour, was the place where, until comparatively recently, would-be immigrants to the United States were detained for investigation prior to entry permission being granted or refused.

Montgomery and Atlanta; but the vast majority remained in New York City.

More Sephardi immigrants arrived after the end of the Second World War; and still more came as a result of the destruction of the ancient Jewish communities of the Islamic world following the establishment of the State of Israel in 1948. There are now about one hundred and fifty thousand Sephardim in the United States, the vast majority in and around New York.

The immigrants who arrived in New York in the 1920s and the 1930s, and who settled in Harlem and the Lower East Side, had great difficulty in adapting to life in America. It is no exaggeration to maintain that most did not; and it was not until the 1950s that their children and grandchildren adjusted fully to their new environment.

Divided amongst themselves by language — they included Ladino, Arabic, Turkish and Greek speakers — they were as foreign in tongue, appearance and temperament to the existing Sephardi establishment of New York as they were to the millions of Ashkenazim who had also entered America during the same period.

Many Ashkenazim found it hard to accept that the Sephardim, who knew no Yiddish, were even Jewish. As neither Sephardi or Ashkenazi immigrants could yet speak English, they were not even able to talk to each other. Indeed, a group of Ashkenazim from the Lower East Side once petitioned the Mayor to remove the unruly 'Turks in our midst' — only withdrawing

130 Medical examination
Immigrants being examined at Ellis Island.

131 David de Sola Pool
He left London in 1907 to become
Minister of Shearit Israel, where he served
until his retirememt in 1956. Dr. de Sola
Pool was an author and historian as well as
an active communal leader. He edited and
translated the Sephardi prayer books.

their request on learning that the 'Turks' were really Sephardi Jews.

The grand Sephardim of Shearit Israel worried so much that they might
be confused with the newcomers that they persuaded H.I.A.S. to change
the name of one of its committees from the 'Committee for Sephardic
Jewish Immigrants' to the 'Committee for Oriental Jewish Immigrants'.
They also insisted that the immigrants' use of the term 'Sephardic' to
describe their various organisations was inappropriate and must be changed
to 'Oriental'. This attitude greatly offended the immigrants who, though
acquiescing, must have pondered the fact that whilst many of them were
pure-blooded Spanish-speaking Sephardim, the members of Shearit Israel
were partly Ashkenazi by descent. (Note: 'Sephardic' — spelled in that way
— is the version of the adjective used in the U.S.A.)

To be fair to the old Spanish and Portuguese congregation, both its
members and its spiritual leader, Rabbi David de Sola Pool, did their best
to help their poorer brethren. Free 'overflow' services were organised for
them in the social hall of Shearit Israel's synagogue and few calls for help
were ever turned down. Its Sisterhood, in particular, made strenuous efforts
to help the newcomers by operating a Neighborhood Settlement House and
synagogue on the Lower East Side, and by organising all kinds of social
and educational activities. Eventually the synagogue, Brith Shalom, became
completely independent of its parent body.

Dr de Sola Pool and the lay leadership worked long and hard to integrate
the Orientals, stressing repeatedly that they all shared a glorious common
heritage. But their good intentions — sometimes insensitively or even
clumsily expressed — were often misunderstood and resented by the
immigrants, who reacted fiercely against any suggestion of 'charity'. Indeed
so prickly were they in their inordinate pride that they usually succeeded
in offending those who most sought their benefit.

With hindsight, it is now not difficult to appreciate the misunderstanding

132 Hester Street
The heart of the immigrant district on the Lower East Side of New York City, 1899.

caused by the great differences in background, culture, education and economic circumstances between the rich 'grandees' of Shearit Israel and the poor but proud immigrants. At the time, the Orientals regarded the attitude of the established Sephardim as patronising; whilst the Spanish and Portuguese were continually exasperated by the behaviour of those they tried so hard to befriend. Happily, some Orientals did join Shearit Israel as devoted members; and there are now no remaining traces of former quarrels.

Even more important for the Sephardi immigrants was the constant Ashkenazi denigration of their life-style and lack of ambition to integrate themselves into the larger American community. In Ashkenazi eyes, the Sephardim were very slow to learn English and acquire citizenship. They seemed to care little for education — either for themselves or for their children — preferring to loiter in coffee shops, play cards and smoke water-pipes. They were accused of treating their women as slaves. They took no part in the struggle to unionise the exploited immigrant workers; nor were they interested in the politics of the aspiring Jewish masses of New York. Even their Hebrew pronounciation was strange and their synagogue chants untuneful. Compared to the millions of Ashkenazim, with keen ambition to better themselves by rapidly becoming American, the Sephardim seemed an insignificant and indolent minority.

Indeed the Sephardi immigrants do appear to have been singularly ill-equipped by their Ottoman education to adapt comfortably to American life. Much of the Ashkenazi criticism, quoted above from the Yiddish newspapers of the day, was valid to some extent. Many Sephardim certainly did lack the thrusting ambition of their European brethren. Held at arm's length by the old Sephardi establishment, which insisted on describing them as 'Orientals' or 'Levantines', and rejected by the huge Ashkenazi majority, they turned in on themselves with hurt pride.

Looking back, it is now hard to see why the coffee houses of the immigrants should have so aroused the ire of the American Jewish establishment, or why Shearit Israel's minister should have railed against their bad influence. The coffee houses must have provided much-needed comfort to their frequenters — with their tastes, smells and sounds of home. To quote directly from Rabbi Marc Angel's 'The Sephardim of the United States of America: An Exploratory Study':

After the day's work the men would go to the cafe, their only outlet for recreation and social intercourse, and their one escape from the bleak tedium of daily life. They would sip Turkish coffee, tell jokes, gossip, complain, discuss politics, read the Judeo-Spanish papers, laugh, cry and dream. The coffee house, a regular feature of the communities in the Levant, had always been popular with the working people and always unpopular with the rabbis.

Like their ancestors on first quitting Spain, the newcomers huddled together in tight little groups derived exclusively from their cities of origin, and on which they could rely absolutely for mutual support in a largely hostile environment. The first Ladino-speaking society, comprising immigrants from Smyrna, was the Union and Peace Society of 1889. This provided burial facilities for its members, High Holyday services in a rented hall and some social amenities.

Other similar societies to cater for Ladino-speakers followed in due course. The principal ones were founded by natives of Constantinople, Monastir, Kastoria, Rhodes, Dardanelles, Gallipoli, Salonika, Angora, Rodosto, Silivria, Tcherlou and Chios. Greek-speaking Jews established the Love and Brotherhood Society of Janina. Immigrants from Aleppo started several societies to cater for their own Arabic-speaking brethren; and those from Damascus established the Helpful Brotherhood.

Joseph Papo, in his valuable book 'Sephardim in Twentieth Century America', gives a detailed account of many of these societies. He explained that to belong to one of them was a badge of honour and a passport to the homes of all its members — for they admitted only those in good health and with impeccable morals. Members could rely on each other for help and would no more think of looking to an outsider for assistance than they would consider responding to such a request themselves.

Each society had a written constitution. Papo describes that of the Ahavat Shalom of Monastir (Love of Peace Society of Monastir), printed in Ladino. The Society was established in 1907 for the following purposes:

> To visit the sick, to bury the dead, to provide Jewish religious education to members and their children by providing Synagogue and Talmud Torah services following the Sephardi Minhag...
>
> Membership to be open to every Jew eighteen years of age and over, of good health and character, and who is married according to Jewish religious laws; any member entering a marriage contrary to these laws is to be stripped of membership...
>
> At the death of a member, all members will be taxed one dollar each, to be remitted to the spouse or nearest relative for the erection of a tombstone. The following services are to be rendered in the case of death: a mortuary cleansing of the body, a coffin, a hearse, two cars for the use of the family, a burial plot, and religious services.

A number of Ladino newspapers were started in New York; but few survived for any length of time. Bitter quarrels and communal indifference were the main causes of their early collapse. Only La America (1910-25) and La Vara (1922-48) lasted for long enough to have a marked effect on the immigrant society; and they both campaigned ceaselessly for greater Sephardi unity, and for closer understanding of the American/Ashkenazi world beyond.

Indeed, for all their virtues, the societies' jealous guarding of their own independence much impeded progress by the Sephardim in finding their own place in New York society. In 1916 for example, Joseph Papo quotes that no fewer than twenty nine immigrant Sephardi services were being held in New York. Twenty four were on the Lower East Side, within a stone's throw of each other: four were in Harlem; and one was in the social hall of the Spanish and Portuguese Congregation. Of those, three were for Greek-speakers, four for Arabic-speakers and twenty one for Ladino-speakers.

The Ladino press repeatedly stressed the scandal of having so many poorly conducted synagogues without adequate rabbinic or educational facilities. It urged Sephardim to pool their resources and establish one or two central synagogues under the direction of respected rabbis. But though several attempts were made, all ended in failure. All attempts by the immigrant Sephardim to attain some kind of organisational unity also foundered because of the entrenched attitudes of the societies and their leaders.

Even the search for a Chief Rabbi to unite the disparate groups met with little success in the early days. A commission, set up in 1917 for that purpose, was recommended to select a candidate with command of 'Hebrew, Spanish, Turkish, French, Greek, Arabic and, if possible, English'. A suitable rabbi was located in Turkey. But controversy immediately broke out concerning both his credentials and also whether the community yet had the infrastructure necessary to support such an appointment. In any

133 Shearit Israel's present Synagogue
Opened on Central Park West, New York
City, in 1897.

event, war with Turkey prevented his arrival; and no Chief Rabbi was in fact appointed until 1941.

It was not until 1941 that a leader finally emerged with sufficient charisma to unite all Sephardim. This was Rabbi Nissim Ovadia, formerly Sephardi Chief Rabbi of Paris, who had escaped from Nazi-occupied France. A leader, organiser and spiritual guide, Rabbi Ovadia stressed that Jewish learning, education and religious observance were the pillars required to support a renaissance of Sephardi culture in America.

His message was taken up with enthusiasm by a newly emerging lay leadership and by the Sephardi press. Public meetings were held, funds donated and much enthusiasm generated. Even the Arabic-speaking Syrian Jews and the Greek-speaking Jews, who had held aloof from previous efforts at unity, joined the other societies in pledging their full support. The Central Sephardic Jewish Community of America was inaugurated with Ovadia as its Chief Rabbi.

The Central Community's aims were ambitious. It sought to engage in most types of communal activity, particularly those connected with worship in accordance with traditional Sephardi custom, religious education and the formation of a Beth Din. But it also offered assistance in the field of immigration and the acquiring of American citizenship, in employment and in welfare. Unfortunately Rabbi Ovadia died the following year. His place was taken by Rabbi Isaac Alcalay, the former Chief Rabbi of Yugoslavia and another refugee from Nazi oppression.

Despite the shock of Rabbi Ovadia's death, the Central Community continued for a while and did much good work. Its periodical, called The Sephardi and written in English, had a circulation of about four thousand. It lasted for sixteen years. A professional social worker was appointed to liaise between needy Sephardim and Jewish social service agencies. A Youth Director was engaged. A Central Location Service was established to assist Holocaust survivors to find their relatives. Much of value was also achieved in the field of Jewish religious education, and in the establishment of the Sephardic Jewish Center of the Bronx. The building of the spectacular Sephardic Jewish Home for the Aged in Brooklyn, opened in 1951, absorbed much energy and is still regarded as one of the great successes of communal endeavour.

The Central Community foundered eventually, partly because of the attitude of the societies — which reverted to one of jealously guarded autonomy — and partly because of growing apathy within the community. It became harder and harder to raise the necessary funds to finance its activities; and as these declined, so did enthusiasm and support.

Only two of the original immigrant congregations still remain in the Bronx. Most of the others dispersed as their members prospered and moved out of their original neighbourhoods. Apart from Brooklyn, to be discussed in more detail below, the (Conservative) Emet Veshalom Congregation of Cedarhurst in Queens — the bulk of whose membership originates in Monastir — is now the largest of the former communities. The original Congregation of Shearit Israel, with its splendid traditions, now numbers about five hundred famililies and includes members from all over the Sephardi diaspora.

All Sephardi leaders in New York, and in North America as a whole, accept that an effective system of education is vital to secure continuation of Sephardi consciousness in circumstances where Sephardim have become a small minority, widely dispersed amongst far more numerous Ashkenazim.

In recent years, much of value has been and is being accomplished by the Sephardic Studies programme of Yeshiva University, which trains rabbis, hazanim and teachers for the community and does its best to stimulate interest in Sephardi history and culture. This work was reinforced in 1985, when the Center for Sephardic Studies was established at the City University of New York. Sephardi House, attached to the Shearit Israel Synagogue of New York, also does a great deal to promote awareness and knowledge of Sephardi culture.

In survival terms, the thirty thousand strong Syrian Jewish community of New York must be the most unusual in the entire Sephardi diaspora. Its members, who originally came to New York from Aleppo and Damascus, were joined later by more recent immigrants from Egypt, Beirut and Israel — mostly also with their roots in Aleppo or Damascus. Though outwardly assimilated to life in America, the community has carefully preserved the customs and social patterns of its origins; and this seems likely to continue for the forseeable future. Its history has been well documented in the two books 'Magic Carpet: Aleppo in Flatbush' and 'Aleppo Chronicles' by Joseph Sutton, from which much of this account is derived.

The lives of the Syrian newcomers to New York in the early years of the twentieth century were little different from those of the other Sephardi immigrants already described. They too were desperately poor. They too settled on the Lower East Side. If anything, being Arabic-speaking and knowing no Ladino, they must have felt even more isolated than their fellow Sephardim, who at least had their own newspapers and coffee shops. Like other immigrant groups, they too founded their own small synagogues as soon as they were able; and then strongly resisted all attempts to merge into a unified Oriental Jewish Community.

But there the similarity ends. As the Syrians inched their way up the economic ladder — from peddling textile goods, to running small shops and then on to owning large stores — their mutual ties strengthened rather than loosened.

Members of the community tended to live together in the same neighbourhood and to move together as a group as soon as their means permitted. The first step in their migration from the Lower East Side was to cross the East River to Williamsburgh. A few years later, they moved on again to Bensonhurst, an area of Brooklyn with reasonably priced family houses. In the early 1940s, the Syrian community migrated en-masse to the Flatbush district of Brooklyn, around Ocean Parkway, where it has remained.

Not only do the Syrian Jews choose to live close to each other, but they also holiday together. Even the less affluent families do their best to take

134 Jewish Woman of Aleppo, 1873
Note that this (married) woman is wearing an elaborate wig.

their children to where they will meet and eventually marry other Syrian children. Bradley Beach in New Jersey was the first vacation spot chosen by the community. It was later replaced by the more elegant Deal, not far away. In fact, Deal has now become a smaller replica of Flatbush, with some five hundred Syrian families in permanent residence, eight synagogues, a Jewish school and an intensive social life centred round their club. Even commuters to New York travel on special buses, where those who wish can recite their morning prayers together.

The Sha'are Zion Synagogue on Ocean Parkway, the luxuriously appointed mikveh (ritual bath) and the nearby Sephardi Community Centre are at the heart of the Syrian-Jewish community of Brooklyn. A number of shops and restaurants, selling and serving traditional Syrian food, are also situated nearby.

Sha'are Zion is the leading synagogue of the several founded by Jews from Aleppo. There are also synagogues in Flatbush for those who came from Damascus, from Egypt, from Beirut, as well as one which attracts Iraqis, Moroccans and Yemenis. There is no problem about attendance, with each synagogue able to run at least one morning service on weekdays, and Sha'are Zion hosting four services every morning, with times staggered to suit the working hours of the participants. Its 'Early Bird' Sabbath morning service, which starts at 6.30 a.m., is used by some of the less observant shopkeepers.

The Flatbush community is a self-contained society that stubbornly maintains the closely-knit family and social patterns of Aleppo and, so far, has made few concessions to the cultural climate of New York. Its members are driven by ambition to succeed in business; and this urge takes precedence over most other aims in life apart from family cohesion and religious observance. Higher secular education is not very greatly valued. Until recently, very few of the young people entered the professions after leaving university.

Perhaps the most important factor in protecting the community's traditional way of life against erosion from cultural influences from the outside is the close attention given to children and youth. A network of Jewish schools, ranging from the middle-of-the-road to the ultra-orthodox in religious terms, is attended by the vast majority of its children — estimated at about ninety per cent. After school years, the lavishly equipped and staffed Sephardi Community Centre, with its swimming pool, gymnasium, library and social activities, ensures that much youthful energy is directed inwards rather than to the world outside.

Another factor that may have assisted survival is the absolute ban on out-marriage, first imposed in 1935 and standing to this day. In terms of a Decree endorsed by all its rabbis and religious institutions, no convert to Judaism, from whatever source or for whatever reason, is acceptable to the community. In this startling reversal of age-old Jewish custom, the male Jewish partner of a female convert is not eligible to be called to the reading of the Torah in synagogue. His children are refused admission to Jewish schools and cannot marry within the community. After death, he will be denied burial in the Syrian-Jewish cemetery. This policy is justified on the ground that the Syrian out-marriage rate is only one or two per cent a year, compared to that of the Ashkenazim which now exceeds forty per cent.

Several reasons have been advanced to explain the unique survival of this remarkable community. Those who first settled on the Lower East Side and then graduated in stages to Flatbush and Deal were, on the whole, the poorer Jews of Aleppo — those who had received only a traditional Jewish education and had not been exposed to the European secular influence of the Alliance schools. The original leaders of Aleppo Jewry, members of the wealthier families who knew some French and English and who traded with the West, mostly went to Cairo and to Europe. The old social order, partly based on European education and contacts, was left behind on the other side of the Atlantic; and the struggling immigrant community had to establish its own leadership from those who did best in the new environment.

With standards of Jewish observance unimpaired by secular education from Europe, sufficient Syrian immigrants arrived in New York to build up a cohesive group with critical mass sufficient to enable it simply to transfer its life-style without too much alteration.

The community is now held together by its tightly exclusive social structure, which places strong emphasis on the family. Its members live and take their holidays together. They share a scale of values in which religion and success in business are prized above all else. The absolute ban on out-marriage discourages potential backsliders. But without doubt, the most potent factor of all is the network of Jewish day-schools in which almost all its children are educated.

The Syrian community of New York stands head and shoulders above the other Sephardi groups in terms of its continuation as a distinct group; and its members, so far, have readily accepted the restrictions of their way of life as a price worth paying for that survival.

Gibraltar

The modern Jewish community of Gibraltar dates only from the eighteenth century, even though Jews had lived on the Rock in the fourteenth century and Marranos from Andalusia had also moved there later.

Jewish merchants from Tetuán in Morocco came to settle soon after Gibraltar was first occupied by British forces in 1704. They were joined there by other Jews active in the Morocco trade — from London, Leghorn and Amsterdam — as well as by Marranos from Portugal who seized the opportunity to escape from the clutches of the Inquisition. At its peak in the middle of the nineteenth century, the Jewish community comprised more than half the total population of the Rock; and even now it numbers about six hundred people.

Article X of the Treaty of Utrecht of 1713, in which Spain ceded Gibraltar to Britain, reads as follows:

> And her Britannic Majesty, at the request of the Catholic King, does consent and agree, that no leave shall be given, under any pretext whatsoever, either to Jews or Moors, to reside or have their dwellings in the said town of Gibraltar.

To be fair to the good faith of the British government, in the early days it did strenuously and repeatedly act to enforce that prohibition. It was however constantly frustrated, both by the corruption of its local officials and — more important — by the necessity to maintain supplies of fresh food and building materials for the garrison in times of conflict with Spain. A Jewish presence in Gibraltar has, therefore, been continuous since 1704.

The British garrison of Gibraltar was dependent on Morocco for food and supplies, difficult to ship out from England. That dependence became crucial whenever, as happened again in recent years, Spain imposed a blockade on the colony.

Moses Benatar, a wealthy Moroccan Jewish merchant, wielded great influence with the Sultan of Morocco and acted for many years as his financial adviser and ambassador-at-large. Benatar was determined to block any British commercial arrangements with Morocco that did not allow Jews to live and trade in Gibraltar. His efforts were crowned by the treaty with Morocco of 1721 which, in flagrant contradiction to the Treaty of Utrecht, provided that:

> ... the subjects of the Emperor of Fez and Morocco, whether Moors or Jews, residing in the dominion of the King of Great Britain, shall entirely enjoy the same privileges that are granted to the English residing in Barbary.

By then, the Jewish community numbered one hundred and twenty seven and had opened its first synagogue.

The London government persisted nevertheless in its campaign to rid Gibraltar of its Jews; but was frustrated by the practicalities of the need to maintain the trading link with Morocco and by the venality of its local governors, some of whom accepted large bribes from Jewish merchants for permission to remain. Though this aspect may have been exaggerated, correspondence published by Sir Joshua Hassan in his learned paper 'The Treaty of Utrecht 1713 and the Jews of Gibraltar' indicates very clearly

135 **Jewish hawker from the Barbary States in Gibraltar**
Drawing made in about 1830.

136 Jewish Refugee Camp at Gibraltar
Following a bout of intense persecution in Morocco, about sixteen hundred Jews fled to Gibraltar in 1860. They were housed in tents provided by the Governor and fed by the government, assisted by the Jewish and Christian communities of Gibraltar and by Jews all over Europe.

the exasperation experienced in London at what, for a time, seems to have been common practice.

In 1726, the Spaniards claimed that the Treaty of Utrecht was "null and void" because the British had extended Gibraltar's fortifications and

... had permitted Jews and Moors, enemies of the Catholic religion, to reside in the city.

Spain accordingly attacked and besieged Gibraltar.

It was only after the Great Siege of 1726-7 in which, according to a contemporaneous source,

The Jews were not a little serviceable; they wrought in the most indefatigable manner, and spared no pains when they could be of any advantage, either in the siege or after it,

that the British government began to take less seriously the repeated Spanish complaints about the presence of Jews on the Rock. There were already about one thousand Jewish residents by the time of the Great Siege; and those who remained in the town earned the gratitude of the governor by contributing energetically to its defence. Though London did again order Jews out of Gibraltar, the threat of renewed Spanish blockade ensured that the order was never enforced for fear of upsetting the garrison's Moroccan suppliers.

Because of the strong British link, Gibraltar's Jewish community developed on different lines from those of Morocco. Many Jews were evacuated to London during the Great Siege, where they were helped by the Spanish and Portuguese Congregation and forged strong ties with it. Even before then, Isaac Nieto, son of London's famous Haham, had become its Rabbi and was present at the opening of its first synagogue.

As the Jewish community matured, it contributed to the growing

The Armorial Ensigns of
SIR JOSHUA ABRAHAM HASSAN
G.B.E. K.C.M.G. L.V.O.

College of Arms
MCMLXXXIX

Garter King of Arms

137 Arms of Sir Joshua Hassan

prosperity of the Rock and developed a good relationship with the other residents. To quote from Sir Joshua Hassan's paper referred to above,

Gibraltar has always been notable for the internal peace and friendliness in which people of different religions, customs and interests exist. This has continued and improved; and both Christians and Jews in Gibraltar are proud of the harmony and amity in which all live, each maintaining their own religious observances. It can certainly stand as an example of tolerance and partnership to communities which claim to be more enlightened.

Some Jews lived in great style on the Rock. Aaron Cardozo, who died in 1834, was a friend and confidant of Lord Nelson and helped him in a special mission to secure provisions from the Bey of Oran just before the battle of Trafalgar. Nelson's parting words to him on leaving Gibraltar were:

If I survive, Cardozo, you shall no longer remain in this dark part of the world.

Cardozo was Consul to the Beys of Tunis and Algeria. His former home is now Gibraltar's City Hall.

Another grandee was Judah Benoliel, who died five years after Cardozo. He was Consul of both Austria and the Sultan of Morocco, for whom he negotiated peace with Sardinia. In 1798, Benoliel and Cardozo were publicly thanked before a parade of the garrison for their services in uncovering a plot to betray the Rock to the French.

More recently, Sir Joshua Hassan dominated Gibraltar's political life for over thirty years in his capacity as the city's Mayor and then as its first Chief Minister. He served during a most difficult period in the constitutional development of the colony, and at a time of tension because of the closed border with Spain.

Gibraltar's population was evacuated to England, Jamaica and Madeira during the Second World War of 1939-45. Not all its Jews returned after the war; but for those who did, religious ties had slackened. Out-marriage, facilitated by the ease with which conversion to Judaism could be obtained in Morocco, greatly increased. The people had little Jewish education and, though outwardly religious, they had become lax in their observance.

All this changed radically because of the efforts of one dynamic rabbi, who brought the full strength of his own convictions to bear on solving the twin problems of apathy and assimilation. Rabbi Joseph Pacifici, the son of a prominent Italian thinker and lawyer, was trained at the Ashkenazi Yeshiva of Gateshead in England. He accepted a rabbinic post in Gibraltar in the late 1950s.

Once in Gibraltar, Rabbi Pacifici devoted the major part of his energies to teaching the young. He concentrated on a small number of boys and girls of high ability, guided their thinking and sent them on to yeshivot abroad for more study. The members of this elite group were further influenced in their religious development by prominent Ashkenazi rabbis from the extreme right wing of Judaism.

The young people returned to Gibraltar and eventually became the leaders of the Jewish community. In turn, they made their own impact on its life, transforming the standard of religious observance. Jewish education of a highly "orthodox" variety is now strong. A synagogue is packed each day for morning and afternoon services. No Jewish-owned shop opens on the Sabbath.

To add even greater emphasis to this added dimension, a Kollel was established. This consists of from eight to ten young married Jewish scholars of advanced level. Most happen to be Ashkenazim, because English-speaking Sephardim of sufficient attainment could not be found. The effect of this group, living in the midst of a Jewish community of only six hundred with an already highly developed religious sense, has been to reinforce Gibraltar in its new position as a bastion of strict Jewish observance.

Rabbi Pacifici never flew the Sephardi flag, believing that his primary task was to persuade his pupils to remain Jewish — and only then to be Sephardim. Consequently, though the trimmings of Sephardi culture have been retained, the emphasis has shifted to a rigid 'right wing' brand of Ashkenazi orthodoxy. As a method of reviving a community formerly drifting into apathy, it has been astonishingly successful.

But the loss of some of its distinctive Sephardi ethos has produced tensions in Gibraltar and is regretted by those older people who care deeply for their traditions. The passing of the easy-going Sephardi ways has also been noticed by non-Jewish citizens of Gibraltar, some of whom comment that their relations with Jewish neighbours are no longer as close as previously. The days in which Jews would send sweets to their gentile friends at Purim, and the non-Jews would buy cakes from the kasher baker to give Jews at Christmas, may soon be just a memory.

The lesson to be learned from this revival of intense religious commitment in Gibraltar is just how much can be accomplished by inspirational Jewish education. In this case, the rigorous teachings of Ashkenazi rabbis fell on fertile Sephardi ground, to mutual benefit. Whether or not the same kind of results can be achieved in a more traditional Sephardi way is a question that urgently needs to be asked and answered.

138 **Family of Jewish Refugees** Gibraltar 1860.

London and Manchester

The Sephardi community of England was close to extinction at the end of the nineteenth century. Indeed, an editorial in the Jewish Chronicle put it thus:

A few years ago it was quite the fashion in the Anglo-Jewish Community to look upon the old Sephardi community in Bevis Marks as in a state of irremediable decay... (wondering) when the psychological moment would arrive to direct the attention of the Charity Commissioners to the want of proportion between the vitality of the Congregation and its balance at its bankers.

The appointment in 1887 of an energetic new Haham, Moses Gaster (of Ashkenazi origin), did something to reverse this decline. But Gaster — a brilliant scholar, influential Zionist and powerful personality — clashed repeatedly with the Congregation's lay leadership, unused to a rabbi of his calibre and radical views. He started part-time religion classes in Maida Vale to replace the day-school which had closed shortly before his arrival in London. Unfortunately, his most ambitious project — that of transforming the Montefiore College (previously a retirement home for rabbis and ministers) into a seminary for the rabbinate — started well but ended in failure. Haham Gaster, a disappointed man, resigned from the Congregation in 1919 but retained his leading role in Jewish affairs.

It was the flood of new Sephardi immigrants to England in the early part of the twentieth century that gave the community a new lease of life. That wave of immigration continued sporadically until the final destruction of the ancient Jewish communities of the Islamic world.

There are two large and three small Sephardi synagogues in Manchester. The original Spanish and Portuguese Jews' Congregation of London has survived and maintains three synagogues. London is also host to communities of Jews from many different countries of the former Sephardi diaspora, each one representing another strand of the ancient Sephardi Tradition. Their fascinating stories are described briefly below.

139 Commemorative Service in Bevis Marks Synagogue
The service was held in 1884 to commemorate the hundredth year of Sir Moses Montefiore. The Ashkenazi Chief Rabbi Herman Adler is shown preaching the sermon.

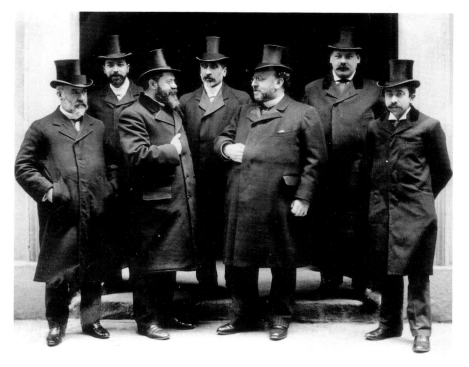

THE MAN OF THE WEEK.

XLIII.—THE REV. THE HAHAM, DR. MOSES GASTER.

"The Giant's Robes."

140 Officials of the Spanish and Portuguese Synagogue, London
In this early twentieth-century photograph, Haham Moses Gaster is shown third from the left, with other officials of the Congregation.

141 Haham Moses Gaster (1856-1939)
In this cartoon of 1908, the Haham of the Spanish and Portuguese Jews's Congregation, London, is shown fitting himself out in the garb of the most illustrious of his predecessors, Haham Nieto.

THE MANCHESTER COMMUNITY

Manchester, with its thriving cotton trade, was the magnet which drew Sephardi merchants from the Ottoman Empire to English shores. The first two permanent settlers arrived in 1843 — Samuel Hadida from Gibraltar and Nissim Levy from Constantinople. They became the nucleus of a small group of younger members of established merchant families, seeking to share in the lucrative trade between Manchester and the Mediterranean, until then wholly in Greek hands.

More Sephardim arrived during the following decades, until by 1872 there were thirty five families in all — from Corfu, Aleppo, Constantinople, Cairo, Gibraltar, Rhodes, and North Africa. They joined the Ashkenazi synagogue but also maintained private prayer rooms, either in their own homes or in hired premises. A Jewish Chronicle reporter declared himself 'delighted with the good order' of the private Sephardi minyan he attended, despite the disparate countries of origin of its members. Of the thirty five families, ten came from Corfu. But to quote from Bill Williams's book 'The Making of Manchester Jewry',

> No group was as stubbornly independent as the merchants of Aleppo, who looked for leadership to Ezra Sharim (Shrem) and founded a social centre in a coffee house attached to Moses Bianco's warehouse .... private Sephardi prayer room in Sharim's house.

That same characteristic of Aleppo Jews was also to be found later in New York, where they settled in even greater numbers and built a vibrant though inward-looking community.

The Manchester Sephardim were led for a time by Isaac Belisha, the grandfather of Leslie Hore-Belisha, who became Minister for War in the late 1930s and lent his name to the 'Belisha' beacons to be found alongside

142 Kiddush Cup
This 19th century English silver goblet was once owned by Sir Moses Montefiore.

each pedestrian road crossing in Britain. Isaac was born in Paris but spent his early years in London. He then set up business in Melbourne, Australia, before moving on to Gibraltar. He arrived in Manchester in 1859 and, with his background and command of English, provided the growing community with a natural spokesman.

The first Sephardi synagogue to be opened in England after the one in Bevis Marks, London, was in Cheetham Hill, North Manchester. Its establishment in 1874 was helped by the London Congregation; and despite the Eastern origin of most of its members, it readily adopted the usages and prayer book of the Spanish and Portuguese Jews and acknowledged the ecclesiastical authority of their Haham. The synagogue lost many members due to the shift of the Jewish population to the south of the city. Eventually the original building was turned into a Jewish Museum in 1984; and its small congregation moved to premises in Salford. It has since been re-invigorated by the accession of an enthusiastic group of new immigrants from Gibraltar and Morocco.

Recent immigrants from Morocco, religiously very observant, also founded the Pinto Yeshivah and synagogue in North Manchester and the small Nefusot Yehudah synagogue nearby.

Movement of Jews from the north to the south of Manchester was responsible for the opening of the Withington Congregation of Spanish and Portuguese Jews in 1904. Like their brethren in Cheetham Hill, the Sephardim of South Manchester modelled their practices on those of the London Congregation, with whom they maintain close ties and whose ecclesiastical authority they accept. Their present synagogue in Queen's Road was opened in 1927 to replace the original building. This large and splendid synagogue, with its decorous services, is also popular with some local Ashkenazim; but it has now begun to suffer from the effect of a further movement of population to even more distant southern suburbs.

Like the two older Manchester congregations, the membership of the Sha'are Sedek Synagogue is composed mostly of Jews whose families originated in Syria, Egypt and Iraq. Literally a stone's throw from the Withington Synagogue, it was founded in 1924 by those who preferred their own traditional Eastern minhag to that of the Spanish and Portuguese Jews. The Synagogue does however maintain friendly ties with the London Congregation and even closer ones with Withington, with which it shares several facilities.

THE SPANISH AND PORTUGUESE JEWS' CONGREGATION, LONDON

The historic Spanish and Portuguese Jews' Congregation of London now has a membership of about seventeen hundred — though some members represent families, and a number of elderly people remain attached for burial purposes only. Fewer than ten per cent of them still bear the Portuguese or Spanish names of the original Marrano settlers or of those

143　Sir Alan Mocatta (1907 - 1991)
Alan Mocatta and Robert Carvalho were
prominent in the leadership of the Spanish
and Portuguese Jews' Congregation of
London from the mid 1940s to the mid
1980s. Both were descended from Marrano
families who came to London from
Amsterdam.

A Nunes Carvalho had attracted the
attention of the Inquisition of the Canary
Islands in the late 1650s; and it is thought
that the family, of Portuguese origin, may
well have fled from Brazil to the Canaries
when the Portuguese evicted the Dutch
from Brazil in 1654. The Carvalhos arrived
in England early in the 18th century.

The Mocattas, whose Arabic-sounding
name suggests centuries-long residence in
Spain, are thought to have left that country
for Italy some years before the expulsion of
1492. They reached England in the 17th
century when Oliver Cromwell was Lord
Protector.

who followed later, the large majority consisting of much more recent immigrants and their descendants.

The Congregation maintains three synagogues. The one in Bevis Marks, opened in 1701, has scarcely altered in appearance with the passing of time; but being far from the residential districts of London, it now attracts only small attendances. A recent project to expand its use to serve also as a religious and part-time educational centre for all Jews working in the City of London has made an encouraging start. The second synagogue, opened in Maida Vale in 1896, is the present focus of communal activity. The Congregation's third synagogue, in the suburb of Wembley, opened in 1977. It was originally intended to serve refugees from Egypt; but it soon attracted younger married members of the parent congregation who settled in the locality, as well as other Sephardim from the Middle East.

A great achievement of the years following the Second World War of 1939-45 was the transformation of the Judith, Lady Montefiore College from a home for retired ministers to a teachers' training college. This was accomplished by Haham Solomon Gaon, who inspired a fruitful partnership between the College, the Spanish & Portuguese Jews' Congregation and the Torah Department of the Jewish Agency.

The new institution opened its doors in 1951. Its aim was to provide the whole Sephardi diaspora with a steady stream of teachers, hazanim and rabbis; and it succeeded well in that task. The College drew most of its pupils from the dissolving Jewish communities of North Africa. It provided them with the basic secular education they lacked, as well as with the religious knowledge necessary for their future careers — and indeed, many Sephardi schools and synagogues throughout the world today are led by its former graduates. The College seldom attracted pupils from England however; and it was obliged to close in the early 1980s when its supply of recruits from North Africa finally came to an end.

In an unusual burst of activity in the 1970s, the Old Peoples' Home, formerly the Community's hospital, was enlarged and transferred from the decayed East End of London to new, purpose-built premises in suburban Wembley. The Wembley synagogue was built. The Communal Centre attached to the synagogue in Maida Vale was extended and refurbished. The Montefiore College was re-housed. And a new cemetery was opened in Edgwarebury to replace the one in Golders Green, then reaching the limit of its capacity.

Traditional Sephardi services are lovingly and meticulously recited in the three synagogues of the Congregation, and much attention is devoted to ceremonial forms inherited from the past. The Congregation is rich in historic treasures and possesses fascinating archives.

At times, the leadership of the Congregation seems over-burdened by the complex network of committees and associated charities which have accumulated over the years, and by elaborate rules and procedures which appear increasingly irrelevant to most of the present membership.

Several past attempts to promote the unity of London's Sephardim under some kind of umbrella organisation all failed. This was due partly to

144 Rabbinic Blessing
In the photograph taken in 1986 Rabbi Kadoorie, the famous Kabbalist from Jerusalem, is shown blessing the children of the Jewish Preparatory School. With him are Rabbi Abraham Levy and Rabbi Abraham David.

indifference, partly to the fierce spirit of independence of the newer Sephardi groups, and partly to the clashes of personality that, sadly, seem inevitable in such circumstances.

The decision of the Spanish and Portuguese Congregation not to elect a new Haham, after the retirement of the last incumbent in the mid 1970s, is another factor that has weakened both its prestige within the Anglo-Jewish Community and its role as standard-bearer for the other Sephardi groups in England. In the past, the Haham acted together with the Chief Rabbi of the Ashkenazim in a representational role. He may have been seen as the junior partner but he was there. Also, whether formally or not, the Haham's authority was acknowledged by most Sephardim in England and the Commonwealth. However well it may deal with its technical tasks, the present Joint Ecclesiastical Authority of the Congregation (comprising the Communal Rabbi and the Ab Beth Din) lacks both the charisma and the cohesive power of the traditional office of Haham.

Over-emphasis on buildings, aesthetics and traditional forms has left the Spanish and Portuguese Congregation remarkably ill-equipped to understand and face the underlying problems of the day. Large groups of Sephardim in suburbs other than Wembley have been neglected, both in means of worship and in the education of their children. Many have joined local Ashkenazi synagogues. Assimilation is now rapid to the secular world beyond the community; and people are fast being lost, not only to their own particular Sephardi tradition but even to Judaism itself.

Like their brethren all over the diaspora, the original Sephardi congregation of London has been slow to realise that it is now faced with the basic problem of survival. It has also been slow to grasp the lessons of the past — when neglect of Jewish education led to a faltering of commitment and brought it close to extinction.

The recent wave of Sephardi immigration to London, now ended, may well be the last; for the historic centres of the Sephardi diaspora are empty.

The leading Sephardi community of England is beginning to realise that the sudden increase in its numbers is not necessarily a sign of health nor a ground for complacency. This may be its last chance to build a firm foundation for the meaningful continuation of the Sephardi tradition in England.

THE BAGHDADI COMMUNITY

The first Jews from Baghdad arrived in Manchester in the 1880s. Though a Sassoon had already established himself in London in 1858, the Sassoon family, fabulously wealthy and well-integrated into Anglo-Indian society, was in an entirely different category from that of the humbler pioneer merchants straight from Baghdad.

The members of the tiny community, being Ottoman subjects, were interned as enemy aliens on the outbreak of the First World War of 1914-18. Only one managed to obtain an early release, the others remaining in custody for the duration of hostilities.

Other Baghdadi Jews followed in the years between the First and Second World Wars, swelling the Sephardi communities of both Manchester and London. The last wave of all came to London between the 1950s and the 1980s, after the extinction of the Jewish community of Baghdad.

The immigrants from Baghdad form a closely-knit group. They have preserved their own very special identity far longer than the other groups of Sephardim, who merge more readily with each other and with the Ashkenazim. Unlike their Sephardi brethren, the Baghdadi Jews were for many years very reticent about their origins. Their identity was jealously guarded — but only in private social groups and never in communal institutions, which they were content to leave to others. It is claimed that there are now several thousand Jews of Iraqi origin in and around London.

It was only comparatively recently that Jews from Baghdad started to come forward to take their proper place in the Anglo-Jewish Community. A magazine called 'The Scribe', founded and run by Naim Dangoor, suceeded in re-awakening the pride of the Baghdadi Jews in their ancient heritage by linking it directly to the glorious traditions of Babylonian Jewry. Several of their extremely successful businessmen, led by Davide Sala, now contribute generously to Israeli and other Jewish causes; and they are widely courted as a result. An Iraqi synagogue, open in London for High Holyday services, draws large congregations. And perhaps most important of all, David and Sami Shamoon with other Iraqi benefactors have enabled a Jewish preparatory school, run on Sephardi lines, to be established in London.

THE TURKISH COMMUNITY

The 1920s also saw a big influx of other Sephardi immigrants from the old Ottoman Empire to England — both to London and Manchester. The ending of the First World War, and the convulsions caused by the break-up

145 The Holland Park Synagogue
This was opened in 1928, primarily to serve the needs of the growing Turkish community of London.

of the Empire, were primarily responsible for this acceleration of immigration.

A small number of Jews from Constantinople (Istanbul), Salonika and Smyrna (Izmir) — mainly dealing in oriental carpets — visited England for the Franco-British Exhibition of 1908 and subsequently settled in London. They organised their own services in hired premises, at first for the High Holydays only and later also for Sabbaths.

The tiny community came under suspicion on the outbreak of war with Turkey and Germany in 1914, its members being supposed by the British government to be loyal subjects of Turkey. Several heads of families were directed to work as road repairers and then interned as enemy aliens when they refused. It was in the struggle to obtain their release from internment that the first step was taken to unite the different groups into a single community. The internees were finally freed after the issue of a certificate by the Haham of the Spanish and Portuguese Jews' Congregation to the effect that they were members of a Sephardi congregation.

The city of Salonika was stripped from Turkey and handed to Greece after the end of the war; and Salonika, Istanbul and Smyrna were all badly damaged by great fires. Large numbers of Jews left, some finding their way to England, where they joined compatriots already in residence. The two dominant groups, one from Salonika and the other from Istanbul, formally came together in 1924 with the aim of building a single synagogue. In the subsequent appeal for funds, it was stated that about seven hundred Sephardim were by then living in the neighbourhood of Holland Park and Shepherds Bush in West London.

An attractive synagogue was built in Holland Park, London, and opened in 1928. The community was helped in this by a generous grant from a

146 The founders of the Holland Park Synagogue
A marble tablet in the vestibule of the synagogue, recording the names of its founders.

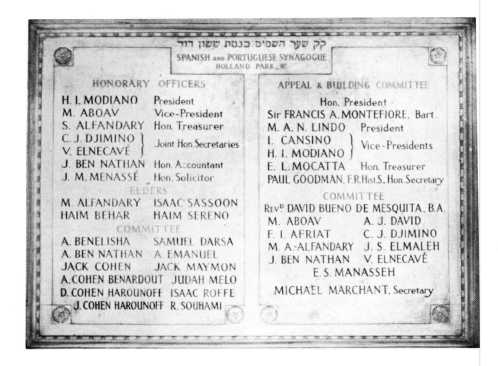

charitable fund and by a large loan — repaid in full — from the Spanish and Portuguese Jews' Congregation, whose Haham they gladly acknowledged as their religious authority.

In the Synagogue's early days, the two founding groups to some extent maintained their separate identities — with Jews from Istanbul sitting on one side and those from Salonika on the other. Prayer books from the original communities were used at first. These were replaced in 1950 by the standard Spanish and Portuguese books (Hebrew and English) — plus a specially printed supplement, partly in Ladino, which includes the special prayers belonging to the community's own age-old tradition. Ladino still survives in spoken use among some of the older members and has recently been undergoing a revival.

All original distinctions have long since broken down. The membership of the Holland Park Synagogue is now drawn widely from most of the ancient communities of the Sephardi diaspora and also includes some Ashkenazim. Happily though, some vestiges of the music of Turkish Jewry, its traditional hazanut and forms of prayer, remain in use to this day.

THE INDIAN COMMUNITY

The first member of the Sassoon family of Bombay arrived in London in 1858. He was followed in due course by other Sassoons, immensely rich and soon on easy terms with members of the Royal Family. The Sassoons entered into English life with gusto. They married into the aristocracy, owned racehorses and contributed a government minister and a famous poet to their adopted land.

A trickle of immigrants from Bombay and Calcutta, including members of other leading Jewish families, followed the Sassoons to England. They continued to arrive in London until the outbreak of war in 1939.

Those early immigrants mostly joined the Spanish and Portuguese Congregation. David Sassoon held services in his house in Bruton Street, London; but he was also a member of the Spanish and Portuguese Congregation, whose practices and standard of religious observance he criticised in his private diaries. Other Sassoons served on its governing body.

India had always treated its Jews with respect and tolerance, never persecuting or discriminating against them in any way. But having lived in India under the British flag since 1798, the Baghdadi Jews of Bombay and Calcutta viewed the ending of the British Raj with unease. So too did the other Jewish communities of India — the Bene Israel and the Jews of Cochin.

India was granted its independence in 1948; and that was the signal for departure. Most left for Israel which also attained independence in the same year, for London and for Sydney, Australia. A few also made their way to Los Angeles, New York, and Canada. Once the exodus had started, it was maintained by family ties and by the success stories of those who had left

147 Reuben Sassoon (1835-1905)
Cartoon by Spy, 1890. Contrast this with
the picture (on page 74) of his father,
David Sassoon, who never wore European
clothes.

and made good abroad. It continued steadily until very few Jews indeed
were left in India.

The Indian Jewish community of London, which received its largest
influx of immigrants during the late 1940s and early 1950s, now numbers
between two to three thousand people. They mostly live in Stamford Hill,
Ilford, Golders Green and Hendon.

They first established three synagogues, one in Stamford Hill, one in
Golders Green and a smaller one in Ilford. More recently, two additional
small synagogues have opened, one in Golders Green and the other in
Hendon. All are attended by former members of other Eastern communities
as well as by those of Indian origin. The Stamford Hill synagogue is
particularly impressive with its Indian-style furnishing and its large walk-in
Echal (Ark), into which women enter for private petition and prayer after
the end of the services. The synagogue service and music used are those
most familiar to Indian Jews.

The community also imported many of its customs and food to England. Women, who formerly employed cooks, now pride themselves on their own mastery of Indian cuisine. A typical anecdote in Esmond Ezra's 'Turning Back the Pages' concerns his father, who burst into tears on his arrival in London when he first saw Esmond's sister cleaning her house. He declared that he never thought he would live to see his own daughter having to scrub and clean. It took a very long time to persuade him that almost every English housewife did the same.

The immigrants have by now settled down to life in London, though the older members still experience pangs of nostalgia for the past — and in particular for the close, extended family life they enjoyed in Calcutta and Bombay, and which they see fast disappearing for ever.

THE PERSIAN AND BUKHARAN COMMUNITY

The extraordinary story of the Jews from Meshed (Mashad in Arabic) in the north of Iran, and the tenacity with which they clung to their ancestral faith despite much hardship, is described in Part Two of this book.

One of the first immigrants from Meshed to reach London, via Istanbul and Jerusalem, was a dealer in oriental carpets. He arrived at around the turn of the twentieth century.

In 1914 Mashadi Jews in Jerusalem were ordered to take up Ottoman citizenship or face deportation. Many refused and were sent to Cairo, then under British control. Some eventually reached London in the 1920s, where they formed the nucleus of a small community. Mostly working in the carpet and fur trades, they gravitated to Stamford Hill, London. There, joined by Jews from Bukhara, they first held services in a private house before establishing their own permanent synagogue in East Bank.

A closely-knit group, passionately devoted to their faith, they set up their own remarkable 'hevra' (brotherhood) — in which each man undertook to pay a voluntary tax to the community amounting to 0.1% of his turnover in business or 10% of his turnover as a broker. This was a system of complete trust in which books of account were not inspected; but it worked. The money went towards maintaining their own community in London as well as to assist poorer brethren overseas.

Though the Bukharan Jews split off in 1930, many more Mashadis came over to London soon after, again swelling the numbers. The Bukharans were too few to build their own synagogue in London; and they joined existing congregations, though still maintaining their group identity and looking to their community in Jerusalem for spiritual inspiration as they still do.

One or two families from Teheran also settled in London and Manchester in the inter-war years.

The Mashadi community did well in London. On the outbreak of war in 1939, many families evacuated themselves to Torquay where, in co-operation with local Ashkenazim, they established a synagogue in a converted church. An Ashkenazi rabbi ministered to their joint needs; and

148 Bukharan Wedding in Jerusalem

he was so well liked by the Persians that he returned with them to Stamford Hill after the war.

Some Mashadis departed for the United States in the post-war years, attracted by business opportunities there; but others came from Iran, Israel and elsewhere to fill their places. A new Persian Synagogue was built in Stamford Hill in 1965. But this was a little too late, as by then many Mashadi Jews were already moving away to Hendon and Finchley in North-West London.

Always a pious community with strong internal cohesion and close family ties, the Persians were welcomed warmly by the Ashkenazi synagogues of North-West London, which did their best to accommodate them. Their numbers were greatly increased in the 1980s after the overthrow of the Shah of Persia; but the newer immigrants did not all have the same dedication to traditional Judaism as did the original Mashadis.

The community is very much alive today and numbers from four to five hundred people. The Ashkenazi synagogue in Kinloss Gardens, Finchley, provides premises for them to hold their own Mashadi services on the High Holydays; and the community is now seeking to build a new synagogue for itself in North-West London. Its social activities include an active youth movement. Only a handful of Mashadis still live in Stamford Hill; but their synagogue there flourishes — and is used by other Eastern Sephardim from many different countries of origin.

THE ADEN COMMUNITY

Though the Jewish community of Aden was one of great importance in the twelfth century, it had dwindled to insignificance by the time of the British occupation of the town in the middle of the nineteenth century.

The opening of the Suez Canal in 1869 brought prosperity to Aden, for its port occupied a key position on the route to India and the Far East. Its population grew rapidly — and so too did its Jewish community because of immigration from Egypt, India, Turkey and places even further afield. By 1947 nearly five thousand Jews were living in Aden. The British presence, and close contacts with Europe, forged a society markedly different from those in the rest of the Arabian Peninsula.

Several thousand Jewish refugees from the Yemen were also sheltering in a camp in Aden in 1947, waiting hopefully to enter Palestine. The refugees were helped by the local Jewish community in so far as that was possible. Eventually the Yemeni Jews were air-lifted to Israel from Aden in the dramatic rescue project known as Operation Magic Carpet. This caught the world's imagination because of the simple faith that enabled the primitive Yemeni Jews — many of whom had never seen an aeroplane in their lives — to climb aboard the transport planes without fuss, secure in knowledge of the prophesy that God would deliver them from bondage 'on eagles' wings'.

Aden was a duty-free port, where ships stopped on journeys to and from India and the Far East. Many of the shops at Steamer Point, close to the docks, were in Jewish hands; and that was the main occupation of the

149 Yemenite immigrants en-route for Israel
In operation 'Magic Carpet' in January 1950, the American Joint Distribution Committee chartered planes to fly the Yemenite Jews from refugee camps in Aden to Israel.

wealthier members of the community. The others were small traders, with shops on the main road bordering the Jewish quarter and in the bazaar. There were also some merchants engaged in importing and exporting goods through the port.

The Jews lived in the Crater District. This was actually the crater of an extinct volcano, connected to Steamer Point by a tunnel through the mountain. The Jewish quarter contained four streets — named One, Two, Three and Four. Though a kind of ghetto, it was a voluntary one. Its houses were large and comfortable, often in multiple occupation. They were wholly owned by Jews, who preferred to live close together. Those who remember what they regarded as 'a good life' in Aden still speak nostalgically of the old days.

There were two Jewish day-schools, one for boys and one for girls, and many synagogues. The main synagogue, Magen Abraham, could seat a thousand people; and its Echal (Ark) contained no fewer than two hundred and seventy Sifrei Torah (Scrolls of the Torah).

In 1947, three days after the United Nations voted to partition Palestine

150 The Adeni Synagogue of London
In this recent photograph, the Chairman of the community is shown holding a Sefer Torah.

151 Bride and Bridegroom in Morocco.

into Jewish and Arab states, a violent pogrom erupted in Aden. Over one hundred Jews perished. The British authorities were blamed bitterly for not doing more to protect the community from the predicted violence.

That was the signal for Jews to start leaving; and not even the personal intervention on the spot of the President of the Board of Deputies of British Jews could restore sufficient confidence to save the community. Only one hundred and fifty Jews remained in Aden to witness the anti-British riots of 1967; and they too left later that same year.

By 1960, fifty families had settled in London where they established their own synagogue and social centre in Stamford Hill. The community now numbers between five and six hundred committed families, consisting of those who came direct from Aden and others who arrived later via Israel.

Many Adenis subsequently moved from Stamford Hill to the Golders Green and Hendon districts of North-West London, posing their community with the same kind of difficulty in surviving as a distinct group as that being faced by the Mashadis who have also moved away from their original centre in Stamford Hill.

THE MOROCCAN COMMUNITY

Attracted by economic opportunities, small numbers of Jews from Morocco and North Africa settled in England from the eighteenth century onwards and merged with the general Sephardi community. This was made easier by the fact that some Jews, especially from Mogador in Morocco, had acquired British protection in the nineteenth century and were able to travel abroad on British passports.

Though many Jews fled from Morocco after the establishment of the State of Israel in 1948, few if any found their way to English shores. Most of the wealthy and educated went to France, Spain and America, and the rest to Israel.

Several hundred Moroccans came over to London in the 1960s, again for economic reasons. Though not institution oriented, they maintained their close family ties and formed the nucleus of a small community. They were joined in the 1980s by a fresh wave of immigration, this time from Israel, of some of the children of those who had originally left Morocco for Israel.

The community now numbers several hundred people. In 1989 it opened its first synagogue in borrowed premises in Hendon, where it holds regular services conducted by a Moroccan hazan. Many of its members also belong to other synagogues, both Sephardi and Ashkenazi, to whom they look for other facilities.

Moroccan Jews of even more recent origin have established two small synagogues of their own and a yeshivah in North Manchester.

Uniquely for Jewish émigrés from an Islamic country, the former Moroccans in London maintain cordial relations with their country of origin. Friendly messages have been exchanged between some of its leading members and the King; and both the Moroccan Ambassador and the Israeli Ambassador attended the formal opening of the community's synagogue.

THE EGYPTIAN COMMUNITY

Several thousand Jews from the ancient communities of Cairo and Alexandria made their homes in England following the Suez crisis of 1956 when life became impossible for them in Egypt. Many of the refugees settled in the north-western suburbs of London, where they quickly formed The Maimonides Group for mutual encouragement and support.

On their arrival in London, some of the Egyptians joined the Spanish and Portuguese Congregation. This did its best to welcome the newcomers and help with their religious and social needs. Synagogue services were organised in temporary premises; and in 1964, the Wembley Sephardi Congregation was established for them as an integral part of the parent congregation.

The new community soon became popular with other Sephardim from Iraq, North Africa and other places. It also attracted many children of the 'English' Sephardim who had moved to the Wembley area on marriage. A permanent, purpose-built synagogue — still part of the Spanish and Portuguese Jews' Congregation, London — was opened in 1977.

More European in education and outlook than most other immigrants from the Near East, the Egyptians assimilated well into the existing communities — mainly joining the Spanish and Portuguese synagogues in Wembley and Maida Vale, the Eastern Synagogue in Golders Green and the Neveh Shalom Community (also in Wembley). Though not preserving a separate institutional identity, their presence has certainly enriched the life of London's Sephardim.

THE NEVEH SHALOM COMMUNITY

In late 1969 David Kamhi, the Rabbi of the Spanish and Portuguese Wembley Congregation resigned, together with a group of members formerly from communities of Eastern Sephardim. They wished to use their own familiar minhag in London and to develop and worship in a manner different from the more formal ways of the Spanish and Portuguese Jews. They then established their own independent Sephardi Congregation, also in Wembley.

Acting with vigour and a strong sense of purpose, the new congregation attracted about fifty families, mainly from Eastern communities — from Turkey, Egypt and the Sudan, from Iraq and Iran. It soon found the means to obtain its own synagogue by buying, reconstructing and extending two adjacent houses.

Neveh Shalom managed to survive the tragically early death of its founding Rabbi; and now numbers over one hundred and twenty families. It runs its own religion classes. Members pride themselves on their close family ties, which have produced a caring community under whose auspices they much enjoy meeting and praying together.

THE JEWISH PREPARATORY SCHOOL

A Jewish primary school, run on Sephardi lines, was opened in the Maida Vale area of London in the early 1980s. It was founded as an independent charity by the Communal Rabbi of the Spanish and Portuguese Congregation in his personal capacity, with the assistance of three generous donors from the Baghdadi community.

The school has done well and now has over one hundred and twenty pupils. It is run in accordance with the Sephardi practice of combining the best of traditional Jewish and secular education. Many of the parents, Sephardim and Ashkenazim, have joined the Spanish and Portuguese Synagogue as a consequence of their childrens' education and because of the commitment it has inspired.

A splendid synagogue, attached to the school, hosts the High Holyday services of the Iraqi community, conducted partly under the auspices of the nearby Spanish and Portuguese Synagogue.

THE FUTURE

There is new awareness that education for all ages, and at all levels, is the key to ensuring the survival of the Sephardi tradition in England.

Several Sephardi rabbis, including some from the Eastern communities, now run small-scale but significant programmes of higher Torah learning as well as general adult educational projects. The Jewish Preparatory School does valuable work. Improvements to religion classes for children are already producing results. These are all encouraging signs that the community is becoming more aware of what is at stake and that, this time, the challenge will be met.

152 **The Future**
Pupils of the Jewish Preparatory School, London, late 1980s.

List of maps

Compiler: Lucien Gubbay
Cartographer: John Mitchell

List of illustrations

Abbreviations

B.H. Beth Hatefutsoth. Museum of the Diaspora, Tel Aviv.

I.M. Israel Museum, Jerusalem.

B.M. British Museum, London.

A.R. Alfred Rubens's collection.

A.L. Collection of Abraham and Estelle Levy.

S & P. Spanish & Portuguese Jews' Congregation, London.

Cover

Front
TREE OF LIFE. Worked by Estelle Levy

Back
DAMASCUS KETER. Jewish National and University Library, Jerusalem

Colour plates

Illustrations

Permission from the various owners and copyright-holders, where traceable, to reproduce the pictures is acknowledged with much gratitude.

Selected Bibliography

Main sources of information and quotations

The Sephardim: A Problem of Survival
Abraham Levy

A History of the Marranos
Cecil Roth
Jewish Publication Society of America. 1959

Marranos in Portugal
Vestry Office, Bevis Marks, London. 1938

Sabbetai Svi, The Mystical Messiah
Gershon Scholem
The Littman Library

Quest for the Messiah
Lucien Gubbay
The Book Guild, Lewes, Sussex. 1990

The Jews of Islam
Bernard Lewis
Routledge and Kegan Paul. 1984.

The Western Sephardim
edited by Richard Barnett and Walter Schwab.
Gibraltar Books. 1989.

The Scribe
Exilarch's Foundation, London. Vol. 36, Sept. 1989.

Magic Carpet: Aleppo in Flatbush
Joseph Sutton.

Aleppo Chronicles
Joseph Sutton.
Thayer Jacoby. New York. 1988.

Aleppo and Devonshire Square
Ralf Davis.
Macmillan. London. 1967.

The Jews of Calcutta
Flower Elias and Judith Elias-Cooper.
The Jewish Association of Calcutta. 1974.

Turning Back the Pages
Esmond Ezra.
Brookside. London. 1986.

On the Banks of the Ganga
Ezekiel Musleah
The Christopher Publishing House, Mass. 1975.

Jews in Twentieth Century Egypt
Jacob Landau.
New York University Press. 1969.

Jewish Life in Turkey in the Sixteenth Century
M.S. Goodblatt.
Jewish Theological Seminary of America. 1952.

The British in the Middle East
Sarah Searight.
Weidenfeld and Nicholson. 1969.

French Jews, Turkish Jews
Aron Rodrigue.
Indiana University Press. Bloomington and Indianapolis. 1990.

Jewish Rhodes
Isaac Levy.
Judah L Magnes Museum, California. 1989.

A History of the Jews in North Africa (two vols.)
H. Z. Hirschberg.
E.J. Brill, Leiden. 1974 and 1978.

Between East and West: A History of the Jews of North Africa
A Chouraqui.
Jewish Publication Society of America, Phliladelphia. 1968.

The Responsa of R.Simon Zemah Duran
I. Epstein.
Oxford University Press. 1930.

The Sephardi Community of Amsterdam
F.J. Dubiez.
Portuguese Synagogue of Amsterdam.

Bevis Marks Records
Vestry Office, Bevis Marks, London.

The Other Jews
Daniel Elazar
Basic Books, New York. 1989.

Sephardim in Twentieth Century America
Joseph Papo.
Pele Yoetz Books, San Jose, California.
Judah L. Magnes Museum, Berkeley, California. 1987.

The Treaty of Utrecht 1713; and the Jews of Gibraltar
Sir Joshua Hassan.
Jewish Historical Society of England. 1970.

The Sephardim of the United States: An Exploratory Study
Marc Angel.
American Jewish Community. New York. 1973.

The Making of Manchester Jewry
Bill Williams.
Manchester University Press. 1976.

Index

Main entries are in heavy type.